The Defamation of Pius XII

THE DEFAMATION OF PIUS XII

Ralph McInerny

St. Augustine's Press
South Bend, Indiana
2001

Manufactured in the United States of America.

1 2 3 4 5 6 07 06 05 04 03 02 01

Library of Congress Cataloging in Publication Data
McInerny, Ralph M.
      The defamation of Pius XII / Ralph McInerny.
              p. cm.
      Includes bibliographical references and index.
      ISBN 1-890318-66-3 (alk. paper)
      1. Pius XII, Pope, 1876–1958 – Relations with Jews.
      2. Judaism – Relations – Catholic Church. 3. Catholic Church
      – Relations – Judaism. 4. Holocaust, Jewish (1939–1945)
      5. World War, 1939–1945 – Religious aspects – Catholic
      Church. 6. Christianity and antisemitism – History – 20th
      century. I. Title.
BX1378 .M396 2000
282'.092 – dc21   00-010831

O the mind, mind has mountains; cliffs of fall
Frightful, sheer, no-man-fathomed. Hold them cheap
May who ne'er hung there.
Gerard Manley Hopkins

Table of Contents

THESIS

Since the heroic efforts of Pius XII during World War II are a matter of history and the attacks on him are risibly easy to dismiss, the question becomes: Why is this good man being defamed? Who are those attacking the man who behaved most nobly during the darkest period of the twentieth century? Anti-Catholicism has been called the anti-Semitism of the liberal. It has now become the trademark of the Culture of Death.

Overture

Eugenio Pacelli was elected pope in 1939, took the name of Pius XII, and reigned for almost twenty years until his death in 1958. As the Vicar of Christ on earth and the successor of St. Peter, a pope's principal job is to evangelize the world. God so loved the world that he sent his only begotten son to save it from its sins. That is the Good News the Church was formed to spread. The Holy Father is a primarily spiritual leader, but just as God became incarnate in Jesus, the Church is *in* the world, though not *of* it. Thus it is no small matter that the papacy of Pius XII took place during World War II and continued into the Cold War that grew up between the awkward allies who had defeated Hitler and the Axis Powers.

It is a simple fact that no political or religious leader emerged from World War II with a nobler and more heroic record than Pius XII. Vatican City is located in a country which had a Fascist dictator, Mussolini, who eventually allied himself with Hitler. Mussolini's regime may have looked less menacing than Hitler's, but it was totalitarian. When Mussolini was forced to resign in 1943, German troops rushed in to fill the vacuum, occupying Rome and surrounding the Vatican. These were the hostile circumstances in which Pius XII reigned until the liberation of Rome by Allied forces in 1944. Bombs actually dropped on Vatican City, whether German or American bombs was never clear. But American forces did level Montecassino on their march toward Rome.

The moral problems posed by an unlimited war, predicated on the unconditional surrender of Hitler, were huge – the bombing of cities, the blurring of any distinction between combatant and civilian, the violation of the most elementary precepts of natural law. Added to this, were the dreadful racial policies of the Third Reich. Hitler was a satanic figure motivated by seething resentment of Germany's defeat in World War I, a dream of an Aryan people occupying the land mass of Europe for a thousand years. Standing athwart this goal – apart from the military might of the allies – were two things: Christianity and the Jewish people.

Hitler declared war on the church from the beginning.

He vowed to rid first Germany and then Europe of "inferior races," most notably the Jews.

The measures taken against German Jews prior to the outbreak of hostilities were a matter of public knowledge. The brain drain of Jewish intellectuals from Nazi Germany and Austria enriched the universities of Britain and the United States. The occupation of Austria and Czechoslovakia by German troops was supinely agreed to, but the invasion of Poland brought a declaration of war on Germany by Britain and, more reluctantly, France, and World War II was on.

Nazi activities in occupied territories were more difficult to monitor than they had been in peacetime Germany. But the network of papal diplomats, and the presence of the Church throughout Europe, brought the incredible news to the pope, and he both condemned what he characterized as the extermination of peoples and announced it to the world. Again and again and again.

The identification and condemnation of Nazi atrocities continued throughout the war. It was accompanied by efforts to protect the innocent victims of a diabolical regime. The Catholic Church, under the leadership of Pius XII, is credited with saving nearly a million Jews from certain death during the war. This is an achievement not even approached by other heroic efforts. It was gratefully acknowledged during and after the war by Jewish leaders who knew what the pope had done.

Jewish criticisms of Jewish efforts to rescue the Jews in Nazi occupied Europe are seldom juxtaposed to the unfounded attacks on Pius XII. But surely if Pius's efforts are to be criticized, it must be asked . . . compared to whose?

Saving nearly 1 million Jews, glorious as this was, was only one of Pius XII's personal and pontifical achievements. Nonetheless, after his death, grumbling in the Church about his defense of the Deposit of the Faith against Modernist tendencies became more audible, and with the call for the Second Vatican Council, the pre-conciliar Church became the *bête noire* of liberal and progressive Catholics. It has been suggested that this was one of the disposing conditions for the success of an amazing assault on Pius XII that was launched in 1963.

The turning point was the play, *The Deputy*, by Rolf Hochhuth. In it, Pius XII is portrayed as the dark opposite of his historical self. Hochhuth's Pius XII is silent about the treatment of Jews, connives in their deportation from Rome and Italy, and might as well be the Nazi Hochhuth himself once was – Nazi youth, at any rate. The play flies in the face of historical facts and represents a slanderous attack on a holy and heroic figure. Hochhuth wrote a similarly slanderous play about Winston Churchill which received the treatment it deserved. But his defamation of Pius XII has passed from the realm of sick fantasy into that of received opinion. The latest contribution to the sorry genre inaugurated by Hochhuth is John Cornwell's *Hitler's Pope*.

For more than three decades, historians have patiently shown that such portrayals of Pius XII are devoid of any historical basis. All the Vatican documents covering the period are now available in twelve volumes, but far from putting the matter to rest, there is a continuing buzz that the Vatican is hiding something and is engaged in an effort to save Pius XII from the truth about his papacy. Many of the attackers are anti-Semites and ex-Nazis, others are disenchanted Catholics (e.g., James Carroll, a former priest; Garry Wills, former Jesuit seminarian; and John Cornwell, a self-described "Catholic agnostic"). Most dismaying of all have been those Jews who have joined in the attack on a man who was their main protector during the darkest hour of European history.

Pius XII was a good and holy man. He was a heroic defender and protector of Jews during World War II. The evidence for this truth is massive, the testimonies are many, the facts are unchangeable. All efforts to show the opposite have been conclusively refuted. The question is *not* whether Pius XII acted heroically during World War II and was instrumental in saving hundreds of thousands of Jews from Nazi extermination. The question is *not* whether libels and slanders against this good and holy man can be refuted. The overwhelming question that has to be addressed is this: *Why is this good man being defamed?* Who are those who devote themselves to besmirching the reputation of Pius XII? What are they really after? What is their fundamental objective?

The Didache taught that there are two paths, one of light, the other of darkness. John Paul II has spoken of a Culture of Death and a Culture of Life. During World War II, Pius XII courageously walked the path of light. He stood up against the Culture of Death and defended the Culture of Life. The Nazis he condemned are no more. Their totalitarian twin,

THE DEFAMATION OF PIUS XII

the Communists, have withered away as the state was supposed to. But the Culture of Death is still among us, stronger than before. Those who opposed Hitler now occupy countries which have espoused under other names his genetic atrocities. The moral relativism and nihilism of the West, which have permitted the Culture of Death to flourish among us, recognizes its main enemy. That enemy is the Catholic Church. For such foes, Pius XII is merely a target of opportunity. Their aim is the natural law which, as Pius emphasized from the beginning of the war, was violated by the Nazi racist policies. The Culture of Death is an equally systematic assault on the natural law of which the Catholic Church is the chief custodian. Hence the libel and the defamation of the Church. That is the thesis of this book.

1

Youth

1876	March 2. Born in Rome to Virginia Graziosi and Filippo Pacelli.
	March 4. Baptized Eugenio Maria Giuseppe Giovanni.
1878	February 20. Leo XIII elected.
	Began formal schooling, kindergarten, then elementary school.
1886	First Communion.
1891	Student at Ennio Quirino Visconti Lyceum.
1894	October. Entered Capranica Seminar, taking classes at Gregorian University.
1895	Illness causes him to continue studies at home.
	Registered at Sapienza School of Philosophy and Letters and at the Papal Athenaeum of St. Appolinaris for theology. Received bachelor and licentiate degrees summa cum laude.
1899	April 2. Ordained priest.
	Curate at Chiesa Nuova.
	Continued studies for doctorate in canon and civil law at Apollinaris.

The Popes and the Pacellis

Eugenio Pacelli was born on March 2, 1876, of a family long associated with the Vatican and the papal court. His grandfather, Marcantonio Pacelli, had been minister of finance for Pope Gregory XVI and minister of foreign affairs under Pius IX from 1851 to 1870. His father,

Filippo, was a lawyer in the Congregation of the Sacred Rota. The Pacellis were "Blacks" because they sided with the pope; "Whites" were Romans who took the side of the king. The family's parish church in Rome was the Chiesa Nuova where the body of St. Philip Neri is buried. Pius was baptized Eugenio Maria Giuseppe Pacelli in the Church of St. Celsus, by an uncle, Monsignor Giuseppe Pacelli.

There was a proximity both spatial and professional between the Pacellis and the Vatican. The family apartment, when Eugenio was born, was an elegant but unheated twelve rooms on the third floor of a building at 34 Via Orsini, in the Ponte section of Rome, in the shadow of the Vatican, but a mile from St. Peter's Square. Shortly after his birth, the family moved to the Via della Vetrina. Half a dozen years before Eugenio's birth, his grandfather had witnessed the seizure of the papal states by the Italian government. It was the term of a process that had begun in 1848 when revolutionary forces entered Rome. Count Pelligrino Rossi, whom Pius IX had named his prime minister in 1848, was assassinated by revolutionaries on November 16, when he went to negotiate with them in the Cancelleria. A mob then converged on the Quirinal Palace, where a committee presented an ultimatum to Pius IX, demanding that he agree to a democratic ministry. The crowd grew impatient and set fire to the papal palace; the pope's secretary of Latin letters, Monsignor Palma, was shot as he stood at the pope's side. Pius IX had little choice if he were to prevent blood from running in the streets of Rome. He fled to Gaeta, a humiliating event, and did not return to Rome until April, 1850. It is scarcely surprising that Pius IX took a new and colder look at the political and social changes sweeping through Italy and Europe. After the loss of the papal states in 1870, the pope became a voluntary prisoner in the Vatican. Pius IX suffered a posthumous outrage as well. When his funeral cortege approached the church of St. Lawrence Outside the Walls – a church that would be accidentally destroyed by American bombers on July 19, 1943, their target being the city's railway center – the mob threatened to seize the casket and throw it into the Tiber.

Pius IX was pope when Eugenio was born. Giovanni Maria Mastai-Ferreti, as a young priest, had spent two years in Chile with a papal mission, administered a Roman hospice, was named bishop of Spoleto, then cardinal, and was elected pope in 1846 at the age of fifty-four. When he was elected, he was thought to have liberal sympathies because he advocated administrative changes in the government of the papal states and expressed sympathy with Italian nationalism. One of his first acts as pope was to declare a political amnesty and introduce reforms in the papal states, establishing somewhat reluctantly a bicameral assembly. His popularity soared, but it soon became clear that Pius IX had no intention of ceding the temporal sovereignty of his office. It was when he refused to put the authority of the papacy behind the effort to expel Austria from Italy that the mood changed, leading to the assassination of his prime minister, Count Rossi, and Pius's own flight to Gaeta when a Roman republic was declared. Pius appealed for help, and with the aid of French troops papal rule was reestablished in Rome. This ignited national aspirations, and the papal troops were defeated by Cavour by 1860, causing the loss of the papal states, leaving Pius with the city of Rome and the immediately surrounding territory. He reigned under the protection of the French until the Franco-Prussian War of 1870 brought about the occupation of Rome by Italian forces. This left the pope with only the Vatican City as his temporal domain. Pius's reaction was to confine himself to the Vatican as a prisoner, and he never again set foot outside it. He forbade Catholics to take part in the political life of an Italy that had dealt so severely with the papacy. The pope himself lived in a state of spiritual siege. In the Syllabus of Errors, Pius IX enumerated the ways in which the path of the world diverged from that of the Church. Vatican I, the ecumenical council called by Pius IX, defined the infallibility of the pope when teaching on matters of faith and morals. If Pius IX discerned the growing social and philosophical threats to the faith, he was less clear as to what to do about it. The declaration of papal infallibility by Vatican I caused defections from the Church and brought about a wave of anti-clericalism in Europe. Bismarck's *Kulturkampf*, which Pius denounced, made it clear that the battle was ultimately a spiritual one. For all that, Pius remained an attractive personality, admired even by his political opponents. He was pope longer than anyone before or after, reigning from 1846 to 1878. Cardinal Ferrata reported the pope remarking in a melancholy way: "Everything around me has changed; my system and my politics have had their day, but I am too old to change direction. That will be the work of my successor." His successor, Joacham Pecci, was elected when Eugenio Pacelli was two years old.

Leo XIII

Pecci took the name Leo XIII and reigned from 1878 until 1903. More than a fifty-year stretch of time united the outlooks of Leo and Pius IX.

Leo had held office in the papal states as well as serving as papal nuncio in Belgium. Visits to Cologne, London, and Paris gave him personal acquaintance with a rapidly industrializing Europe. Recalled from Belgium, he was named bishop of Perugia but was more or less *persona non grata* in Rome because he favored better relations between the Church and the ambient world. As pope, he continued principled efforts to work with an increasingly secularized culture but without any fundamental break with the outlook of Pius IX. His naming John Henry Newman a cardinal was in many ways the signature of his papacy. Newman had defined what he meant by the liberalism he opposed in an appendix to his *Apologia pro vita sua,* but for all that Newman saw Catholicism as what the modern world needed and, however implicitly, desired. *Aeterni Patris,* in 1879, put forward Christian philosophy, represented chiefly by St. Thomas Aquinas, as providing the principles which would remedy the ills of the times. Leo XIII came to terms with democracy, clarifying how it could be compatible with Christianity and need not be its implacable foe. In encyclical after encyclical, Leo took up modern themes and interpreted them in senses compatible with the faith. With *Rerum Novarum* he became the advocate of social justice and the rights of workers in an industrial world. But Leo was as jealous as his predecessor for the temporal prerogatives of the popes that had been lost along with the papal states. Like Pius IX, he forbade Catholics to participate in Italian politics, but his diplomacy moved him beyond what had seemed the intransigence of Pius. His advice to French Catholics to rally to the Third Republic was met with mixed reactions. An ironic achievement of Leo XIII was to enhance the international prestige of the papacy; the deprivation of the papal states was in effect a liberation. For all that, the Vatican was excluded from the Hague International Peace Conference of 1899.

Pope St. Pius X

Leo XIII was succeeded by the saintly Pius X (1903–1914). The continuity between Pius IX, Leo XIII, and Pius X is manifest: They shared a dim view of trends in the wider world, whatever the nuances of difference with which they addressed them. The realization that the external enemy was making inroads into the Church itself reached its culmination when Pius X condemned modernism. At the heart of modernism was the subjectivism that characterized modern thought. Religious faith was taken to be an inner experience that one might try with varying success to articulate, rather than the graced acceptance of revealed truths which had been clarified and defended by the tradition of the Church. Pius X took this to be not simply another deviation but one so profound that he considered modernism the heresy of heresies.

Such was the ecclesiastical and political context in which Eugenio Pacelli was raised and in which began his priestly life. Romano de Roma, Eugenio Pacelli was born into and lived his life in a city where history is a palpable present. The ancient ruins that had incited Gibbon to write The Rise and Fall of the Roman Empire – a multi-volume attack on Christianity – were all around him. The Middle Ages and Renaissance represent further layers in the historical sandwich that is the Eternal City. But most vividly present to him, physically and through his family, would be the fortunes of the Church and the papacy in the modern world. The suffering of Pius IX were matters of family as well as ecclesiastical lore.

Pius IX had not been the first modern pope to be humiliated by the power of this world. Pius VI and Pius VII had been kidnapped and trundled about like trophies by the mighty of this world. Pius VI died in imprisoned exile in France, the most notable of the victims of the excesses of the Revolution. Pius VII was carried

Vatican Hill

The Vatican hill was named for Numa Pompilius, the king who chose that hill from which to relate his vaticinia, messages from the gods. It was to Rome that Peter came, entering the city by the Appian Way, with Mark his companion, a Jewish stranger in the heart of Empire, come to make Rome the center of Christianity. Church and Empire coexisted until Rome fell in 476. From that time on, the city suffered periodic misery until the Renaissance lifted from the rubble a new and beautiful city. The woman in the Gospel suffered much under many physicians. So Rome has suffered much under Goths, Vandals, and Emperors. When Eugenio Pacelli was born, the wounds inflicted by the unification of Italy were fresh. One of his first acts as pope would be to authorize the excavations beneath the Basilica of St. Peter, which would discover the tomb of the first pope. The boy would live to see the city invaded and the Vatican surrounded by the most savage forces ever unleashed on mankind and the Church.

off to Paris to crown Napoleon but the bumptious Corsican took the crown from the pope's hands and placed it on his own head. After Napoleon's fall, that same pope offered Napoleon's relatives refuge in Rome.

Willingly to School

Eugenio was home-schooled by his mother in his earliest years. With his brother and two sisters, he would gather around his mother in the kitchen where she would read to them, a history of the popes being a favorite. It must have sounded like family history. The mother taught by example as well, visiting the poor and sick. In 1880 Eugenio began his formal schooling with the French Sisters of Providence. The memories of the childhood friends of the eventually prominent are notoriously untrustworthy. When Eugenio went on to the Lyceo Visconti for classical studies, a teacher there later claimed to have been certain the young man would end up on the throne of St. Peter. Little memorable is known of the years of Eugenio's schooling. He was ten when he made his First Holy Communion on October 11, 1886. He swam a little but otherwise engaged in no sport, unless walking be called one. He was an altar boy at the Chiesa Nuova. He was noted for both piety and intelligence. When he was seventeen, the Ministry of Education set as a composition theme the benefits accruing to Italy from the seizure of the papal states. Eugenio vigorously argued the opposite, denouncing the seizure as unjust and condemning the anti-clerical groups that persecuted the Church. In the circumstances, this called for courage. However, he did not suffer for his principled stand and graduated from the Lyceo Visconti with honors that same year. He had arrived at the great crossroads of life when youth confronts manhood.

His older brother Francesco was in law school, his sisters in convent school. It was thought that Eugenio might follow his brother and father and grandfather into the law. Instead, he chose the priesthood, although, after he had acquired doctorates in philosophy and theology, he would go on to acquire a doctorate "in both laws," that is, both Church and civil law. In 1893 he entered Alma Capranica College to begin his seminary training. Residents of the college, founded in 1477 by Cardinal Capranica, followed courses in the Gregorian University. His delicate health caused Eugenio to live at home again for a time, but as a scholar in the Pontifical University of the Roman Seminary, receiving instruction from the Sulpician Fathers.

The seminary course involved six years of study, two years of philosophy, followed by four of theology. As a student of philosophy, Eugenio studied metaphysics and theory of knowledge as well as mathematics, languages, and the natural sciences. The years of theology involved courses in moral and dogmatic theology, canon law, scripture, liturgy, and church history. Eugenio's passage through this process was marked by the degrees of baccalaureate, licentiate, and finally the doctorate. In 1895, Eugenio received tonsure, formally removing him from the lay to the clerical state. Through the years of theology he received some of the Holy Orders, first the minor orders – porter, lector, exorcist, acolyte – and then the three major orders – subdiaconate, diaconate, and priesthood. When he became a subdeacon in the spring of 1898 he bound himself to the ministry of the Church forever and promised celibacy. It was a solemn moment.

> You ought to consider attentively again and again to what burden you, of your own accord, this day aspire. For as yet you are free, and it is lawful for you at will to pass over to worldly pursuits. But if you receive this Order, you will no longer be at liberty to recede from your resolution, but you will be obliged to serve God perpetually, and with his assistance, to observe chastity, and you will be bound to the ministry of the Church forever.

These were the words of the ordaining bishop. Then the names of the *ordinandi* were called out. "Eugenio Pacelli." "*Adsum.*" ("Here I am"). He was now a man of the Church forever. The diaconate was conferred on him the following fall and on April 21, 1899, he was ordained priest in the Basilica of Santa Maria Maggiore. He said his first Mass in the Borghese Chapel of the Basilica on April 22 where there is a picture of the Blessed Virgin said to have been painted by St. Luke. The newly ordained priest was twenty-three years old. He held doctorates in philosophy and in theology. He could speak German, French, Polish, and English. Pope Leo XIII personally congratulated him on his academic accomplishments. He was as well an accomplished musician, his instrument the violin.

Don Pacelli

Don Eugenio Pacelli began his priestly life as an assistant to the pastor of the Chiesa Nuvoa, the church that he had known through his life as the parish church of his family. The Chiesa Nuova is located on the Corso Vittorio Emmanuele, which runs from the Piazza Venezia to a bridge that crosses the Tiber to the Via Conciliazione, which runs into St. Peter's Square. Across the Corso from the Chiesa Nuova lies the Campo dei Fiori, the Farnese Palace, and the Palazzo della Cancelleria, where Count Rossi was assassinated. Not far away was the Piazza Navona and the Pantheon. This setting, familiar to Eugenio from his childhood would now be where he entered into his pastoral ministry, the care of souls.

At the same time, he was pursuing the study of canon law at St.

Apollinaris from which he would receive a third doctorate, in both laws, civil and canonical. Given his academic accomplishments and the involvement of his family in Vatican affairs, it is not surprising that in February 1901 Cardinal Rampolla asked Leo XIII to appoint young Pacelli to the Congregation of Extraordinary Ecclesiastical Affairs. Cardinal Gasparri told the young priest he understood his desire to be a pastor, but to serve the Church is also to serve souls. Of course the young priest went where he was sent, becoming an attaché, the first level of employment in the Congregation. He had entered onto a path that would lead him, after a long and distinguished diplomatic career, at home and abroad, to the throne of St. Peter.

The city in which he lived, his studies, family lore, would have made him keenly aware that beneath the pomp and ceremony of the Vatican lay the simple fact that the Bishop of Rome was the successor of St. Peter. And every pope must be prepared for rough treatment by the world. Peter had been martyred, crucified as was the Lord whose vicar on earth he was. Young Father Pacelli had more than a bookish knowledge of how the popes of modern times had been treated. The mission of the Church is to bring the Good News of salvation to the world, but the world is not always receptive, indeed at times is openly hostile to a truth that goes against its own grain.

It is noteworthy that Pius XII himself lived in what could be called a time of assassination. The assassination of Czar Alexander II, which was to have such terrible consequences for Russian Jews, occurred in 1881. In 1894, Carnot, president of the French Republic, was assassinated, just as the Dreyfus Affair was about to cause tumult in the nation. It was not until 1906 that Captain Dreyfus was rehabilitated. In 1898, Elizabeth, Empress of Austria, was assassinated. In 1900 Humbert I, King of Italy, was assassinated. President McKinley was assassinated in 1901, and Alexander of Serbia and Draga, his queen, in 1902. To these personal tragedies must be added the wars that raged while Eugenio grew up, culminating in World War I. Nor could the young priest have been unaware of the depredations of the Church in France, the dispersal of congregations and the secularizing of education. The modern world was a bloody place whose spirit was increasingly inimical to the Church.

2

Diplomat

1901   Research assistant in Office of Congregation of Extraordinary Ecclesiastical Affairs.

1903   August 4. Pope Pius X elected.

1904   Papal Chamberlain, with title of monsignor.

1905   Domestic Prelate.

1908   Offered professorship in canon law at Catholic University of America; refused in deference to Pius X's wishes.

1910   Represented Holy See at coronation of George V in London.

1911   March 7. Appointed assistant secretary of the Congregation of Extraordinary Ecclesiastical Affairs.

1912   June 20. Appointed pro-secretary of state.

1914   February 1. Appointed secretary of the Congregation of Extraordinary Ecclesiastical Affairs.

1914   September 3. Pope Benedict XV elected.

1917   April 20. Appointed nuncio to Bavaria.

May 13. Consecrated bishop and elevated to rank of archbishop.

May 28. Presented his credentials to Ludwig III, King of Bavaria.

1920   June 22. Named first apostolic nuncio of Germany.

1922   Feb 6. Pius XI elected.

1924   March 29. Signed concordat with Bavaria.

1925   January 15. Concordat ratified by Bavarian Parliament.

Moved residence from Munich to Berlin.

1929   June 14. Concluded concordat with Prussia.

August 14. Concordat ratified.

December 16. Recalled to Rome and created cardinal.

Young Father Pacelli made some early journeys outside Rome. In 1896, prior to his diplomatic career, he went as secretary of Father Phillip Lais to a meeting of astronomers in Paris. He would visit Paris again in 1904 and continue on to Belgium in company with a relative. In Rome, he heard confessions at the Chiesa Nuova, his confessional number 4 near the door of Saint Philip Neri, and he also taught moral theology at the Institute of the Assumption on the Corso d'Italia. However inevitable his career may look retrospectively, there was a time early in his priesthood when Eugenio Pacelli might have dedicated himself to pastoral or to academic life rather than becoming one of the stars of the Vatican diplomatic corps.

A Long Apprenticeship

The congregation in which Father Eugenio Pacelli began his Vatican career in 1901 had its origin in the difficulties the Church encountered as the result of the French Revolution. In 1793, Pope Pius VI established the Congregation of Ecclesiastical Affairs of France. His successor, Pius VII changed its name to the Congregation for Extraordinary Ecclesiastical Affairs. In 1809, Pius VII was kidnapped from the Quirinal Palace and carried off to France, beginning an exile that would last until 1814, when he was allowed to return to Rome. This tragic episode was proof that the Church was right to be anxious about where the Revolution was heading. When he changed the name of the congregation, Pius VII was acknowledging that the winds of change, not all of them favorable to the spiritual mission of the Church, were not confined to France. Pacelli's mentor in the Vatican was Cardinal Rampolla, the secretary of state, but he also assisted Cardinal Gasparri in the revision of canon law that would appear in 1917. This required putting order into what could be gleaned from documents, ranging from papal bulls to pontifical decrees, dating from the beginning of the Church up to the twentieth century. This exacting and important task was not a publicized one, but it involved some five thousand collaborators around the world. The scholarly skills of Father Pacelli were soon as evident as his aptness for a diplomatic career. In 1902, he was named professor of canon law at a Roman university, but Gasparri persuaded him not to take it. In 1908, he was offered a professorship in Roman law at the Catholic University of America, and again Gasparri dissuaded him from accepting. Thus, on two occasions, his career might have altered profoundly. But he was destined for diplomacy, something he himself must have recognized when he submitted to Gasparri's advice. In 1911 he was in the papal party that attended the coronation of George V in London.

Pacelli slowly matured under experienced Vatican diplomats and several popes. His career began when Leo XIII was pope and continued under the papacy of Pope St. Pius X and Benedict XV (1914–1922). On June 24, 1914, Pacelli as secretary of the Congregation for Extraordinary Affairs, established a concordat with Serbia. On the 28th, in Sarajevo, the archduke was assassinated. Cardinal Merry del Val had said it was too late in the year for war, but Pius X, who had only a few months to live, cautioned against over-optimism. *Ecco la scintilla*, said the saintly pope. Sarajevo was indeed the spark that would set off one of the bloodiest wars in history. Pius X died that August.

Cardinal Della Chiesa had served in the Vatican diplomatic service but was appointed archbishop of Bologna by Pius X in 1907. Pius named him a cardinal in 1914, just in time, as it happened, for the conclave in which Della Chiesa was elected and took the name Benedict XV.

After 1917 Monsignor Pacelli began to teach in the Pontifical Academy of Noble Ecclesiastics, where future diplomats were trained. It had been founded by Clement XI, when nobles were picked as diplomats, but over time it had opened its doors more widely to those "from distinguished families in comfortable circumstances." The academic course included: ecclesiastical diplomacy, political economy, diplomatic forms, languages. Don Pacelli taught diplomatic form (*stile diplomatico*), and he was considered an effective teacher. His mentor was Cardinal Rampolla who was succeeded as secretary of state by Cardinal Merry del Val, when Pius X assumed the Throne of St. Peter. Pius X gave his expression to the mission of the Vatican diplomatic service.

> Whoever judges things dispassionately will realize that the Sovereign Pontiff cannot separate politics from the Magisterium that he exercises in faith and morals. Moreover, because he is the chief and director of what is a perfect society, the Church, that is to say, the Pope, must be willing to enter into a relation with the rulers of states and the governors of republics, for lacking such a relation, he would not be in a position to assure Catholics everywhere and in all places security and freedom. [Pope St. Pius X, November 9, 1903]

Cardinal Merry del Val, when asked what the principles of Vatican diplomacy were answered, "The New Testament." Pacelli served under Merry del Val and at the same time continued to work with Cardinal

Gasparri on the codification of canon law. Moreover, he devoted himself to the care of souls for several hours each day, hearing confessions and teaching sacred doctrine at the Chiesa Nuova and elsewhere. It was as if he resisted having his life too narrowly circumscribed by his bureaucratic tasks.

When Benedict XV was elected in 1914, he made Cardinal Gasparri his secretary of state, a post he would hold until 1929. Monsignor Pacelli was named undersecretary of state, a post he held during the horrendous days of World War I. Pacelli witnessed the fate of Benedict XV's efforts to restore peace. The Vatican was, of course, neutral in the conflict, and this led to suspicion on both sides, each of whom thought the pope favored the other. In France, Leon Bloy, godfather of Jacques and Raissa Maritain, called him Judas XV, while Charles Maurras of Action Française supported the papal peacemaking efforts. In Germany, Ludendorff was dismissive of Benedict's efforts, but then so was Clemenceau in France. Benedict XV's peace plan was distorted as it was reported and dismissed as in every way unfavorable to France. The French wanted the pope to take their side and condemn German bombing of churches and the burning of the cathedral of Saint-Quentin. How could the pope preserve neutrality in the face of such sacrileges?

Much of the diplomatic work of the Vatican must have seemed equally unproductive. The Church enters into pacts and concordats with civil states in the interest of Catholics in those states. Eugenio Pacelli was to negotiate many such concordats in the future, but perhaps he never forgot the adage, *Historia concordatorum, historia dolorum* (the history of concordats is a story of sorrows). Often the Church has sacrificed privileges, property, jurisdiction, in the interests of the salvation of men's souls. Pius XI said in 1929 that "he would negotiate with the devil himself if the good of souls demanded it."

The long apprenticeship Monsignor Pacelli had served in the Vatican can be seen as preparation for the heavy task that was now given him. His family now lived at 19 via Boezio, near the Piazza Cavour, and there his father died on November 20, 1916. On April 20, 1917, Pope Benedict appointed Monsignor Pacelli nuncio to Bavaria. Thus he became a wartime ecclesiastical diplomat. At the same time he was named titular archbishop of Sardes and was consecrated by Pope Benedict XV in the Sistine Chapel, with his family in attendance. He was forty-one years old. The pope of World War I had thus raised to the episcopacy and assigned the daunting task of representing the Church in ravaged Germany to the man who would be the pope of World War II.

The Secret of Fatima

On the very day that Eugenio Pacelli was made an archbishop three children in Fatima, Portugal, had the first in a series of apparitions of the Blessed Virgin Mary. She told them many things that were unintelligible to them, but that was because she intended for them to pass the message on. What would three illiterate country children make of the claim that there would be a revolution in Russia when the present war was over and, unless men repented of their sins and turned to God, another and worse war would fall upon the world? Did they even know what or where Russia is? Were they aware that the world was then at war? The answer to both questions is likely no. But they understood the plea for prayer and penance.

On June 26, 2000, Cardinal Ratzinger, prefect of the Congregation for the Doctrine of the Faith, released what had for decades been known as the "secret of Fatima." This was the conclusion of the account the only surviving seer, Sister Maria Lucia, had written of what the Blessed Virgin had revealed to her and the two other children in 1917. The first two parts of the secret had been made known; only the third had been held back. The first part tells of the glimpse of hell they were given.

> Our Lady showed us a great sea of fire, which seemed to be under the earth. Plunged in this fire were demons and souls in human form, like transparent burning embers, all blackened or burnished bronze, floating about in the conflagration, now raised into the air by the flames that issued from within themselves together with great clouds of smoke, now falling back on every side like sparks in a huge fire, without weight or equilibrium, and amid shrieks and groans of pain and despair, which horrified us and made us tremble with fear. The demons could be distinguished by their terrifying and repulsive likeness to frightful and unknown animals, all black and transparent. This vision lasted but an instant. How can we ever be grateful enough to our kind heavenly Mother, who had already prepared us by promising, in the First Apparition, to take us to heaven? Otherwise, I think we would have died of fear and terror.

The second part was this:

> We then looked at Our Lady, who said to us so kindly and so sadly: "You have seen hell where the souls of poor sinners go. To save them, God wishes to establish in the world devotion to my Immaculate Heart. If what I say to you is done, many souls will be saved and there will be peace. The war is going to end: but if peo-

ple do not cease offending God, a worse one will break out during
the Pontificate of Pius XI. When you see a night illumined by an
unknown light, know that this is the great sign given you by God
that he is about to punish the world for its crimes, by means of war,
famine, and persecutions of the Church and of the Holy Father. To
prevent this, I shall come to ask for the consecration of Russia to
my Immaculate Heart, and the Communion of reparation on the
First Saturdays. If my requests are heeded, Russia will be converted, and there will be peace; if not, she will spread her errors
throughout the world, causing wars and persecutions of the
Church. The good will be martyred; the Holy Father will have
much to suffer; various nations will be annihilated. In the end my
Immaculate Heart will triumph. The Holy Father will consecrate
Russia to me, and she will be converted, and a period of peace will
be granted to the world.

Devotion to Our Lady of Fatima spread throughout the world. The faithful followed Mary's express wish that they attend mass and receive
communion on the first Saturday of five consecutive months. Penance
and prayer, particularly the rosary, was the message for the world. But
interest in what had not yet been told of the account Sister Maria Lucia
had written mounted, and there was much speculation over what it contained. The second part of the secret predicted World War II, spoke of
the persecution of the Church, and twice spoke of the Holy Father, who
would be persecuted and suffer much. Pope Paul VI visited Fatima, but
it was not until Pope John Paul II that the consecration was made, on
March 25, 1984.

On May 13, 1981, there was an assassination attempt on the life of
John Paul II in St. Peter's Square. The pope attributed the failure of the
attempt to "a mother's hand that guided the bullet's path." The bullet
that might have taken his life has been set in the crown of Our Lady of
Fatima. What was in the long-awaited third part of the secret?

After the first two parts which I have already explained, at the left
of Our Lady and a little above, we saw an Angel with a flaming
sword in his left hand; flashing, it gave out flames that looked as
though they would set the world on fire; but they died out in contact with the splendor that Our Lady radiated toward him from her
right hand: pointing to the earth with his right hand, the Angel
cried out in a loud voice: "Penance, Penance, Penance!" And we
saw in an immense light that is God, "something similar to how
people appear in a mirror when they pass in front of it," a Bishop
dressed in White "we had the impression that it was the Holy

Father." Other Bishops, Priests, men and women Religious going up a steep mountain, at the top of which there was a big Cross of rough-hewn trunks as of a cork-tree with the bark; before reaching there the Holy Father passed through a big city half in ruins and half trembling with halting step, afflicted with pain and sorrow, he prayed for the souls of the corpses he met on his way; having reached the top of the mountain, on his knees at the foot of the big Cross, he was killed by a group of soldiers who fired bullets and arrows at him, and in the same way there died one after another the other Bishops, Priests, men and women Religious, and various lay people of different ranks and positions. Beneath the two arms of the Cross there were two Angels each with a crystal aspersorium in his hand, in which they gathered up the blood of the Martyrs and with it sprinkled the souls that were making their way to God.[1]

If the third part did not refer to the failed attempt on Pope John Paul II, then worse things are in store. Of course all this lay in the distant future. But popes did not need to wait until the end of the Second Millennium, or the Third, to be sorely tested.

Mission to Munich

Archbishop Pacelli left at once, going by way of Switzerland, with a stop at the monastery at Einsiedeln. He arrived in Munich on May 24, 1918, and on the 28th presented his credentials to King Louis III of Wittelsbach. At the time, Munich, located in the most Catholic part of the country, was the only permanent diplomatic post the Holy See had in Germany.

The Munich Archbishop Pacelli came to in 1917 had a population of 170,000 citizens and a university that was then the third largest in Germany. The see was called Munich-Friesing and was formed in 716 by Saint Corbinian. Friesing, during its long history, had known war and schism. When the papal nunciature was established in Munich in 1786, the Congress of Ems had been called to deal with the schism. A concordat between Pius VII and King Max Joseph in 1817 brought about some measure of peace and tranquility. Dioceses were dissolved, among them Friesing, and the Archdiocese of Munich-Friesing established. The situation was chaotic when Archbishop Pacelli arrived. No wonder. World War I was in its third year. Poverty and want, spawned by war, were everywhere, and a disposition toward socialism and communism began to emerge, in Germany generally, but particularly in Munich. In Germany as a whole, there were some 40,000 apostasies a year as opposed to 8,762 converts. When losses due to mixed marriage were added in, there was an annual loss to the Church of some 70,000 souls in Germany. Munich was harder hit than other areas.

One of Archbishop Pacelli's first tasks was to present to Kaiser Wilhelm Benedict XV's proposals for peace. He managed to meet with the chancellor, but it took some weeks to secure a meeting with the Kaiser at Kreuznach. The pope's peace proposals have been summarized (by Charles Hugh Doyle) as follows:

1. Replacement of material forces by moral forces of right.
2. Disarmament.
3. Settling of international disputes by arbitration.
4. True freedom and community of the seas guaranteed.
5. Mutual renunciation of indemnities.
6. Evacuation and restoration of all occupied territories.
7. An examination of rival territorial claims, taking into consideration the wishes of the populations.

The conversation was in French, though Pacelli spoke German. Would the Kaiser sue for peace on these terms? He had to consult his government, and a new chancellor accused the Vatican of working for the enemy. The British had informed the Vatican that they would enter into peace negotiations if Germany withdrew from Belgium.

The following day, June 30, Archbishop Pacelli was back in Munich to meet with Charles I, Emperor of Austria. After this flurry of interviews, the waiting began. On September 22, Germany rejected the pope's peace plan. This may have been Eugenio Pacelli's first failure, and it was made all the more bitter because it meant that the mutual slaughter of the armies would continue. Much has been written of the machinations of the two parties. A complication of the discussions arose from the fact that Germany was not a unified state; moreover, political changes were occurring in each of the so-called Central Powers. It was a volatile situation, fueled by nationalism. Papal intervention was welcome only insofar as it could further the military ends of the parties. The pope sought to transfer the discussion to the level of morality and justice. None of the Allies had a representative at the Holy See, and they found it imaginable that the Central Powers would manipulate the Vatican for their own purposes. In the Vatican, at that time, no one thought the Allies would win the war so that the concessions the pope got from Germany – withdrawal from Belgium for example – must have seemed something the Allies could not have achieved militarily.

The Victims of War

Archbishop Pacelli thus failed at his first diplomatic task, although through no fault of his own. Among the lessons he learned from this defeat was the duplicity of some statesmen. Rendering his efforts otiose was the fact that on April 26, 1915, France, Russia, and Great Britain had signed the Secret Treaty of London, which included the following article: "To support such opposition as Italy may make at any proposal in the direction of introducing representatives of the Holy See in any peace negotiations or regulations for the settlement of questions raised by the present war." [article 15] Nor was President Wilson any more receptive to the idea of Vatican help in achieving peace. Countries at war might seek to use the Vatican to achieve their own ends, but they are angered by a Christian judgment on their actions. Archbishop Pacelli had entered a hard school that would prepare him for his own papacy in World War II. After his failure, he spent several months with the Sisters of the Holy Cross at Rorschach in Switzerland.

Thwarted in the effort to bring about peace, the papal nuncio turned his attention in the final months of the war to alleviating the lot of the people. It became his habit to visit prisoners of war, hearing their stories, receiving their petitions, writing letters to their loved ones. From 1914, the Holy See had run a provisory office to gather information concerning prisoners of war. The intervention of the pope was solicited by families of prisoners. After Italy's entry into the war in May 1915, the manner of running the office changed, and heavy reliance was placed on French and German bishops. The pope added to Pacelli's diplomatic duties that of dealing with prisoners. He heard confessions and administered the sacraments to prisoners. And he preached. The pope had urged him to preach peace everywhere, and he did. He distributed packages to prisoners from the Holy Father. At Ingolstadt, in upper Bavaria, in the summer of 1917, he visited a camp where there were ten thousand prisoners of different nationalities. He spoke forcefully but with emotion in French and English, treating guards and prisoners alike. He visited camps at Halle, Celle, Ellwangen, Lechfeld, Minden, Münster, and Ratisbonne. A French prelate, Bishop Fontenelle, said of him that he acquitted his duty in so conscientious a manner that the saving of a great number of human lives was due to him.

Nor was he spared personal suffering: his mother died in 1918. The episcopal ring he wore had been fashioned from jewels his mother had worn at her wedding. He never wore another ring.

In Germany, he attended congresses, meetings of various sorts, the opening of churches, first communions, confirmations, and funerals.

The people began to consider him one of their own bishops, but socialism was already abroad in the land. In March 1917, the Russian Revolution broke out, and there were strikes and agitation in Germany. With the loss of the war, chaos settled over Germany. A republic was declared on November 8, 1918, and Kurt Eisener, a learned Jew, was named president of the socialist government. The Bavarian royal family fled.

Chaos in Germany

With the collapse of the papal effort to bring about a peace, the centrifugal movement of the Central Powers had increased, hardship and soon hunger approaching famine spread through the working classes, strikes were called, political chaos loomed. In the spring of 1917, 125,000 workers in munitions plants called a work halt. More than a year of war remained. The dominance of Prussia made the coming chaos seem inevitable. The malign spirit of Bismarck continued to take its vengeance.

In the face of threatened inner upheaval, the emperor was persuaded to introduce universal suffrage to assuage the almost universal suffering. Hindenburg and Ludendorff launched a desperate offensive on May 27, 1918, and broke through to the Marne. But in two days Foch had thrown them back. The emperor lost all confidence in victory. Austria withdrew from the alliance in September. On November 8, at Compiegne, in the railway car would exercise a seething fascination in the imagination of Adolf Hitler, peace terms were agreed to. The Kaiser, having fled to Holland, abdicated officially on November 9, and the Crown Prince renounced the throne. A socialist became chancellor of the newly proclaimed republic. The new government signed the armistice terms. Judging these socialists insufficiently radical, the Spartakus group, inspired by the Russian Revolution, fought insurrectionist battles in Berlin. Ebert, the socialist chancellor, spoke to Hindenburg, and the insurrection was put down and Rosa Luxemburg, one of the main instigators, killed.

Attack on the Nuncio

These were not simply matters known to the papal nuncio; they invaded his own residence. In Munich, Bolshevist flags began to appear in April of 1919. Civil war threatened, and the diplomatic corps was rattled. During these dark days, hearing of a section of the city where starvation threatened, the papal nuncio gathered up the rice supplies of the nunciature and personally took them to those who were dying of hunger. Armed men burst into the nunciature, and Pacelli was threatened with a revolver and ordered to turn over all money, provisions, and, above all, his car to the rebels. Captain Luca from the Italian legation arrived and took up his stance beside the archbishop. The silent resistance of the papal nuncio sufficed to defeat the invaders. The following day, the commander of the Red Guard threatened to come himself to execute thirteen hostages, claiming his soldiers had been fired upon from the nunciature.

The papal nuncio moved from Munich to Berlin with the declaration of the republic and presented his credentials on June 30, 1920, to Friedrich Ebert, the socialist chief of state of the new government. He became even more familiar with the centers of spirituality in Germany, among them the Abbey of Beuron, where later Edith Stein would spend her Holy Weeks. Despite his love for the Benedictines, he had a Jesuit confessor. And he came to know Augustin Bea, whom he

In Munich, Cardinal Michael Faulhaber, rose courageously to the defense of his city, and came to be called the Iron Bishop. Just as he opposed the Reds in the wake of World War I, so he would oppose the Nazis in 1933, delivering a lecture on "Judaism, Christianism, Germanism," throwing down a Christian gauntlet to the then-triumphant National Socialists. He counseled against fascination with uniforms and the military. In retaliation, his residence was broken into and pillaged.

would later put in charge of a revised Latin translation of the Psalms, having called him to Rome to act as his spiritual adviser. Bea would become a cardinal and play a crucial role in Vatican II.

A general concordat with Germany being unrealistic, Pacelli now devoted himself to concluding particular concordats: Bavaria, 1926; Prussia, 1929. Both in Prussia and Saxony, his efforts saved religious freedom from a tendency toward a state religion. There were fourteen concordats in 1914; by 1922 there were twenty-seven of them. Testimonials to his diplomatic skills are many.

The Weimar Republic

In the chaotic Germany of the 1920s Pacelli saw vast possibilities for regeneration. Freedom was under assault from left and right. Only from Rome could salvation come, Pacelli thought, and the Catholic inspiration must determine Germany's direction. Hence his tireless presence at meetings of German Catholics, at the general assembly of bishops at Fulda – which would be heard from again and again during the dark days of the Nazis – at commemorations of saints. He visited monasteries, hospitals, colleges, schools, factories. In the Ruhr Valley he visited the industrial cities and was photographed in the outfit of a miner after his descent into a mine to see for himself the conditions there.

Eugenio Pacelli was papal nuncio in Germany for twelve years, from 1917 until the end of 1929, when he was recalled to Rome. During that period he had seen the limits of diplomatic efforts when nationalist passion guides thinking; he had seen the rise of new political forces out of the mistakes of previous regimes; he watched the new regime flounder as it sought solutions to the social and economic problems that weighed upon the country. To the East was the looming presence of Soviet Russia, to the West were the republics and democracies Germany was trying to emulate. Everything was in the balance. At the time he was recalled, the Depression was about to be added to the mixture of factors which agitated Germany and were to bring down the Weimar Republic. It is in this light that the tireless efforts of the papal nuncio to stir the Catholic population to a deeper sense of the Church's vision for the world, for social justice, for natural justice, animated the sense that we are all creatures of God. He knew the clergy and bishops well and had found a man of great character and strength in Cardinal Faulhaber. His personal household for the rest of his life would reflect this long stay in Germany. Sister Pascalina Josephine Lehnert entered his service already in Munich, sent by her religious superior. She would remain with him until his death. His spiritual advisors, his confessors, were drawn from people he had met while he was papal nuncio.

Was he any more worried about the specter of the Nazi Party than were German Jews? The party's percentage of the vote would not reach a significant level until a year after Archbishop Pacelli left the country. The Nazi Party was a small and insignificant factor during the time Archbishop Pacelli served as papal nuncio to Germany. Not much more significant than the Zionist party. German Jews were not at the time much interested in or concerned by either of them.

3

Secretary of State

The View from the Vatican

The decade from 1929 to 1939 is one in which Eugenio Pacelli is the right-hand man of Pius XI. But from the time of his ordination, his life had been defined by the papacy – indirectly at first as he moved through the various stages of the Vatican bureaucracy, more directly when Benedict was elected, made him archbishop, and sent him off as papal nuncio to Germany, a post he would hold for twelve years. During that assignment, Benedict died and Pius XI succeeded him. The new pope, an archivist and scholar, was impressed by the precision and elegance of Pacelli's reports and by the depth of analysis. It seems almost inevitable that, when Cardinal Gasparri retired, Pius XI would call Archbishop Pacelli home, create him cardinal, and name him his secretary of state. Much of the diplomatic concern of the Church during the coming decade would be the rise of forces inimical to the Church – communism, which was consolidating itself in Russia and proving to be contagious elsewhere, and, closer to home, fascism – first, that of Mussolini and then the dark figure of Adolf Hitler. More than ever before, Pacelli was a pastor among wolves, a diplomat among barbarians.

Pius X was the only pope canonized since the eighteenth century. Historians find him a bland figure compared with Pius IX and Leo XIII and find his concerns with heterodoxy and modernism quaint. As it happens, those concerns are continuous with the concerns of his two predecessors. If his papacy can seem a kind of interval between the Franco-Prussian War and World War I, his concerns went to the heart of the ideologies which would soon alter the map of Europe. Like his predecessors he saw the dark side of the principles that have, in their happy expression, led to the republics of Europe and the United States. The popes had been chary of those principles when they were first advanced, and indeed their first implementations included as much savagery as spirit. The excesses of the French Revolution are drowned out by the singing of the Marseillaise, but the popes were daily reminded of what the Resorgimento had done all around them. Others might think that mankind had turned a corner of history and was now to advance from height to height, leaving ever farther behind the dark days of popes and kings. But Leo XIII saw darker possibilities ahead and warned against them. A world in which man forgets he is a creature becomes a world in which man cannot survive.

Pius X saw the inroads that the secular spirit had made in the Church itself. His papacy may be seen as a providential pause during which self-examination was possible and discernment as to what strange baggage believers may have picked up from a world essentially hostile to the faith. Pius X reigned for a mere eleven years (1903–1914). Thus he was the pope of Pacelli's first years working in the foreign office of the Vatican. In France, the government began an anti-religious offensive. The Law of Separation annulled the concordat that had been reached with Napoleon, Church property was seized, its revenue stopped. Catholics had been treated worse during the Revolution, perhaps, and the laity was allowed to hold property titles in the name of cultural associations. The government's attempt to laicize the Church could hardly be accepted by the pope. His encyclical denouncing it appeared in 1906. Diplomatic relations were broken and were not reestablished until 1921.

The government turned the property titles over to local government, and priests were permitted their use. The French bishops found causes for optimism in what the government had done, however unjust. In the long run, the Church might better flourish in total independence of the state. The loss of the papal states had grieved Pius IX and made his successors prisoners of the Vatican, but in the long run, good had come out of evil, and the pope was stronger when he no longer had the concerns of a temporal ruler. In modernism the pope saw, among other things, the danger of privatizing religious faith, reducing it to a subjective experience, with a consequent disparagement of doctrine and tradition. Such a faith would evaporate, swiftly or slowly. In any case, it was not the faith of a people but of autonomous individuals. By keeping the springs of doctrine clear, Pius X made the work of his successors less onerous.

Benedict XV reigned for eight years, from 1914 to 1922. His efforts to bring about peace between the two groups slaughtering one another in increasingly savage ways were distrusted. The Allies were made up of Orthodox Russia, Anglican Britain, and a France officially antireligious. The Central Powers consisted of a Germany half-Protestant and half-Catholic, Catholic Austria-Hungary, and eventually Italy. So described, it might seem obvious to the superficial eye that the pope had a side. The pope was rigidly neutral, his peace plan dismissed since neither side had any real interest in a conclusion of the war short of victory. With the entry of the United States into the war in 1917, the tide was turned and an armistice forced. The pope was excluded from the peace treaty – it was to emerge that this exclusion was one of Italy's conditions for entering the war – and he came to regard the Treaty of Versailles as a continuation of the war and a "consecration of hatred."

Achille Ratti, a learned man, scholar, and paleographer, once prefect of the Biblioteca Ambrosiana and later of the Vatican Library, because of his linguistic skills was sent to Poland as nuncio where in August 1920 he stayed at his post in Warsaw despite the threat of a Bolshevist attack. Two armies, one led by Stalin, the other by Trotsky, fought their way to the edge of the city before they were beaten back. The diplomatic corps fled, but Achille Ratti stayed at his post. Anyone who imagines that the future Pius XI's concern with atheistic communism was only an abstract theological opposition, would do well to remember those days when as papal nuncio he was in imminent danger of capture by the Red armies. When he was elected pope in 1922, he had first-hand experience of the kind Eugenio Pacelli was experiencing, and would continue to experience, in Germany. It is no mystery why these two men should deplore equally the totalitarianisms that sprang up in the wake of World War I. It is sometimes said that Pius XI was terrified of bolshevism. Given his personal courage in Poland, "terrified" does not seem the right verb. What Pius XI and Cardinal Pacelli saw in communism was an ideology that was in direct conflict with natural law as well as with the Catholic faith. This was the same judgment they made of national socialism. Their concern was the effect of such doctrines on human society. In both cases their fears were tragically realized. Those who find the papal concern with communism excessive, almost amusing, must close their eyes to the inhuman wasteland communism has made of half the world. With Cardinal Pacelli at his side, Pius XI began the difficult task of leading the Church in what has been called the Age of the Dictators.

This is largely the story of what Eugenio Pacelli did.

The Right Arm of Pius XI

Eugenio Pacelli was made a cardinal by Pius XI on December 16, 1929, and less than two months later was named secretary of state to replace Cardinal Gasparri who had retired. For almost exactly ten years, Cardinal Pacelli would be at the side of Pius XI as the pope maneuvered through the dangerous waters which would ultimately bring about the shipwreck of World War II.

A humanism in which man is the measure is a humanism in which man is the eventual victim. Hence the establishment of the feast of Christ the King in 1925. So too the spate of eucharistic congresses around the world, emphasizing Christ's continuing sacramental presence among us. Pius XI issued encyclicals on education (December 31, 1929) and on Christian Marriage (*Casti Connubii*) in December of

1930. *Quadragesimo anno* appeared in May of 1931 on the fortieth anniversary of Leo XIII's social encyclical.

No one can understand the actions of a pope unless he understands that pope's teaching. Efforts to interpret Vatican policy as instances of *realpolitik* must misinterpret it. Pius XI and his secretary of state acted on the basis of the Church's vision of man's ultimate vocation and its implications for what he does in this world. Pius XI was underscoring our creaturely condition: God has made us for himself, and it is folly to imagine that our hearts can be filled by the things of this world. It is only when created goods are sought in the light of the creator of them who is Goodness itself that human beings can become what they ought to be.

The secular society in which the Church must act and believers live had come to disdain those simple truths and substitute their opposites as principles of economics and politics. The pope relentlessly taught the truth and pointed out the errors of the day. He canonized John Fisher and Thomas More to elevate them as models of men who put justice and the faith above expediency. Pius XI was warning the faithful that similar stark choices might be asked of them. John Fisher and

First there was a doctrinal opposition to secularism. His first encyclical called for Catholic Action, that is, urged the laity to bring to bear on their various walks of life the saving truths of Christian revelation. Significantly for what lay ahead, he insisted that the Church's mission involves protecting and interpreting the natural law as well as defending and interpreting the deposit of faith. There is a common human morality, and in calling attention to its demands, the pope speaks to all men, not simply members of the Catholic Church. But the laity must share in these concerns, having the added motivation of Christian love in seeking justice and respect for human dignity. It is noteworthy that in the era when human beings considered themselves most liberated that the Church speaks increasingly of the dignity of the person. Pius XII's motto was "Christ's Peace in Christ's Kingdom." And peace entails recognizing the value of every human life. If only in retrospect, others would wonder that the Enlightenment Experiment, with its stirring cry of Liberty, Equality, Fraternity, should end in the bloodiest wars of human history, in a growing disdain for the value of human life, to a systematic dismantling of the infrastructure of culture and society. Examples range from George Steiner's In Bluebeard's Castle *to Alasdair MacIntyre's* Three Rival Versions of Moral Enquiry *to a recognition as well of the prescience of the popes by Lezsek Kolakowski in* Modernity on Endless Trial.

Thomas More had died as witnesses to the truth; all the other English bishops apostatized. During his long imprisonment, More refused to say one way or another whether he thought Henry VIII's marriage to the widow of his brother was valid. This silence was the legal protection he could afford his family and himself. But his silence was heard all over England.

Dealing with the Nazis

This is the background against which the diplomatic efforts of Pius XI's secretary of state must be seen. Agreements of various sorts were entered into with some twenty states to insure the rights of the faithful. The bitterness of the Law of Separation, passed by an anti-clerical government, was lessened by the settling of some of the tragic effects of that law. Relations between the Church and her "eldest daughter" were thereby improved.

Closer to home was the historic signing of the Lateran Accords, which involved recognition of the Italian state with Rome as its capitol in return for recognition of the four acres of Vatican City as a sovereign state and compensation for the confiscation of the papal states. Popes had not shown themselves in public since 1870. Now, in 1929, after the signing of the accords, Pius XI appeared above the Square of St. Peter and gave his pontifical blessing *urbi et orbi*, to the city and to the world, and one dark era was over. But the Italian head of state with whom the agreement was reached was Benito Mussolini, who had come to power in 1922. Mussolini symbolized the world in which the Church now found herself.

Totalitarianism might have the look of *opera bouffe* in Italy, but this was deceptive. There was no doubt about the regime that had established itself in Russia at the end of World War I. Christians were being persecuted in Russia. *Divini Redemptoris* in March 1937 condemned atheistic communism. The open rejection of God and the supremacy of man, if only in the mass, was overt and unequivocal in Communist ideology. Earlier, in 1933, the Church had signed a concordat with a Germany now under the leadership of Adolf Hitler. This undoubtedly had the effect of lending prestige to Hitler's gangster government and was almost immediately and then repeatedly violated by the dictator. Over thirty-four notes of protest over the course of some three years led to the condemnation of national socialism in 1937 in an encyclical written in German, *Mit brennender Sorge (With burning anxiety)*. Appearing within days of one another, the condemnation of atheistic communism and national socialism put the Church athwart the path of ideologies that considered themselves the voice of modern man.

As a million Jews were banished from public life, persecuted, spoliated, humiliated and their synagogues burned, not a single diplomatic step was taken, not one official protest was lodged, by any of the European States or by the League of Nations. As the moral abyss between Hitlerism and the civilized nations widened, no government stood up for human rights or common decency – none but one. (Lapide, p. 98)

That single exception was, of course, Pius XI. He governed four acres and had a Swiss guard bearing halbardiers and wearing uniforms designed by Michelangelo, but the pope spoke as God's deputy. He and his secretary of state had a clear understanding of what was taking place and cried out the news to the world. "If there is in Christianity the idea of a mystery of blood, it is that, not of race opposed to other races, but of the unity of all men in the heritage of sin, derived from our first father." (Christmas, 1930)

In all, there were eight encyclicals condemning the philosophy of the totalitarians. Non abbiamo bisgno *(July 5, 1931) was directed against Italian fascism.* Acerba animi *(September, 1932) condemned the Mexican persecution.* Dilectissima nobis *(June 3, 1933) condemned the persecution of the Church by the Spanish republic.* Ardenti cura *(March 4, 1937) pointed out that the teaching and practices of national socialism were un-Christian.* Mit brennender Sorge *(March 14, 1937) expanded this condemnation of national socialism, and five days later Divini Redemptoris condemned atheistic communism.* Nos es muy conocida *(March 28, 1937) returned to the troubles in Mexico. Finally, the encyclical on the rosary as the only remedy to war and to the suffering brought on by totalitarianism,* Ingravescentibus meis, *appeared in September of 1937.*

The pope's was a lone voice against these horrors, including the particular savagery of Nazi Germany.

The following month (January, 1931) Cardinal Bertram of Breslau made sure the German people got the message. "In accordance with the open appeal of the Holy Father, the episcopate must speak up against the errors deriving from the false nationalism which recently has been propagated in all regions of our fatherland. It is a grave error to glorify one race and to despise divine revelation and God's own commandments. We Catholic Christians have no race religion."

The Wider world

Nor was this opposition confined to the old continent. In far-off Mexico, the Church was being persecuted, priests hounded and executed. A country whose citizenry was almost entirely Catholic was in the grips of a vicious anticlerical government, and the blood of martyrs flowed. Graham Greene's novel *The Labyrinthine Ways* and travel book *The Lawless Roads* (1939) described the scene.

> This was Tabasco – Garrido Canabal's isolated swampy puritanical state. Garrido – so it was said – had destroyed every church; he had organized a militia of Red Shirts, even leading them across the border into Chiapas in his hunt for a church or a priest. Private houses were searched for religious emblems, and prison was the penalty for possessing them. A young man I met in Mexico City – a family friend of Garrido's – was imprisoned three days for wearing a cross under his shirt; the dictator was incorruptible. A journalist on his way to photograph Tabasco was shot dead in Mexico City airport before he took his seat. Every priest was hunted down or shot, except one who existed for ten years in the forests and swamps, venturing out only at night; his few letters, I was told, recorded an awful sense of impotence – to live in constant danger and yet be able to do so little, it hardly seemed worth the horror.

This passage from *Lawless Roads* gives the seed, Green tells us, of his novel *The Power and the Glory*. The persecution of the Church, particularly of her priests, had become a global phenomenon, nor was it to be restricted to lowly clerics. Bishops and archbishops and cardinals would fall into the totalitarian net. And the Bishop of Rome, not for the first time, would be threatened by the forces of evil. The time was coming when the thought expressed in the passage of Newman that Graham Greene set at the beginning of *The Lawless Roads* would occur to many. Cardinal Newman had described the way of the world,

> . . . the defeat of good, the success of evil, physical pain, mental anguish, the prevalence and intensity of sin, the pervading idolatries, the corruptions, the dreary hopeless irreligion, that condition of the whole race, so fearfully yet exactly described in the Apostle's words, "having no hope, and without God in the world' – all this is vision to dizzy and appall.

The passage rises to this final and fundamental either/or:

> What shall be said to this heart-piercing, reason-bewildering fact? I can only answer, that either there is no Creator, or this living society of men is in a true sense discarded from His presence. . . .

if there be a God, *since* there is a God, the human race is impli-
cated in some terrible aboriginal calamity.

Belloc had said that Europe is the faith, and the faith is Europe.
True perhaps as a historical remark, but the mission of the Church is
global; no one is excluded from the Good News of which she is the messenger. Pius XI, with the troubles of Europe pressing on the gates of the
miniature city-state in which he dwelt, was mindful of the great globe
itself. Hence the judgment on events in Mexico. Hence too his concern
with missionary activities. He canonized Saint Theresa of Lisieux, the
Little Flower, a patroness of sorts of missionaries. And, lest the extended Church seek to Europeonize the mission countries, he consecrated
Chinese and Japanese bishops. The great Jesuit university in Rome, the
Gregorianum, had a faculty of
missionary theology. All human
persons belong to a single species, one race, one human kind.
Christ came to save them all. The
care of souls went on despite the
increasing clamor of political and
military events.

*The eloquent and incessant condem-
nation of the forces that were threatening the world was linked with such
personal gestures as the pope's cordial
reception of the chief rabbi of Milan in
the Vatican on November 19, 1931.
Chief Rabbi DeFano was 82, and the
pope congratulated him on his good
health. The pope had known DeFano
when he was prefect of the Biblioteca
Ambrosiana in Milan, where they had
discussed Hebrew manuscripts.
DeFano thanked the Holy Father for
his appeals against religious persecution. This meeting was reported to
Berlin by the German ambassador to
the Holy See.*

The Concordat with Germany

"The history of concordats is a
history of sorrow," runs the
adage. Shortly after the signing
of the Lateran Treaty, Mussolini
was telling the Italian Chamber
of Deputies that Christianity may
have been born in Palestine, but
it only became Catholic in Rome,
and if it had remained in Palestine would have disappeared without a
trace, like the Essenes. Whereupon he closed down Catholic youth
clubs, organized assaults on the Church, had Church banners destroyed
and priests harried. *Non abbiamo bisogno* was in response to such outrages. Mussolini vacillated in his attitude toward Jews, and his policy
only hardened when Nazi pressure was put upon him. But the situation
in Germany was clear from the beginning.

In Germany, there were heroic figures, but there was weakness and
confusion as well. The bishops of Bavaria on February 12, 1933, pointing out that national socialism, having put race before religion and hav-

ing rejected the Old Testament, even the Mosaic Law, "has taken up a position of the *Kulturkampf* irreconcilable with Catholic teaching." Nazi uniforms and flags were prohibited at divine service. When at Fulda in March this injunction was rescinded, Cardinal Pacelli was furious. On July 20, 1933, a concordat with Nazi Germany was concluded.

It will seem surprising that the Church would enter into an agreement with a regime based on principles it had roundly condemned again and again, thereby lending prestige to Hitler and his government. Of course the concordat was no endorsement of the regime. It was concluded in order to secure human and religious rights in Germany. As has been pointed out, the hope with which the Vatican entered into the agreement was dashed again and again, resulting in those thirty-four notes of protest in the course of some three years.

Pinchas Lapide, putting the concordat in the historical context, observes that in the previous month a Four Power Pact, involving Germany, France, England, and Italy, had been initialed, and it was signed five days before the concordat was reached. Cardinal Pacelli, who had negotiated the concordat, said this to Mr. Kirkpatrick of the British Legation in Rome on August 11, "I had to choose between an agreement on these lines and the virtual elimination of the Catholic Church in the Reich." Throughout the negotiations, Hitler had showed his muscle by arresting ninety-two priests, ransacking sixteen Catholic youth clubs, and closing down nine Catholic publications. Kirkpatrick was struck by the absence of any diplomatic neutrality toward Germany. Cardinal Pacelli deplored Hitler's actions at home, his persecution of the Jews, the reign of terror he had established over the nation. Why sign a concordat with such a gangster? If nothing else, it would be a basis for protesting violations of it which were sure to come.

And come they did. Five days after the ratification, the Nazi sterilization law was passed, a gross violation of the concordat. Five days later, Dr. Erich Klausener, leader of German Catholic Action, was murdered. Over the next four years, hundreds of Catholic priests were arrested, at least 127 were sent to concentration camps, over 200 Catholic organizations were suppressed. All Catholic parties and semi-political organizations were dissolved, Church property was confiscated. It had not been this bad even under Bismarck. By 1939, fifty-five papal notes of protest had been sent to Germany, most of them ignored.

In April of 1933, Edith Stein wrote to the pope asking for a specific encyclical on the Jewish Question. The future saint, martyr at Auschwitz, was concerned with "the indifference of Catholics to the growing vexations against Jews." That Catholics might be drawn into the racist beliefs of the Nazis was already a chief concern of the Church. Pointing out the un-Christian character of the Nazi philosophy was not meant to alter Adolf Hitler; this was directed to the faithful, lest they be confused. That many were is attested by Edith Stein's request. The reply would have to wait until *Mit brennender Sorge*. In the meantime, the Vatican and the German bishops fought the good fight, with rare exceptions. They, like Edith Stein, were caught in the police state Nazi Germany had become. It was for the sake of the Vatican and the German bishops that the concordat was concluded. Unlike the Four Power Pact, which declared the entente, collaboration, and solidarity of Germany, Britain, Italy, and France, the Vatican never wavered from the severity of its condemnation of the Nazi regime.

Cardinal Pacelli on Nazi Ideology

Speaking to 250,000 pilgrims at Lourdes on April 28, 1935, Cardinal Pacelli said, "These ideologues are in fact only miserable plagiarizers who dress up ancient errors in new tinsel. It matters little whether they rally round the flag of social revolution or are possessed by the superstition of race and blood." And in Paris, in Notre Dame, on July 13, 1937, expressing hope for peace, he referred to Germany as "that noble and powerful nation whom bad shepherds would lead astray into an idolatry of race."

In March, the encyclical that pulled out all the stops began, "With burning anxiety and with ever growing dismay we have watched the tribulations of the Catholic Church in Germany." The original had read "with great anxiety" (*Mit grosser Sorge*), but Cardinal Pacelli argued successfully for the more urgent "with burning anxiety" (*Mit brennender Sorge*). Copies were taken on March 12 to the papal nuncio in Berlin by special messenger, and the twelve-page encyclical was read out in all the Catholic churches in Germany on Palm Sunday, March 21, 1937.

The Nazi response was to attack "the Jew-God and his deputy in Rome."

Pius XI received Cardinal Faulhaber and two other German bishops a few days before the publication of *Mit brennender Sorge*, and they thanked him for the encyclical. "Thank *him*," he said, referring to Cardinal Pacelli. "He has done it all. From now on, he will handle everything." And what did the encyclical say?

> Whoever exalts race, or the people, or the State, or a particular
> form of State, or the depositories of Power, or any other funda-

> mental value of human community – however necessary and honorable be their function in worldly things – whoever raises these notions above their standard value and divinizes them to an idolatrous level, distorts and perverts an order of the world planned and created by God; he is far from the true faith in God and from the concept of life which that faith upholds. (n. 8)

National socialism is an idolatry, worship of a false god, a "new order" opposed to the natural created order.

> None but superficial minds could stumble into concepts of a national God, of a national religion; or attempt to lock within the frontiers of a single people, within the narrow limits of a single race, God, the creator of the universe, King and Legislator of all nations before whose immensity they are *as a drop of a bucket* (Isaiah 40,15) (n. 11)

Many observers of Nazi meetings and rallies had noticed the quasi-liturgical form they took. The encyclical warned against the secularizing of fundamental aspects of faith.

> The term "revelation" must not be debased to mean the suggestions of "race and blood, for the irradiations of a people's history." This is sheer equivocation. Faith is to hold as true what God has revealed, not in a confidence in the future of one's own people. "To substitute the one for the other and demand on the strength of this to be numbered among the faithful followers of Christ, is a senseless play on words, if it does not conceal a confusion of concepts or worse. (n. 23)

At the most fundamental level, national socialism is in conflict with common morality. "It is in the light of the commands of natural law, that all positive law, whoever be the lawgiver, can be gauged in its moral content and hence, in the authority it wields over conscience. Human laws in flagrant contradiction with the natural law are vitiated with a taint which no force, no power can mend." (n. 30) This makes the Third Reich illegitimate; its laws do not bind conscience, and its overthrow would be justifiable.

In retrospect, some have found statements of the Holy See wanting in rhetorical flair, as if some unused trope would have changed the course of history. No one misunderstood the encyclical at the time or the moral forcefulness and unequivocal clarity with which it made its points. The Germans were furious. *Voelkischer Beobachter* said that the German government "had to consider the Pope's encyclical as a call to battle . . . it calls upon Catholic citizens to rebel against the authority of the Reich." The Gestapo confiscated all the copies of the encyclical it could and closed down and expropriated twelve shops for having printed it. An intemperate note of protest was presented by the German ambassador. Joseph Goebbels's propaganda machine had earlier made the only inference that could explain the pope to a racist. Pius XI was said to be half-Jewish, his mother a Dutch Jewess. Pius XI called and raised. "Spiritually we are all Semites." This was not mere oratory.

Fascism's crude political parody of theology had tried to sever the New from the Old Testament. This is impossible. The Church began with communities of converted Jews, meeting first in synagogues. When official Judaism drove them out, the message was carried to the gentiles. The New Testament is unintelligible without the Old – how would one understand Christ's claims that he fulfilled the biblical prophecies of the Messiah? The long liturgical tradition of the Church, the *ecclesia orans*, has had the Psalms of David as its central prayer. Down through the centuries, choir answering to choir, these timeless songs have echoed in the vaults of monastic churches and other religious houses, the chant itself a heritage from Judaism, have formed themselves soundlessly on the lips of priests.

The previous spring, on April 30, days before Hitler was due to arrive in Rome on a state visit, the pope withdrew to Castel Gandalfo in the Alban Hills, saying that "he could not breathe the air of Rome." He had described the preparations for the visit to Mussolini's ambassador as an apotheosis of a confessed enemy of the Church and Christianity and asked if the visit did not violate the concordat with Italy. The pope ordered the Vatican museums closed for the occasion and

Reminding his listeners of this vast heritage, Pius XI remarked on September 6, 1938, "Whenever I read the words The sacrifice of our Father Abraham, *I cannot help but be deeply moved. Mark well, we call Abraham our Patriarch, our ancestor. Anti-Semitism is irreconcilable with this lofty thought, the noble reality which this prayer expresses. Anti-Semitism is inadmissible; spiritually we are all Semites." These words flew across the world to the pages of* The New York Times *in which they appeared on December 12, 1938.*

forbade any Nazi emblems to appear on any of the one thousand churches of Rome. While Hitler and Mussolini were dining in Rome, the pope spoke at Castel Gandalfo to a general audience. "Sad things are happening, Many sad things, Both far and nearby. Nothing could be less suitable or less timely than to fly, on Holy Cross day, the banner of an alien cross hostile to that of Christ." *Osservatore Romano* completely ignored Hitler's coming. In the course of July, three papal condemnations of racism appeared in the pages of *Osservatore*. "Human dignity consists in the fact that we are a single great family, the human genus, the human race – that is the Church's answer, that in our eyes is the true racism."

The One Sure Voice

In November 1938, the infamous *Kristalnacht* took place. In October 1938, Poland planned to revoke the citizenship of thousands of its Jewish citizens who were living in Germany, and this prompted the Germans to undertake a swift repatriation of the Polish Jews before the deadline. This was the prelude to the events of November. The story came out during the Eichmann trial on April 25, 1961.[1] The father of Herszl Grynszpan testified that his son, in despair at the prospect of his father being sent back to Poland, assassinated a German diplomat in Paris, thus providing the Nazis with a pretext for the night of broken glass, *Kristalnacht*, a terrifying night when Jewish shops and properties were vandalized, windows broken, contents destroyed. The message was frighteningly clear. First the property, next time the proprietor. At the pope's urging, Cardinal Van Roey of Belgium, Vedier of Paris, Shuster of Milan condemned this savage display of racism and the blood myth. Cardinal Faulhaber provided a truck so that the chief rabbi of Munich could save the Torah Scrolls before his synagogue was vandalized.

Pius XI died on February 10, 1939. Mussolini said, "This stubborn old man is now dead."

During these dark days, the one sure voice that was raised in protest against violations of natural law was that of the Catholic Church. The historical record is there for all to see. Nor was it unappreciated at the time. In Geneva, in January 1939, the Jewish Congress issued the following statement.

> *We record the Jewish people's deep appreciation of the stand taken by the Vatican against the advance of resurgent paganism which challenges all traditional values of religion as well as inalienable human rights upon which alone enduring civilization can be found. The Congress salutes the Supreme Pontiff, symbol of spiritual forces which under many names are fighting for the re-establishment of the rule of moral law in society.*

The statement appeared in The New York Times *of January 17, 1939.*

The tributes were fulsome. Again, Jews marked the special concern the pope had shown for their tragic plight. The *Alliance Israelite Universelle* said on February 13, "Never shall we forget the kindness and courage with which the late pope has defended all the victims of persecution, irrespective or race and religion, in the name of those eternal principles whose noble spokesman he has been on earth." *Time* Magazine, on December 23, 1940, published the quietly eloquent words of the world's most famous scientist.

> Only the Church stood squarely across the path of Hitler's campaign for suppressing the truth. I never had any special interest in the Church before, but now I feel a great affection and admiration because the Church alone has had the courage and persistence to stand for intellectual truth and moral freedom. I am forced thus to confess that what I once despised I now praise unreservedly.

> Albert Einstein

4

A Pope in Time of War

Pius XII reigned from 1939 to 1958, a long papacy, during which his Magisterium steered the Church through the choppy waters left by the modernism controversy at the beginning of the century and prepared the Church for the council that would be convened by his successor, John XXIII. Pius introduced liturgical changes. He gave a new charter to biblical studies. In 1950, in the encyclical *Humani Generis*, he cautioned against the course some theologians were taking. He gave prudent and prescient advice to the medical profession. But all his many accomplishments as pope have been eclipsed by concentration on his wartime words and deeds, which are scrutinized in support of lies so large they would have embarrassed Joseph Goebbels himself. The vilification of Pius XII was begun by the Nazis shortly after his election as pope.

The only response to falsehood is the truth. In this long chapter, I will put before the reader the actual wartime record of Pius XII. Since later controversy has turned on what he did for the Jews persecuted by Hitler, that will be emphasized. I will rely as much as possible on Jewish historians and the contemporaneous record, so the reader can see what was, what is, and what was acknowledged to be by those who benefited from it, a magnificent and noble – and successful! – campaign to save as many Jews as possible.

One of the saddest aspects of recent controversies is the wedge they threaten to drive between Catholics and Jews. World War II was a time of unprecedented cooperation between Catholics and Jews. Pius XII put his papal nuncios at the disposal of Jewish organizations that sought his help and urged his bishops to apply in their own dioceses the principles of Christian morality and natural law.

In order to give a balanced picture of the rescue work undertaken by Pius XII and his cardinals and bishops and nuncios – to say nothing of ordinary Catholics who took in Jewish refugees to save them from the clutches of Adolf Eichmann – I will alternate accounts of what Pius XII did, year by year, with accounts of the activities of the Jews themselves to save their fellow Jews in Europe.

Pius XII's own statement of his wartime policy was formulated on September 14, shortly after the German armies had invaded Poland. "We will not cease to watch attentively so that We may give all the assistance within Our power and as opportunities allow: especially to motivate once again the people, today inflamed and divided, toward concluding a peace that is honorable for all . . . and then, for as long as this is not possible, at least to alleviate the terrible wounds that have been or will be inflicted in the future."[1]

1939

Habemus Papam

When Pius XI died, William L. Shirer left his post in Berlin and went to Rome to cover the conclave. (His *Berlin Diary*[2] begins in 1934.) "Rome, March 3. Eugenio Cardinal Pacelli is the new Pope, elected yesterday, and a very popular choice all around except perhaps in Germany." The *Berlin Lokal Anzeiger* declared that "The election of Cardinal Pacelli is not accepted with favor in Germany because he was always opposed to Nazism and practically determined the policies of the Vatican under his predecessor." As the dark specter of war gathered over Europe, Pius XII continued to point out the incompatibility of national socialism and Christianity. The Germans invaded Poland on September 1. *Summi Pontificatus*, his first encyclical, appeared in October. It went to the heart of the matter: "We should take the opportunity of paying homage to the King of Kings and Lord of Lords as a kind of Introit prayer to Our Pontificate, in the spirit of Our renowned predecessor and in the faithful accomplishment of his designs, by consecrating them all to the spread of the kingdom of Christ." He looked about and saw an age, whatever its technical progress, that was beset by spiritual emptiness and interior poverty. The world "had abandoned Christ's cross for another which brings only death."

Eugenio Pacelli was sixty-three years old when he was elected pope and took the name of Pius XII. Since he began work in the Vatican as a young priest, he had been groomed, however unconsciously at first, for the papacy. Pius XI had made it clear that he thought Cardinal Pacelli would make an excellent pope.[3] Perhaps no one else had experience to equal his in the problems that now faced the Church. He had spent twelve years in Germany and had seen that country reel from defeat in war through the Weimar Republic and a twenties that far surpassed in mindless pursuit of diversion and pleasure the same decade in the United States. Post-war Germany had been impoverished, and it would feel the impact of the Depression as severely as any other country. The scene was set for the emergence of such a figure as Adolf Hitler, although while Pacelli was in Germany Hitler had yet to emerge as a political force to be reckoned with. The rise of Hitler took place when Eugenio Pacelli was acting as Pius XI's secretary of state, and he had followed the phenomenon with foreboding. The concordat of 1933 was entered into with distaste for the Nazi government but with the conviction that only by the concordat could the Church weather the coming storm. Pius XI had seen the Communist threat first-hand when he was papal nuncio to Warsaw, when the Red Army had threatened to do what it only managed to do some twenty years later after it had allied itself with Hitler. In Munich, Cardinal Pacelli had been confronted by the raw violence of the revolutionaries of the left when they first fired on his residence and then broke in and threatened him with drawn pistols. He had stared them down, much as Achille Ratti in Warsaw had refused to desert his post as the armies of Trotsky and Stalin bore down on the city and the rest of the diplomatic corps fled. The two men saw in fascism a similar assault on the natural law and on the Church. The 1937 encyclical, *Mit brennender Sorge,* was largely the work of Cardinal Pacelli. The final version was finished when the German cardinals were called to Rome. That it was issued in German was meant to facilitate its dissemination to the German people, to whom it was to be read from all the pulpits on Palm Sunday. The almost simultaneous appearance of the encyclical on atheistic communism was misunderstood as in some way subordinating the menace of nazism to that of communism. But the two isms shared a denial of principles which the Church was committed to defend.

Despite his long diplomatic experience, despite his decade as secretary of state, Pacelli as Pius XII was a new figure to many. Tall, thin almost to the point of emaciation, his air was said to be aristocratic. There is little doubt that he was conscious of the dignity of the office to which he had been called, and as the years passed he became more and more assimilated to his role as Bishop of Rome, successor of St. Peter, the Vicar of Christ on Earth. According to his associates, he was anything but autocratic in private, reveling in lively exchanges, laughing with the abandon of a happy child. Unlike Pius XI, he did not smoke nor did he tolerate anyone smoking in his presence. In private as in public, he was always in his white soutane with a high Roman collar. Even when asked to sit in his presence, those who reported to him were inclined to stand. For all that, he was wont to say that he was unworthy of the office he held.

His Daily Schedule

His daily schedule was daunting. He rose at 6:15 except in winter when he rose fifteen minutes later. He exercised every morning so his trim figure was not simply a genetic gift. He said his Mass at 7:45, attended by his secretary and his valet, after which he breakfasted. Private audiences began at 9, followed by meetings with his staff. A general audience or religious ceremonies followed at 12:15. He lunched at 2 and then took a forty-five minute nap. 3:15 found him walking in the Vatican gardens, always following the same route. The walk was exercise as well as relaxation, and during it he read. He spent an hour and a half in his private chapel, from 4:30 to 6 P.M. He consulted with his staff until 8:30. He listened to music during his evening meal and then worked until retiring at 1 or 1:30. This was his regimen throughout his papacy.

As often as not he was alone, for that is how he preferred to work, having been brought dossiers and documents by his staff. He read rapidly, grasped issues swiftly. He had his personal library maintained by three Jesuits and located between his office and his private apartment. He was kept au courant on many things but without the illusion that he was expert at the many things that interested him. Besides Italian, he had other languages – German, French, English – and had at hand a battery of dictionaries he called his "lay breviaries." The style of his documents was at once precise and elegant. Bossuet was his model. His telephone, which he liked to use, was white.

This routine did not favor improvisation, and he was uncomfortable when the need arose to speak without preparation: In this he was unlike both his predecessor and his successor, Pope John XXIII. His immediate staff consisted of two monsignors, but the redoubtable nun he had brought back from Bavaria, Sister Pascalina (Josephine Lehnert), a Franciscan, along with two other sisters of her order, presided over the daily life of the pope. Unlike any other person in his entourage, Sister Pascalina moved freely about his apartment and his office without concern for protocol. She retained the pope's confidence because she was completely self-effacing, shunning journalists and photographers. After the pope was dead, in 1982 Sister Pascalina published a memoir of her years of service to Pius XII. She was not the only one he had brought from Germany to serve in the Vatican. The Jesuits who worked for him were German, and his confessor, August Bea, was also German. At the suggestion of the French cardinals who had admired him as papal nuncio in Paris, Pius named Luigi Maglione as his secretary of state, but Maglione never became for him what he himself had been for Pius XI, and Pius often bypassed him to consult with others.[4]

A Letter to Hitler

Pius XII began his papacy among the ruins of all the efforts he had made in the service of his predecessors. Fascism had grown strong and brazen in Italy now, as well in Germany. Germany annexed Austria in March, and the Austrian bishops, with Cardinal Innitzer of Vienna at their head, had welcomed the return of Austria to the Reich. This deserved and received censure from Rome. Pius XI had called Pacelli back from vacation on October 30, 1938, when Mussolini had introduced a severe new law against Jews. Hitler's visit to Rome brought on a discussion as to whether the Vatican should withdraw in protest from the concordat with Germany. The provocations had been enormous. But what would be the effect of withdrawing from the concordat? A complete rupture with Germany would make communication with bishops difficult and deprive the Vatican of channels of information. Such a withdrawal had been tried in France at the time of the persecution. And at the present the lack of a nuncio in Mexico put the Vatican at a great disadvantage.

Sent as papal delegate to the Eucharistic Congress in Budapest, Cardinal Pacelli gave a prophetic address. Souls were undernourished, there was anemia of the spirit, and a moral infection, and the only cure was to turn to the living sources that nourished the epochs of faith. Without the affirmation of man's religious foundation and the provision of solid moral bases, man was on a slippery slope. The Berlin-Rome axis brought Mussolini more and more under the influence of the partner least likely to change. The anti-Semitic laws were a flagrant violation of the Lateran Accords.

Pius XI warned Mussolini that if he continued to persecute Catholic Action the pope would show him what fighting meant.

In France, the submission of Charles Maurras, facilitated by the pope's mercy and the intervention of the Carmel of Lisieux, brought the conflict with Action Française to an end. Maurras's monarchist movement had attracted many Catholics, among them Jacques Maritain, since it seemed to pit the tradition of French Catholicism against the secular and anti-clerical French government. The condemnation of Action Française confused and angered many, among them Georges Bernanos. Maurras and many of his followers defied the condemnation for years before submitting to it.

With the death of Pius XI and the election of Pius XII, the new pope entered into a discussion with his cardinals as to whether to not to make yet another try to stop Hitler. Was it still possible to stop the rush toward war? Would it make sense to seek to influence the dictator one more time? The record of the preceding decade gave no cause for optimism, as the new Pius XII knew better than anyone. But could a failure to try be justified? The custom according to which a newly elected pope informed heads of state of his election provided the occasion and a carefully written letter was the result.

> Honorable Sir,
>
> Having been elected to the pontifical throne as the result of the vote of the College of cardinals, We thought it a duty of Our charge to make known to you by means of this letter, in your capacity of head of state, Our election.
>
> At the outset of Our pontificate we wish to assure you that We have an intimate affection for the German people consigned to your care and with a paternal feeling We ask for them from the all powerful God the true good that religion feeds and reenforces.
>
> Recalling many years during which, as papal nuncio, We labored to organize the relations between the Church and the State in a reciprocal agreement and effective collaboration to the advantage of the two parties and to assure further advantageous developments, a goal at which We aim particularly now with all the

ardent desire that the responsibility of Our office charges Us, inspires Us and makes possible for Us.

We are confident that this ardent desire on Our part, which is strictly linked to the well being of the German people and the effective strengthening of order, can, with the help of God, be happily realized.

In this expectation, We implore for you, most honorable sir, and for all your people, the protection of heaven and the blessing of almighty God.

Given at Rome, at St Peter's, March 6, 1939, the first year of Our pontificate.

Pius XII, Pope

It was a wasted gesture, as doubtless Pius XII knew it would be. But by making it, the onus for the continued attacks on the Church in Germany must clearly rest on Hitler. Moreover, channels of communication with German bishops remained, and these proved to have more than ecclesiastical significance in the years ahead. Hardly had the triple crown been placed on his head than the threatened catastrophes began.

The German army moved into Prague. Mussolini invaded Albania. And then on August 23 the Nazi-Soviet Pact was announced, uniting the two giants of political depravity and anti-human philosophy. This paved the way for the invasion of Poland, first by the Germans from the west, then by the Russians from the east. Finland had been invaded. The Second World War was under way. What Pius XII, during his years as nuncio, during his years as secretary of state, had sought to stave off was upon him half a year after he had been installed in the Chair of St. Peter. His motto was *Opus iustitiae pax.* Peace is the work of justice, the effect of justice.

Peace Follows on Justice

In keeping with his motto, Pius XII sought to head off the impending war. Hitler had already made military moves with impunity, from reclaiming the Saar Valley, the annexation of Austria, and moving into Czechoslovakia. Hitler had played on the desire of the democracies for peace and what seems the hopelessly naive inter-state parleys, from which Britain and France emerged in the illusion that they had secured the peace. Pius XII sought to bring the great powers together and secure a peace based on justice rather than the perceived self-interests of the parties. Having been gulled and lied to by Hitler, Britain and France gave their guarantee to Poland: If Germany invaded, they would declare war. Mussolini, dazzled by Hitler's successes, occupied Albania on Good Friday, April 7, 1939. On Easter Sunday Pius addressed the root of present troubles – the misery of so many, an evil distribution of natural resources, lack of trust among nations, the violation of treaties, the arms race. He might have been pointing to causes whose effect in the circumstances seemed inevitable.

But Pius XII meant to go beyond mere words. He proposed bringing the bickering nations together in a conference. Mussolini was sounded out and liked the idea. Pius decided to invite France, Germany, England, Italy, and Poland to air and settle their disputes. On May 3, telegrams were sent. Mussolini had assured Pius's envoy that the proposal would meet with approval. France did not quite refuse but did not accept. Hitler told the papal nuncio in Berlin, Archbishop Orsenigo, that there were problems that could only be solved by conflict now. Then he threw a tantrum about Britain's guarantee to Poland. Poland declined. The British thought the idea should be postponed. In short, the answer was, Thanks a lot, but no thanks.

Through the summer the clock ticked on. German troops were massing at the Polish border; there were strange tourists coming into Danzig from Germany. And then on August 21, the announcement that the two countries whose political philosophy was antithetical to Christianity, Germany and Russia, announced that they were signing a non-aggression pact. Intimations of this had been picked up by Vatican diplomats earlier, but leftists around the world were shocked that the adversaries of the war in Spain should now be allies of a sort. It was as if the last impediment to conflict had been cleared away.

At this point, expressing in prospect a hope that many would express in retrospect, the British saw the pope as the last best hope for peace. "Halifax hoped that in such a case the Pope would bring the full weight of his authority through a final appeal to reason. The following day Osborne returned to Monsignor Tardini with his suggestion for a solemn radio message in which Lord Halifax was placing his last hope."[5]

Pius may not have given up all hope, but he advised prudent caution in others. "In April 1939, Pope Pius XII invited me for an audience and offered to help me leave Italy and gain admittance to any country I chose," recalls Professor Guido Mendes, a famous lung specialist. "When I mentioned Palestine, the Pope promised to intervene with the British authorities and secure a certificate of immigration. Montini (now Pope Paul VI) dealt with the matter, and as a result my entire family arrived in Palestine in 1939."[6]

Vilification Campaigns

The vilification of the new pope began immediately. In Germany a pamphlet called *"General und Kardinal"* appeared, attributed to the widow of General Eric von Ludendorff, claiming that, despite his ostensible enmity toward the Fatherland, Pacelli actually espoused national socialism, as had her late husband. This little screed is the precedent for what has become a genre of increasingly venomous lies about Pius XII in the decades since his death. Nor were the attacks confined to Germany. Rumors were spread among Italian workers that the pope had wanted war, that he provided money for its continuance from the funds raised to help the needy, that he had done nothing for peace. Pius was familiar with this kind of attack on the Vatican from World War I. But this was a calumny more monstrous and absurd. Pius addressed a gathering of workers on this subject in June of 1943 and spoke about such charges. He saw the attack as one against religion. His tone is the almost bewildered one of a man accused of doing the exact opposite of what he had been doing throughout his official life. As for what he has done, "We have the witnesses of Our heart and lips which do not contradict one another: Our acts do not deny Our words and in Our conscience We know the falsity of all that the enemies of God attempt perfidiously to trouble workers and the people." And there is of course the unadorned historical record of what he has said and what he has done. But the facts have never stopped calumny when there are receptive ears to hear it.

Of course Pius XII earned and probably sought criticism from the Nazis. "When the Jewish professor and cartographer, R. Almagia lost his chair in 1939 as a result of Italy's racial laws, Pius XII not only gave him employment in the Vatican Library, but had him prepare the publication of an artistic reproduction of "A Map of the Danubian States" (originally drawn in 1546), a copy of which the nuncio in Berlin presented to Ribbentrop in February 1940 "on behalf of the Pope."[7]

The British government's White Paper of May 17, 1938, limited and eventually stopped Jewish immigration into Palestine. The *S.S. Struma* with 769 Jewish refugees from Nazi Europe on board, sank at sea after having been refused entry into Palestine and into a Turkish port. A senior official of the British Immigration Office commented: "How dreadful, but it is perhaps the best thing that could have happened."[8]

In German-occupied Poland, the Church was a first target in removing all opposition to the Nazi philosophy. "When in September 1939, the Germans executed 214 Polish priests, imprisoned another 1000, exiled Cardinal Hlond and a number of bishops, and closed down several churches, 'the Vatican Radio,' Guenter Lewy tells us, 'told the story to the world.' But when reprisals for these publications made things progressively worse, 'Cardinal Sapieha, the Archbishop of Cracow, repeatedly pleaded with the Pope to stop the protesting, as it only made things worse.'"[9] And the slaughter continued. "During October and November, 214 Polish priests were executed, among them the entire Cathedral Chapter of the bishopric of Pelplin. By the end of 1939, approximately 1000 Polish clergymen had been imprisoned, many in the newly constructed concentration camps."[10]

It is against the cascade of historical events that plunged the world into war that Pius XII's first encyclical must be read. Pius XII reminded the world that before God there is neither Jew nor Greek nor Gentile – all are one. This sound, traditional, and, *salva reverentia,* trite teaching brought a stiff complaint from the German embassy in Rome. The BBC broadcast it without changing a word.

In Poland, Jew and Catholic had their brotherhood brought home to them by the Nazis. "In a German military report written in Bromberg as early as November 17, 1939, we read of the 'extermination of Polish priests' – on the same page where 'the removal of all local Jews' is reported as completed."[11]

Cardinal Suhard interpreted the pope's first encyclical for his flock. "The Pope, moreover, concurred publicly with this interpretation of the encyclical, in his public reply to the French Cardinal Suhard of November 21, 1939: 'With you we think that . . . the French may rightly rejoice to see confirmed in the encyclical certain principles which they legitimately cherish; and to see in it reproved certain ideas which they reprove, and to hear certain procedures which they condemn, accused of being the main source of present evils."[12]

As the Nazis took over, what would become a tradition in war-time France began – the sheltering of Jewish refugees. As one example out of many, there was Paul Claudel, who noted in his *Journal* for September 3, 1939, that they agreed to take in eight refugees.[13] Claudel, distinguished poet and dramatist, as well as career French diplomat, had been in the group sent to represent his country at the coronation of Pius XII. His *obiter dicta* about high churchman and statesmen, heroic and the opposite, during the war, are worth searching for in his *Journal.*

Writing in *The New York Times* for October 30, 1939, Anne O'Hare McCormick said this, "The central theme of his long encyclical is the function of the State in the modern world, and that is the crux of the struggle of our time. The dictatorship of today is not simply a form of government, it is a form of life, a usurpation of every human and divine right, a growth of power so abnormal that it is like a tumor pressing on the whole social body and preventing other nations from functional normality." In the same issue, readers were told that Pius XII's encyclical denounced the violation of treaties, the ruin of Poland and the forcible transfer of populations. The pope was determined to fight against the Church's pagan enemies and defend the rights of the family and the individual against dictatorial encroachments.

Pius closed 1939, the first of his pontificate, with a Christmas message broadcast over Vatican Radio. It did not require keen hearing, only the ears with which to hear, to catch the contemporary relevance of what the pontiff had to say to the world when he spoke of "that universal love which is the compendium of Christian ideals, and therefore offers a way also for *those who . . . do not participate in our faith.*"[15]

1940

Poland to its discredit had participated in the dismemberment of Czechoslovakia and now she had learned, as Russia too would learn, that one needed a very long spoon in order to sup safely with Adolf Hitler. The German armies swept into Poland, displaying the new kind of warfare it called *Blitzkrieg.* This consisted in falling on unsuspecting or unprepared opponents without a declaration of war, terrorizing the population with Stuka bombers, and rolling across the countryside in tanks with infantry behind them. Lightning war indeed. The thunder sounded only after one had been blinded by the flash of cannon and fireworks of the bombs. For all that, the Poles at first thought that occupation by Germany would be less horrible than life under the Red Army. Poles who survived to make the comparison, subjected first by Germans, then by Russians, saw little to choose between their diabolical policies.

Already in October and November, reports came into the Vatican telling of the slaughter of priests. No wonder that Pius had acceded to Cardinal Hlond's plea that he mention what was happening in Poland in his first encyclical.

> The blood of countless people, even noncombatants, gives rise to a harrowing funereal lament, especially over Poland, a dearly beloved country. Because of its glorious attainments on behalf of Christian civilization, attainments indelibly inscribed in the annals of history, Poland has a right to the world's human and fraternal sympathy, and confident in the powerful intercession of Mary who is the *auxilium Christianorum*, it awaits the hour of its resurrection in justice and peace.[1]

That resurrection would be delayed longer than anyone at the time could have imagined. But now in January, Cardinal Hlond submitted a report to the pope on the dreadful happenings in Poland.

On January 2, doubtless mindful of the coupling of the extermination of priests and the removal of Jews, Pius's concern was not restricted to clerical or Catholic victims of the Nazi onslaught. On January 2, the United Jewish Appeal for Refugees and Overseas Needs, in Chicago, offered the Holy Father $125,000 dollars to help in Vatican rescue operations "of all those persecuted because of religion or race."[2] A rescue near at hand had been the employment of Professor Almagia in 1939 to work on old maps in the Vatican Library, thus immunizing him from the Fascist anti-Semitic laws. On January 25, Pius received Almagia in private audience and thanked the Jewish scholar in writing for "his splendid work." The pope's appointment of two Jews to the Vatican Academy of Science as well as the hiring of Almagia were reported by *The New York Times* in the editions of November 11, 1939, and of January 10, 1940.

In Germany, the Security Service grumbled about the effects of Pius's first encyclical.

> Whilst the Catholic clergy has been reticent during the first months of the war, it has displayed more activity during recent months, mainly under the influence of the papal encyclical *Summi Pontificatus*. The attitude of the priests in this respect shows such great unanimity, that there must have been central instructions.... . From various reports it transpires that part of [German] clergy has declared that they would welcome it if Germany should lose the war.[3]

With Poland occupied by Russians and Germans, the Church faced the problem of how to administer dioceses under such conditions. Some dioceses were without bishops simply because successors had not yet been named when war broke out. Cardinal Kakowski of Warsaw had died; the archbishop of Cracow, the redoubtable Adam Sapieha, had sent in his resignation for reasons of age; Cardinal Auguste Hlond, the primate of Poland, had fled with the government to Roumania and then come on to Rome. Three of the bishops arrested by the Germans died in camps: Kozal in Dachau, Goral in Oranienburg-Sachsenhausen, Wetmanski in Auschwitz. Along with the clergy, lay members of the Polish elite were arrested and executed, removing any competition to German governance. When the Holy See sought permission for Cardinal Hlond to return to Poznan, it was refused: The cardinal was considered to be an enemy of Germany.[4] The papal nuncio in Warsaw had also fled with the government, and now Polish bishops began to deal with the nuncio in Berlin, Archbishop Orsenigo, who was granted authority to do so. German efforts to secure control over the Church in the countries they occupied was summarily repelled.[5]

The papal nuncios in occupied countries would play multiple roles in the dark days ahead. As representatives of the Holy See, their primary task was to monitor the Church in their country of assignment – they communicated to the bishops, the bishops communicated with them. If the country had a concordat, the nuncio was there to protest any breach of it. As the horrors of German occupation became clear, the nuncios became representatives of the natural law as well as of the Church. Increasingly they were recognized as the last best hope of the oppressed, not least of the Jewish people. Pius XII, through his nuncios, did more to rescue Jews from the Nazi extermination machine than all other efforts combined. His reward has been calumny and defamation, sometimes even by the descendants of those who owed their lives to his efforts. Because of the pope's patronage of Almagia, Hitler's minions reacted. "'Jewish journals report with a certain joy,' *Der Stuermer*, Streicher's notorious hate-sheet wrote on May 2, 1940, 'that the relations between the Church and the Jews are good, and that even the Pope employs a Jew in his library.'. . . From fragmentary evidence it appears that Pius dealt personally with 150 to 200 of such refugees between 1939 and 1944."[6]

Vatican Radio

The nuncio in Berlin, Orsenigo, reported on February 24 the Reich government's complaint about Vatican Radio broadcasts. Vatican Radio had been established by Pius XI, and it was to prove an indispensable instrument for getting information out to the world as to what was going on in occupied Europe. Contemporary listeners, friend and foe, got the message. So too, while a little thing in itself, yet symbolic, was Pius's patronage of a concert by the Polish pianist Miecislav Horszowski at the Pontifical Institute of Sacred Music, on March 3, the first anniversary of his election as pope. The program consisted of Chopin's most patriotic pieces, and all income was to go to the relief of Polish war victims. The pope was heard to say: "Poor Poland is being crucified between two thieves."[7] Invited to attend a special concert of the Berlin State Opera that Mackensen, German ambassador to Italy, sought to arrange a year later, the pope not only refused but demanded that a paper that had written of the concert as if it had occurred with him present, retract its story. The Polish concert, on the other hand, had been prominently featured in *Osservatore Romano*.

The Vatican newspaper and radio were to be a constant bone of contention with the Germans as they had long been with Il Duce. Conditions of the Church in Poland were broadcast to Germany, and a denunciation of German policy there went out in all languages. "Conditions of religious, political, and economic life have thrown the Polish people, especially in those areas occupied by Germany, into a state of terror, of degradation, and, we dare say, of barbarism, much akin to what the communists imposed on Spain in 1936."[8]

When Ribbentrop called on March 11, Pius XII repeatedly protested against the treatment of Jews, but Ribbentrop responded by speaking of the invincibility of the Reich and the inevitability of a German victory. This invitation to join the winning side did not get the response Ribbentrop may have expected. "The Pope heard him out in stony silence, opened his drawer and began a recital – in perfect German – of all the racial persecutions and violations of the concordats, both the German and the Polish ones, committed by the Nazis, quoting the dates and particulars of all major crimes. The audience ended with a curt nod from Pius. Ribbentrop is said to have felt faint when he left the Pope."[9]

Count Ciano, Mussolini's foreign minister, told the Italian ambassador in Berlin, Dino Alfieri, what Pius had said to him. "Come what may, he concluded with determination [the quote is from Alfieri's memoirs], even if they arrest me one day and send me to a concentration camp, we have no fear. Each one of us has to answer for his deeds one day before God.' Ciano added: 'Pius is ready to let himself be deported to a concentration camp, rather than to do anything against his conscience.'"[10] Over-dramatic? Martin Bormann in 1940 had prepared at

Hitler's personal request what was called "Operation Pontiff." The pope was to be kidnapped and put under arrest in a monastery in Germany, while a Nazi papacy was put in place.[11] Pius said to Dino Alfieri, who had begged him to be more careful in his pronouncements: "We were not afraid of guns pointed at us once; we shall fear them even less the second time. . . . We ought to speak words of fire against the atrocities in Poland, and the only thing which restrains us, is the knowledge that words would make the fate of those wretches even worse."[12] Nor was it only the Nazis who had to be taken into account. Pius XII wrote to the bishop of Berlin, whom he often consulted on German affairs: "from bishops as well we receive plaints, nay cries of anguish, because of the reports by Radio Vatican."[13] The Germans also worried what the reaction of the Italian people would be if Italy entered the war on Germany's side.[14]

Blitzkrieg West

On April 9, Germany invaded Denmark and Norway, meeting no resistance from Denmark, and that of Norway was more of an annoyance than a deterrent. It did not slow down the Nazi schedule. On May 10, the Netherlands, Belgium, and Luxembourg were invaded by German forces. In Britain, the feckless Chamberlain was replaced by Winston Churchill. On May 14, the Germans invaded France. The Netherlands had surrendered its forces, and on May 28 the Belgian Army followed suit. Then 340,000 British, French, and other Allied forces were driven to the channel port of Dunkirk, and, in one of the most remarkable military feats of the war, were rescued to a man, brought to England in any craft that sailed. On June 10, Mussolini declared war on France and Britain. Paris was occupied on June 14. Only a month had elapsed from the time German troops crossed the French border and when they goose-stepped down the Champs d'Élysées. On June 22, Hitler dictated an armistice to the French in the very railway car in which the German defeat of 1918 had been settled. Afterward, the Führer danced a jig of triumph outside the railway car.

These were dark days for the world, and darker for Britain. France, its ally, was now occupied by the enemy. Britain was woefully unprepared for war. The rescue at Dunkirk stirred the pulse, but Churchill was not deceived. Should Britain sue for peace? John Lukacs has argued that Churchill's successful persuasion of his cabinet that the war must be fought made the first days of June the most decisive of the war. The first bombing of London took place on September 7. Japan joined the Axis of Berlin and Rome.

In slightly more than a year, the map of Europe had been completely altered. Germany controlled the continent. Its non-aggression pact with Russia had protected its eastern rear when it turned West to roll through country after country. When Ribbentrop spoke to the pope of the invincibility of the Reich and the inevitability of a German victory, he seemed to have a point.

The Occupation

In what was emerging as standard German procedure, when the Nazis occupied Holland, "The first step was to ensnare the Jews in a tight network of identification and movement controls by means of decrees signed by the *Reichskommisar* Seyss-Inquart in October 1940 for the definition of the term 'Jew' according to the Nuremberg laws, followed by the registration of 150,000 victims. It drew at once an official protest of the Catholic bishops."[15]

"As soon as the first racial laws were promulgated in July 1940, the Nuncio, Monsignor Andrea Cassulo, issued a protest, and concessions for baptized Jews were wrung from the Antonescu government."[17] "The Vatican lodged repeated protests against these 'so-called racial laws,' which, as Cardinal Maglione, the Pope's Secretary-of-State, stressed in a note to Mussolini's government, dated July 25, 1940, 'cause a good deal of suffering, desolation and ruin.'"[18]

Situated in a country that had allied itself with the Nazi juggernaut that had swept the

On June 5, 1940, some 500 Jews embarked at Bratislava on a leaky Danube steamer headed for Palestine. Four months and untold deprivations later, their ship tried to enter the port of Istanbul. When the Turkish coast guard refused to admit them, their ship headed southwest – to be captured two days later by an Italian patrol boat, which led to their imprisonment in a camp on Rhodes. When rumors spoke of an imminent handover to the German authorities, Herman Herskovich, the son of one of the group leaders, managed to reach Italy, and in Rome obtain an audience with the Pope. The latter's intervention resulted in the transfer of all 500 refugees to a hastily improvised camp in Southern Calabria near the tip of the Italian boot. That is where we found them, most of them, sound and thankful, on December 23, 1943, the day after our Palestinian unit landed at Taranto.[16]

continent of Europe under its iron wing, with seemingly little prospect that any effective military opponent would arise to liberate the subjected countries, Pius XII manfully went about his Father's work. In far-off America, the pope's words and actions were fully appreciated. "No keener rebuke has come to Nazism than from Pope Pius XI and his successor, Pope Pius XII," said Louis Finkelstein, provost, Jewish Theological Seminary of America.[19] These efforts did not go unnoticed by the Germans. Von Bergen, Germany's ambassador to the Vatican, reported to Berlin on August 7: "Councillor Teixidor of the Spanish Embassy to the Holy See recently remarked during a conversation that the papal Secretariat of State had recommended the requests for entry visas of various Jews who wanted to emigrate to Spain."[20]

Atrocities in Poland

Poland remained the principal theater of horror. The Germans were engaged in an effort to sever the Polish church's connection with Rome.[21] "As of October 1, 1940, in the archdiocese of Posen alone 74 priests had been shot or died in concentration camps, and 451 were being held in prisons or camps. Of the 441 churches of the archdiocese, only 30 were still open for the Poles."[22] Administrative problems created a nightmare for the Vatican, but far more anguishing were the plaints of the Polish people that reached the pope. The victims in Poland could not know of the series of protests made by Orsenigo, the papal nuncio in Berlin, on behalf of the pope. Written protests went to Ribbentrop on August 28, September 2, and September 29. Yet another protest on September 13 was occasioned by the activities of Greiser. Unaware of this, Catholic Poles thought the Church was indifferent to their fate.

One of the agonies Pius XII was to suffer throughout the war was that his countless protests against the outrages inflicted on the innocent were not heard by those on whose behalf he spoke or brought about reprisals on them. But Catholics in Poland recognized and did their duty to Christ, even though his vicar's efforts were often concealed from them. "Emmanuel Ringelbaum, the chronicler of the Polish holocaust, notes in his diary on December 31, 1940, that priests in all of Warsaw's churches exhorted their parishioners to bury their prejudice against the Jews and to beware of the Jew-hatred preached by 'our common enemy,' the Germans."[23]

The Vatican was of course officially neutral. Condemnations of Fascist and Nazi persecution of the Church and of such innocent victims as the Jews were not, of course, a prelude to declaring war and unleashing the Swiss Guards on the Italian and German armed forces. With the loss of their temporal sovereignty, the question of popes going to war was moot, but even if it had not been, what was the other side the pope might have joined? The countries on the continent of Europe had fallen like bowling pins before the German invader. Britain was being bombed by the Luftwaffe and seemed in imminent danger of invasion herself. These were the stark circumstances in which Pius XII acted during 1940. All he had was the moral authority of his voice, and he had to use it in such a way that he did not worsen the matters he condemned. The bishops and nuncios brought him information denied to those living in the still-peaceful areas of the world, but Pius let the world know what was happening under the German occupation. And his voice got through.

This was particularly the case with the Christmas Message with which Pius brought 1940 to a close. Surrounded by hostile forces, surveying a Europe under the iron heel of Hitler, without prospect that there would be any military reversal of the German victories, the pope laid out the principles on which the political order must be based. Hatred must be renounced, treaties must be faithfully respected, there must be a spirit of law and collaboration among the nations. It was an eloquent recalling of the principles of social and political justice, and it must have seemed to have zero relevance to the world to which he spoke. In the message, Pius XII expressed his joy over having been able to help a great number of refugees, *especially non-Aryans.*

Those who had escaped the reach of Hitler understood. Albert Einstein said at the end of 1940: "Only the Catholic Church protested against the Hitlerian onslaught on liberty."[24]

History, it has been said, is a technique that makes us eyewitnesses of past events. It should not overlook the contemporary statements on those events.

1941

In 1941, Pius XII led a Church which, so far as Europe went, operated in countries occupied by forces totally inimical to Christianity and indeed to the principles of the natural law. That Germany, a Christian country by and large, had permitted itself to turn over the reins of government to Adolf Hitler remains one of the great mysteries of the twentieth century. Many colluded in or acquiesced to his rise to power who were unclear or perhaps disbelieving of the ideology that drove the World War I corporal, who was determined to reverse the verdict of 1918, and then some. *Mein Kampf* was there to be read; doubtless it sat on the shelf in many German homes. The scholar in his study, reading the book all these years later, forgetful of the booming, buzzing confusion in which most deeds are done, may marvel at the fact that *Mein Kampf* had not been generally seen as the blueprint for what was to follow. But it was another book that should have deterred the German people from giving their allegiance to Adolf Hitler. How could a Christian nation. . . .

However it came about, with whatever degree of guilt or innocence, once Hitler was in power, the German people were in his power every bit as much as the people in occupied countries. The prospect of any change in the map of Europe that Hitler had redrawn was bleak throughout the new year. In Africa, the British had driven the Italian army out of Egypt in 1940, and the British fleet was asserting itself in the Mediterranean. Rommel's *Afrika Korps* would soon become a household word as he swept across the sands of North Africa. But the Germans invaded the Isle of Crete, and it was surrendered on June 1 in an action immortalized by Evelyn Waugh in *Sword of Honour.*

The Holy See noticed that, with respect to racial refugees, it was becoming increasingly difficult to get them out of German-controlled territories. Moreover, the word "deportation" was being used instead of "emigration." Cardinal Innitzer reported to the pope from Vienna that there had been an indiscriminate deportation of sixty thousand Jews from his city, eleven thousand of them Catholics of Jewish origin. "No consideration is given to age or religion." The cardinal apologized for the indignation expressed in his appeal. "Perhaps it will be said that my proposals are too audacious and daring. But whoever knows our inability to offer aid and who is aware of the indescribable suffering of the victims will understand my boldness and will also understand that assistance, if it is to be effective, must be supplied as soon as possible."[1] Cardinal Maglione's response on February 6 summarized all that had been done, lest Cardinal Innitzer be unaware of Vatican efforts on behalf of Jews, whether Catholic or not, and sent two thousand dollars. To what efforts did Maglione refer? "These efforts included interventions to mitigate racial laws, to obtain the release of Jewish internees, to improve the condition of prisoners, and to provide economic aid to families. Encouragement was also given for the formation of national committees to assist refugees and for the issuing of visas allowing immigration to North and South America."[2]

Innitzer said that the committee formed in 1939 had not been very effective, and he lamented the condition of Jews who had become Catholics. They were apostates and renegades in the eyes of other Jews; with conversion came an end of all financial aid from Jewish sources. But the cardinal had been edified by these converts. "Numerous Catholics being sent to Poland undergo their harsh fate with a courage worthy of admiration, and they go to the uncertain fate of their exile with a Christian heroism that edifies the Jews of the Mosaic rite."[3]

The Delasem (*Delegazione Assistenza Emigranti Ebrei*) was unable by its regulations to help refugees who did not belong to the Hebrew religion.[4] On July 25, Delasem officials informed Archbishop Borgongini of Genoa of these restrictions. "Even with the best of intentions, it is impossible for us to extend our ordinary activity to refugees who do not belong to the Hebrew religion." Fortunately, Pius XII did not operate under a similar restriction.

Under Nazi Occupation

Occupied Holland was to show a nobility and courage that contrasts dramatically with what that land has since become.

In February 1941, as a preliminary *ballon d'essai*, the Nazis pro-
voked the first of a series of anti-Jewish riots in the city of
Amsterdam, where 70,000 of their future deportees resided. They
counted on the usual stage-managed pogrom carried out by local
rowdies, directed by a few expert SS men, They did not expect the
Jews to strike back. Nor did they expect the tough boys of the
adjacent Jordaan quarter in Amsterdam to march in serried ranks
to the center of the Jewish quarter and to fight – and beat – the
goons who attempted to engineer anti-Jewish riots. Slowly, the
Jews of Amsterdam, aided by their Christian neighbors, stormed
back at the invading hoodlums. A savage battle raged for hours,
until the attackers were forced to give ground and retreat. But it
was a pyrrhic victory. Ten days later a new outbreak of violence
gave the Germans the excuse they needed to seize and deport the
first 425 Jews to a concentration camp.[5]

Pius was informed by his bishops of these events, and Pinchas Lapide
thinks he might have drawn the same conclusion as that drawn by the
Israel Digest: "The abortive strike of February 25, 1941, did not
improve the situation of the Jews in Holland – in fact the protest action
resulted in a tightening of German anti-Jewish measures."[6]

In occupied Roumania, the Antonescu government was under pressure from the Nazi Richter to prevent Jews from trying to escape persecution by intermarriage or conversion.

Again Antonescu backed down halfway, but to close all loopholes
Richter had a law promulgated on March 21, 1941, forbidding
Jews to change their religion. The Vatican immediately instructed
Cassulo to protest this violation of the concordat which nullified
Roumania's hitherto liberal religious laws. Antonescu promises
the Nuncio "to clarify matters," but the results, of course, were nil.
Cardinal Maglione, Pius' Secretary of State, refused to give up;
and two protests later, the following Roumanian reply was sent to
the Pope on July 28: "Jews who convert to the Catholic faith will
be entitled, in the religious sphere, to all rights guaranteed by the
concordat."[7]

The Papal Nuncios

The work of Pius XII's nuncios became increasingly vital. Angelo
Roncalli, the future Pope John XXIII, kept up an incessant pressure on
events in Greece. "In brief, the Gestapo struck before rescue work could
be properly organized and only some 12,000 out of the 70,000 Jews of
Greece eluded the Nazi dragnet. How a goodly number of the survivors

were saved by Roncalli's compatriots is described by Rabbi Michael
Molho and Joseph Nehama, the co-authors of the standard work on the
destruction of Greek Jewry."[8]

"The new Italian Consul General Castrucci came to Salonika when
the drama of the deportations reached its climax. He at once saw the
danger and acted swiftly. Apparently he had secret instructions from
Rome. *The incessant pressure of the Vatican* brought on second
thoughts in the Fascist government, and the racist laws . . . remained virtually only on paper."[9]

When Pinchas Lapide, in his role as Israeli consul, paid his respects
of Roncalli in 1946, the Patriach of Venice, as he then was, cut off the
expression of gratitude. "'In all those painful matters," he said, raising
his hand in deprecation, "I referred to the Holy See and afterwards I
simply carried out the Pope's orders: first and foremost to save human
lives.'"[10]

On June 22, Hitler invaded Russia. The non-aggression pact had
served its purpose, permitting him to drive to the channel; now he could
turn eastward and deal with Stalin. Communists and fellow-travelers
had been thrown into confusion when Stalin signed a non-aggression
pact with Hitler, invaded Poland with his new partner, and set upon
doughty little Finland as well, where he got far more of a fight that he
expected. With the German invasion of Russia, a clamor went up from
the Left; the old adversaries from Spain were reestablished. The war
was once more a war against fascism.

One of the most tragic effects of Hitler's breach of the non-aggression pact and invasion of Russia was that it made the tyrant Stalin seem
a useful ally. If Russia could keep Hitler busy, until England and perhaps others were ready to counter the changes Hitler had made on the
continent, why not? Whatever pragmatic arguments might be fashioned,
Stalin was a ruthless tyrant whose hands were already dripping with the
blood of at least 10 million of his own subjects in the artificially induced
famine of the early 1920s. The butchery of nuns and priests in Spain by
the Communists was overlooked even by such Catholics as Jacques
Maritain and François Mauriac, bewitched by propaganda about
Guernica and the atrocities of Franco. No atrocity is defensible. Perhaps
as Georges Bernanos and Simone Weil concluded, there was no good
side in Spain. But the over-attack on the Church and the massacre of her
ministers and religious turned atrocity to sacrilege. The heroes and
heroines of those days have been acknowledged by John Paul II, who
has placed some of them officially on the calendar of the saints. Pius

XI's encyclical on atheistic communism appeared in 1938 and doubtless had Spanish Reds as much as Russia in mind, insofar as in this case there was any real distinction between them.

Given the Church's experience with and condemnation of communism, there are fanciful types who imagine that, after June 22, 1941, at least, the pope was backing Hitler, hoping he would defeat the forces of atheistic communism. And there were Nazi efforts to portray Operation Barbarossa, as the Russian venture was called, as a kind of crusade, with Germany the paladin of Christian civilization. The Nazi effort to enlist the pope in such a bogus description of what Germany was after in invading Russia, of course, failed. But retrospective innuendo continues. A first and obvious antidote to it is to remind oneself of the condition of the world at the end of June 1941 and the ecclesiastical and humanitarian problems the pope faced in German-occupied countries as well as in Germany itself.

Doubtless there were those who hoped Germany and Russia would destroy one another – not the countries or their captive citizens, but the evil men who led them both. That Russia, the invader of Poland, should now be the ally of Britain, which had made the invasion of Poland a *casus belli*, was something worse than irony. The alliance might have begun as grudging pragmatism, but it ended with mindless chatter about Uncle Joe, the thug who outsmarted Roosevelt and Churchill at Yalta, and ended with most of Hitler's spoils under his mailed fist. Churchill coined the phrase "The Iron Curtain" when Stalin cut his captured east off from Western Europe, but he and Roosevelt prepared the stage on which that curtain fell.

Words and Deeds / Words v. Deeds

One immediate consequence of Operation Barbarossa was that Roumania sided with Germany in the war. Massacres of Jews became an almost daily occurrence. "In June 1941 when the Roumanians sided officially with Germany in the war against Russia, massacres of Jews became an almost daily occurrence. . . . The historian Dr. Theodore Lavi writes: 'Towards the end of 1941 when news arrived of the desperate flight of the deportees in Transnystria, the Chief Rabbi, Dr. Shafran, in secret appealed to Queen Helena. She contacted Monsignor Cassulo, the papal envoy and the doyen of the diplomatic corps, and in accordance with his advice, she persuaded Antonescu . . . to have aid sent to the deportees in Transnystria."[11] Vatican comments on such horrors may seem from a distance of more than a half century cautious and careful, perhaps to a fault. But the style of such comments was not dictated by any want of agony at what was happening but at the realization that a more perfervid rhetoric would harm the very ones one sought to help. On June 29, 1941, he said that he refrained "in solicitude for those who suffer, from revealing in detail their unspeakable sufferings and persecution."[12]

If the public statements of Pius XII did not ring with Ciceronian flights or demands that *Germania delenda est*, this was intentional, however agonizing it was to speak with measured but unmistakable condemnation. All over the world, where the pope's messages were heard, they were understood. More importantly, perhaps, he spoke through the deeds of his nuncios and bishops on the front lines of a war that Pius correctly saw as a war against the Church and the common morality the Church was entrusted to defend. In this he had read the Nazis accurately.

Martin Bormann prepared in June 1941 a top-secret memorandum addressed to the Gauleiters and Nazi leaders. "The ideas of National Socialism and of Christianity are irreconcilable," he wrote. "The Christian churches are built on the ignorance of their believers. . . . National Socialism rests on scientific foundations." Unsurprisingly, Hitler liked the memorandum. After the war, Hitler said, every country could elect its own pope. "The Christian-Jewish pest is now approaching its end," he said to Alfred Rosenberg.[13]

Some Catholics objected to the way in which the Nazis constantly tied them to the Jews, but Pius XII was not among them, any more than his predecessor had been. Pius XI had recognized that Christians are spiritually Semites. When Eugenio Pacelli was elected he was called by a strident Nazi paper "The Deputy of the Jew-God." But it was not only the common fatherhood of Abraham that linked Jew and Christian. Their common humanity provided the basis for moral laws which applied to all, believer and non-believer alike, and the Church had the duty of defending the natural as well as the divine law. This is why, in pleas for the common rights of the innocent, there was no need to make special mention of Jews. The Church must come to their defense as to that of any other innocent victim. But again and again, Pius XII did make special mention of Jews, since, among the innocent targets of the Nazi ideology, they were specified as the most dangerous of all.

Did Nazis tremble at papal condemnations of what they were doing? Not the Nazi governor general of Poland. "The propaganda against these cruelties leaves me perfectly cold. . . . I could not care less about such indignation, whether it comes from the Americans, the French, the Jews, or even the pope."[14]

Father Blet tells us how the Vatican felt its way through the various phases of the Nazi program of anti-Semitism. If the establishment of an information service so that families might communicate with prisoners met with opposition in Berlin, cooperation with the Red Cross was smooth, eased by the Swiss Catholic Mission which had been established in World War I for prisoners of war. By the end of 1943, 120,000 prisoners were listed and 43,000 packages had been forwarded to the camps.[16]

But what were the Nazis' intentions concerning the Jews? "The Nazi authorities first appeared to seek a solution to the Jewish question by expelling Jews from German territories. And so assisting these Jews meant finding countries willing to accept them. The Holy See began with the fate of baptized Jews, for this group was in very great need since Jewish relief organizations were often unaware of them."[17] The effort to help Jews emigrate began in November 1938, when a letter was sent to the pope's representatives around the world – in the Americas, in Ireland, in Africa and the Near East. In January 1939, another circular letter was sent to all the archbishops in free countries asking them to create national relief committees "to assist non-Aryan Catholics." "The next day Pius XI wrote to the two cardinal archbishops in the United States and Canada, recommending to them the Jewish scholars who were forced to leave Germany."[18] Father Blet adds that the Dutch Committee excelled all the others until the German occupation put it out of business. In Germany itself, the St. Raphael Society had great success in aiding Non-Aryan Catholics to emigrate, but it was shut down by the police in July 1941.

Archbishop Orsenigo, the papal nuncio, sent the pope this report: "A few days ago I succeeded at last in going to Berchtesgaden where I was received by Hitler," Monsignor Orsenigo, the papal nuncio in Berlin, reported to Rome. "As soon as I touched upon the question of Jews and Judaism, the serenity of the meeting was broken at once. Hitler turned his back to me, went to the window and started drumming on the panes with his fingers . . . still I went on, voicing our complaints, Hitler, all of a sudden turned round, went to a small table from which he took a water glass and smashed it to the ground with fury. In the face of such diplomatic behavior, I had to consider my mission as terminated."[15] A symbolic re-enactment of Kristalnacht? Perhaps the very thought of Jews made Nazis want to break glass.

One of the resettling projects was for Roumanian Jews to be settled in Spain. "In the summer of 1939 a certain Dr. Kirschberg presented the Vatican with a plan to populate the Portuguese colony of Angola with Jews."[19] Other places ranging from Venezuela to Alaska were proposed, but the Vatican backed a plan to help Jews emigrate to Brazil, "which brought about real though, to be truthful, limited results."[20] With the help of Cardinal Faulhaber of Munich and the St. Raphael Society, the plan was set in motion. The United States had made immigration more difficult, requiring a wait of three or four years, but Brazil was willing to give three thousand entry visas. Allegedly, Faulhaber was unable to obtain them. The plan finally got under way in March 1940, but as Blet remarks, the results were not great. There would be notable successes in subsequent years, particularly when emigration was known to thwart rather than fulfill Nazi plans for the Jews.

Cardinal Innitzer in Vienna, with personal experience of what was happening, appealed to the Vatican on May 20. "The situation of the non-Aryan Catholics continues to become very bleak; on the one hand, their misery constantly increases; on the other hand, the possibility of assisting them constantly decreases; above all, it is no longer possible to obtain visas so that they might leave. Twenty-thousand non-Aryans have gone from Vienna into the General Government, and among them are a thousand Catholics whose situation is hopeless. So it is almost impossible to help them."[21] Archbishop Orsenigo, the papal nuncio in Berlin, had forebodings. "As is easily supposed, this suppression of news leaves the gate open to the most gruesome suppositions as to the fate of the non-Aryans. Unhappily, there are rumors, difficult to control, of catastrophic journeys and even of large massacres of Jews." The awful truth was beginning to be known.

But papal concern for the victims of war could no longer be confined to the East, now that France and Belgium and the Netherlands were under the Nazi yoke, to say nothing of the Protestant lands of Scandinavia – save Sweden, of course, the Switzerland of the north. Occupied France came under the racial laws imposed by the Germans – compulsory registration, the marking of Jewish business establishments, curfews, the Jewish badge. All this was soon to be seen as the prelude to deportation and death. It was a bitter thing that France, the first country that had extended civil rights to Jews, should now be forced to treat them so. Marshal Pétain took counsel with the representative of the Holy See about the anti-Semitic laws. Leon Berard, replied:

We know from history that the Church has often protected Jews against the violence and injustice of their persecutors, and that at the same time it relegated them to the ghettoes. St. Thomas in his *Summa Theologia* sums matters up: The Jews must be tolerated in the exercise of their religion; they must be protected from religious coercion . . . but it would be unreasonable for a Christian state to allow the Jews to participate in the government and thus subject Catholics to their authority. It follows that it is legitimate to forbid them access to public office. The Vatican has expressed the desire that the precepts of justice and charity be observed in the application of the law.[22]

Lapide takes pleasure from the thought that "the prince of scholastic philosophers helped to save the Jews of the city wherein he had studied theology" seven hundred years earlier. It might even be called a bonus of the Thomistic Revival initiated by Leo XIII. Berard is a somewhat faulty Thomist, however. Applying the notion of a "Christian State" to modern France just won't work. The natural law, present in Thomas's injunction of toleration and the dignity of Jews as human beings, obliges Christians, and everyone else, to treat Jews as such. But even faulty Thomism is better than none.

The behavior of the Portuguese to Jewish refugees was favorably noted. "The help offered to Jewish refugees from Nazi occupied countries in Portugal by the local non-Jewish population was emphasized at a press conference by the Director of Refugees Committee. The comparatively small Jewish community in Lisbon would have been unable to cope with the refugees that poured into the city after the collapse of France, had not the Portuguese come immediately to their assistance."[23]

The horrors of Nazi medicine were felt first in the fatherland, and Bishop von Galen won the admiration of the pope for preaching against the loathsome practice of euthanasia. "Praising Bishop von Galen, who had openly preached that "euthanasia is murder," Pius XII wrote to the bishop of Berlin on September 30, 1941, that "his three sermons have afforded us solace and satisfaction, the like of which we have not felt for a long time." "Conversely, on September 30, 1941, he chided the Bishop of Berlin for the vagueness of the joint pastoral letter adopted by the Fulda Conference of German Catholic bishops: 'It is a truth that many have wished that the pastoral letter would reveal a little more of that Catholic self-confidence which animates the three sermons of the Bishop of Muenster.'"[24]

Papal pressure was exerted on Slovakia, emphasizing that it is natural law as well as specifically Christian principles that are at stake.

"Upon prodding by the Nuncio, the Slovak episcopate had already sent on October 7, 1941, a collective protest to President Tiso – their brother of the cloth – in which they stated that 'the so-called Jewish Code violates natural law and the liberty of individual conscience.'"[26] "As a result of the papal interventions, Karl Sidor went to Bratislava, where he spoke with President Tiso. 'The President assured me that he had intervened in order to mitigate these ordinances,' he reported to the papal Secretary of State, on his return to Rome. Sidor also went to see Tuka, to complain, on be-half of the Vatican, that the Slovak Government had still not replied to the Vatican's note of protest dated November 12, 1941. Tuka's answer according to Sidor: 'The Prime Minister has not yet replied as he hoped to give the appropriate explanations in person to the Holy Father.'" On May 8, 1942, the Slovak Government at last replied to the papal note of November 12, 1941: "Slovak Jews will be resettled in various centers around Lublin ... families will remain united. . . . All Jews will remain under the protection of the Reich." "Two days later Monsignor Burzio, the papal Nuncio in Bratislava, went to see the Slovak president in order to stress 'the injustice of these ordinances which also violate the rights of the Church.' Upon receiving the Nuncio's report, the papal Secretary of State instructed him to lodge a written protest with the Slovak government, whilst he himself prepared a note which he handed to Karl Sidor, the Slovak Minister to the Holy See, on November 12, 1941: 'With profound pain the Holy See has learnt that in Slovakia, a country whose virtually total population honors the best Catholic traditions, a 'Government Ordinance' has been published . . . which sets down a special 'racial legislation' containing

There were heroic figures in France as well, notably Cardinal Gerlier of Lyons. "Gerlier defied the authorities with an open letter of sympathy to the Grand Rabbi of France, after a crude Nazi attempt to burn the synagogues of Paris in October 1941. 'Catholics are deeply affected,' he wrote to the Chief Rabbi, 'by the tragedy which has befallen the people of Israel.' Subsequently in a pastoral letter, the Primate of France called upon all French Catholics to refuse to surrender to the authorities the hidden children of deported Jews. Apparently he had no need to ask them to shelter Jews for, as Leon Poliakov, himself a Maquis officer, states: 'Priest, members of the religious orders and laymen were rivals in giving asylum, thereby saving, as Mauriac wrote, the honor of French Catholics. The saving of their honor saved tens of thousands of Jewish lives.'"[25]

various provisions which are in open contrast to Catholic principles,' we read in the papal protest."[27]

Roumania continued to be watched and prodded. "On October 20, 1941, the Nuncio had a lengthy talk with the Roumanian Foreign Minister on his requests for intervention 'not only for Jewish converts, but also for non-converted Jews.' Mihail Antonescu, we learn from Cassulo's reports to Rome, was 'moderate and kind,' spoke of a program to solve the Jewish problem and promised that the government 'would not be lacking in mercy.'"[28] "On instructions from Rome and, it seems, with Roman funds, Cassulo 'used his influence and intervened in every possible place.' On December 5, 1941, he was able to report to the Vatican that the Roumanian government had requested him to place in their hands 'the names of converts and of non-Catholic families who had never participated in any destructive activity. The government added that, as a result of this information, no harm would come to these people.' On ripe consideration, and after consulting Rome, Cassulo turned down their ambivalent request. That he knew the Roumanians only too well was evidenced by the forcible invasion of the central church archives in July 1942 by two police inspectors who demanded access to all records in order to copy 'the names of all converts together with the names of the priests who had converted them.' The Nuncio's hurried intervention and his insistent claim of archival extraterritoriality saved the day – but three weeks later he was forced to submit the lists."[29]

Sometimes the criticism was caromed off other countries. "On November 26, 1941, Bulgarian Foreign Minister Popov had a discussion with Ribbentrop in the course of which he mentioned that the Bulgarian government was encountering difficulties in the enforcement of anti-Jewish legislation, as a large number of countries, including Spain . . . were protesting against the inclusion of their citizens."[30]

Hitler of course was aware of these constant interventions by Pius XII, personally and through his representatives in the occupied countries. This set him musing. "On December 13, 1941, Hitler said: 'The Duce has started with concessions to the Church, whilst he should have better acted in the revolutionary manner like I did. I would like to march into the Vatican and get all that pack out of there. . . . Then I would say: Forgive me, it was all a mistake. But they would have been gone."[31]

The year 1941 had seen an unbroken string of military victories by the Third Reich. But at the end of the year, on December 7, the Japanese attacked Pearl Harbor, the American naval base in Hawaii, causing enormous losses to the naval power of the United States. President

Roosevelt had been giving Churchill every military help a supposedly neutral country could – Lend-Lease – but with the Japanese attack, the massive potential of the United States was enlisted on the side of the anti-Axis powers. Despite the fact that America was brought into the war by an attack on one of her Pacific bases, Roosevelt gave priority to the war in Europe and the defeat of Hitler. Relief for the occupied countries was still years away, but now it became plausible to see their liberation ahead.

The pope's Christmas message in 1941 told the world that the moral ruins of the present time were even worse than the material ones. Force was stifling and falsifying the norms of justice, confusing the notions of right and wrong. Political order "must be based on the unshakable rock of moral law which the Creator has put into the natural order of things: He has engraved it indelibly in the hearts of men." The allusion was to St. Paul; anyone could recognize the traditional doctrine of a natural moral law, which is knowable by all and binding on all, whether religious believer or not. This had become the leitmotif of Pius XII's condemnation of the horrors being committed all around him, including the treatment of Jews. It was just because of a common humanity that the moral law can be invoked in favor of Jews and everyone else. The atrocities of the war were an assault on Christianity. But even more basically, they were an assault on humanity.

His Christmas message in 1941, which "deplored the dishonor to human dignity, liberty and life . . . which cry out for vengeance," was confiscated in Belgium and Holland, and probably elsewhere too, on orders from Berlin.

The Plight of the Jews: Dreyfus and the Diaspora

The Diaspora

The French Revolution and the declaration of the rights of man brought about a radical transformation of the lives of Jews in the Old World. The Jews had been living in isolation from other citizens in the lands where they had settled, since they were considered aliens, not really Europeans. Almost by mutual agreement, Jews were considered different from others and unassimilable into the national life. They were a nation within a nation. In cities, they were segregated into areas, into ghettos. There were more Jews in Poland than in any other nation, and there Jews had their own towns and hamlets rather than urban ghettos, and they enjoyed political autonomy and self-government. In the East, life for Jews worsened at the end of the eighteenth century just as vast new possibilities opened in the West.

The reason for this was the Enlightenment and the revolution it would spawn. There was a Jewish counterpart to the Enlightenment called the Haskalah, whose guiding spirit was Moses Mendelssohn (1729–1786). Mendelssohn was a devout Jew who advocated Jewish assimilation into, rather than separation from, the wider society, adopting its language and culture. The Enlightenment and the Haskalah encouraged a coming together of Jews and Gentiles in an unprecedented manner. The weakening of the hold Christianity had had on that wider culture had something to do with this, no doubt, just as the Haskalah had a secularizing effect on Jews. Many enlightened Jews became Christians – Protestants, by and large – among them members of Mendelssohn's own family. An alternative to this was to adapt Judaism to secular standards. This led to the birth of what came to be called Reform Judaism. This went hand-in-hand with what was called *Wissenschaft des Judentums*, a scholarly interest in Hebrew literature and the recovery of the Hebrew language. The Haskalah has been called the prelude to Jewish emancipation.

In 1790, French Jews were acknowledged to have the same civil rights as all other citizens, and for much of the century following, Jewish emancipation went on apace. Ghettos were abandoned. Jews were no longer a nation within the nation, but citizens on a par with all other citizens. When Napoleon convened the Jewish Assembly of Notables and the Sanhedrin in 1806 and 1807, he wanted to know how Jews themselves regarded their status in French society. The answer was a pledge of exclusive allegiance to France. Politically, Jews were Frenchmen, not Jews.

This became the hallmark of Jewish emancipation in Europe and of course in the United States, where Jews enjoyed equal rights under the Constitution. But if things grew progressively sunnier in the West, the same was not true in the East. Areas of Poland were taken over by Russia and over 1 million Jews were imprisoned in the Jewish Pale of Settlement after the Polish partitions of 1772, 1793, and 1795. Their condition became worse than it had been before.

By the middle of the nineteenth century, there were 3 million Jews in Russia, living in isolation from Christians. Czar Alexander II introduced some reforms in the 1850s and 1860s that gave Jews reason for hope, but when he was assassinated in 1881, anti-Jewish violence erupted into pogroms, and laws restrictive of Jews were passed. There grew up an anti-Semitism unlike any that had been known before. Anti-Semitism became a political ideology, the refuge of many who were unhappy with the advance of liberalism. Jews were said to be at the bottom of economic, social, and political ills. And it was racist. Jews were held to be an unassimilable people, foreign, inferior, alien.

In the 1880s there were 5 million Jews in Russia, which was, we are told, two-thirds of world Jewry. With the rise of violence and legislation against them, Jews began a mass exodus from Russia. Among the countless stories of this period is the first chapter of Raissa Maritain's *We Have Been Friends Together*, which tells of her family's passage from Russia to France.

A surprise soon met Jews who moved from the East to France. France, the birthplace of the Enlightenment, the Revolution, the Rights of Man, had an anti-Semitism of its own, which flared up in the Dreyfus case. Captain Alfred Dreyfus, a Jewish officer, was accused of treason and convicted in the 1890s. He was acquitted early in the next century, but the case provided to be symbolic of the split between those who approved and those who rejected a France based on principles not only secular, but inimical to Christianity. Jews were led to reexamine the whole question of assimilationism. Zionism was born.

Zionism

Among those shocked by the Dreyfus Affair was Theodor Herzl (1860–1904). In 1896 he published a fateful book, *Der Judenstaat* (*The Jewish State*). Herzl was a thoroughly westernized Jew whose Judaism had not been robust. But events had brought on an epiphany, the Jewish Problem. Reversing the whole trend of the recent history of the Jews, Herzl concluded that anti-Semitism plus Jewish unwillingness to surrender their identity created a problem that could only be solved in a radical way. Jews are indeed a people, a *volk*, bound together as the target of anti-Semitism. There is no solution to anti-Semitism. Jews will always be considered unassimilable because they are. Herzl drew what he took to be the obvious conclusion. Only the creation of a Jewish state could solve the Jewish problem.

From 1894 until 1904 Herzl dedicated himself to the task of transforming a vague sentiment among his fellow Jews into Zionism as a political movement. The first Zionist Congress was held in Basel, Switzerland, in 1897 with 200 delegates. Most of the delegates came from a movement that antedated Herzl's, the so-called Hoverei Zion, which had drawn its inspiration from an 1882 tract by Leo Pinsker called *Autoemancipation*. The Hoverei Zion identified Palestine as the intended place for the Jewish nation, and between 1882 and 1903 they were responsible for bringing 25,000 Jews to Palestine. The Hoverei Zion rallied to Herzl. In 1897, Palestine was a province of the Ottoman Empire, so Herzl devoted the last years of his short life to diplomatic efforts with the Turks in an effort to secure a charter that would allow large numbers of Jews to settle in Palestine.

After Herzl's death, Zionists tended to divide into those who favored continuation of diplomatic efforts and those who favored a more practical approach, that is, actually settling in Palestine now. The latter group came into the ascendancy during the years prior to the outbreak of World War I. An office was established in Palestine that acquired land for agricultural development, encouraged economic activity, and in general directed Zionist activities in Palestine. During these years, the second *aliyah*, or wave of immigrants, from Eastern Europe numbered 35,000. Not all remained – indeed half had left Palestine before the war broke out – but those who remained were extraordinary, many of them young in years and socialist in politics. They rejected the *galut*, or exile of Jews from Palestine, and set about creating a society based on social justice. The styled themselves *haltuzim*, or pioneers, and they were dedicated to the renewal of Hebrew culture. Among the members of the second *aliyah* were David Ben Gurion, Yitshak Ben-Zvi, Berl Katznelson, and Moshe Sharett.

In 1914, there were 85,000 Jews in Palestine in forty-three settlements. They said they had come to Palestine to rebuild it and to be rebuilt themselves by it. At this time, there were 127,000 members of the World Zionist Organization, a small minority of Jews worldwide. But in the wake of World War I, Zionism scored a magnificent coup, obtaining from Great Britain an international alliance. The man responsible for this was Chaim Weizmann (1874–1952), a Zionist who combined the aspirations of the two factions, the political or diplomatic type and the practical type. The Balfour Declaration was signed on November 2, 1917.

> His Majesty's Government view with favor the establishment in Palestine of a national home for the Jewish people, and it will use its best endeavors to facilitate the achievement of this object, it being understood that nothing shall be done which may prejudice the civil and religious rights of the existing non-Jewish communities in Palestine, or the rights and political status enjoyed by Jews in any other country.[1]

With the Balfour Declaration, Zionism stepped decisively onto the world stage. Its international center now shifted to London. Unsurprisingly, Weizmann was the undisputed leader of the movement. In 1920 he was elected president of the World Zionist Organization, a position he held, save for an interlude from 1931–1935, until 1946.

In 1918, the British occupied Palestine, and they were granted a Palestine Mandate in 1920. The constitution of the mandate incorporated the Balfour Declaration and underscored the historic connection of the Jewish people with Palestine. The Jewish Agency was formed, which would enlist all Jews in the establishment of a Jewish national home. Britain agreed to assist in this, facilitating immigration to Palestine, and designating Hebrew, along with Arabic and English, as an official language. The Jewish Agency functioned on behalf of the yet-to-be Jewish nation, taking responsibility for settlement, immigration, defense, foreign policy with the mandate and the League of Nations. The implication was that the agency was interim and would be replaced by the Jewish state when it came into existence.

The Balfour Declaration was careful to say that the effort to create a Jewish home in Palestine did not compromise "the rights and political status enjoyed by Jews in any other country." This took into consideration that many Jews, actually the vast majority, chose to think of themselves as citizens of the countries in which they lived, and not as temporary residents destined for eventual removal to Palestine. Indeed, many Jews, perhaps most, were hostile to the whole Zionist project. The very success of Zionism gave rise to anti-Zionism, or at least non-Zionism, among Jews.

Anti-Zionism

Orthodox Jews longed with all their hearts for a return to Jerusalem. "May my arm wither if I forget you, Jerusalem." But this would come about in God's good time and in the way he chose to bring it about. To these devout Jews, Zionism appeared to be a false messianic movement. Jewish liberals and socialists, on the other hand, were sons of the Enlightenment and saw Zionism as reactionary. They saw themselves as members of a religious community, much in the way Protestants and Catholics were members of religious communities, but not as a separate nation.

German rabbis had been in vociferous opposition to the first Zionist Congress. It had been originally scheduled for Munich, but the rabbinic opposition caused its removal to Basel. Zionism was denounced by German rabbis as fanatic and contrary to the Jewish scriptures. As for themselves, they pledged their loyalty to Germany, not Palestine. British Jews reacted against Zionism at the time of the Balfour Declaration. The emancipated Jews of England considered themselves a religious community without any separate national aspirations. Sir Edwin Montagu called Zionism a form of anti-Semitism and caused the Balfour Declaration to speak of 'a' rather than 'the' national home, as well as the language about the civil rights of non-Jewish communities in Palestine. The League of British Jews was an anti-Zionist group formed in 1917 with Lionel de Rothschild as its president.

Zionists were a minuscule minority of Jews worldwide at the end of World War I, and this was emphatically the case in Germany as well. German Jews considered themselves Germans, so far as nationality went, and their religious beliefs did not change that. But the Zionists were a presence in Germany, and their role during the Second World War would prove to be one of the most astonishing stories of all.

If the Dreyfus Affair was the inspiration of Zionism, convincing Herzl that anti-Semitism could never be overcome and that the Jew's best option was to get out of its way and emigrate to a land of his own, it can be said that Herzl misread the significance of Dreyfus. Given the retrial of the captain, given the widespread outrage, given the shame-faced reduction of his sentence, it can be argued that the net effect was a defeat for anti-Semitism. Herzl, a famous journalist in Vienna, suggested no demonstrations. When Karl Lueger, an anti-Semite, was elected mayor of Vienna in 1895, and the emperor twice refused to confirm Lueger as mayor, Herzl urged confirmation. He then proposed a solution to the poor Jewish immigrants who were flooding into Vienna. Entrust the immigrants to him, and he would lead away the unwanted Jews. His offer was refused.

Some years later, in 1902, Herzl went to England to testify on an Aliens Exclusion Bill being debated in Parliament. He proposed that instead of excluding aliens the British should support Zionism. He is reported to have said to Lord Rothschild that he was one of those wicked people "to whom English Jews might well erect a monument because I saved them from an influx of Eastern European Jews, and also perhaps from anti-Semitism."[2] Chaim Weizmann, newly immigrated to England, was already a leading theoretician of Zionism. Looking back on the controversy over the Aliens Exclusion bill, he wrote that whenever the number of Jews in any country reaches the saturation point, the country reacts against them. "This cannot be looked upon as anti-Semitism in the ordinary or vulgar sense of that word; it is a universal social and economic concomitant of Jewish immigration, and we cannot shake it off."[3]

In his negotiations with the Sultan of Turkey, Herzl sought the grant of an autonomous state in return for the World Zionist Organization assuming the Turkish Empire's foreign debts. Seeking more leverage, Herzl met with Kaiser Wilhelm in Constantinople, seeking his intervention with the Sultan in return for Herzl's taking Jews to Palestine. "I explained that we would be taking the Jews away from the revolutionary parties."[4]

When he failed with the Kaiser and the Sultan, Herzl turned next to the Czar of Russia, dealing with Vyacheslav von Plehve, who had organized the first pogrom in twenty years. Most Zionists were opposed to this. Herzl proposed that Jewish taxes be used to finance emigration. His critics magnify remarks of Herzl that he himself might have regarded as negotiating ploys or temporary trade-offs. The Russians wanted to get rid of Jews agitating for civil rights. Zionism, and emigration, could be portrayed as a solution they would accept. However unsuccessful during his lifetime, Theodor Herzl was dedicated to an idea he clearly thought would be beneficial to his fellow Jews. That he might describe it differently to them than to those whose political support he sought is scarcely surprising.

After World War I, Zionism saw itself and was seen by others as the foe of bolshevism. At the Versailles Conference, on February 23, 1919, Chaim Weizmann spoke about the Jewish problem. "There was, I said, no hope at all of such a solution – since the Jewish problem revolved fundamentally round the homelessness of the Jewish people – without the creation of a National Home."[5]

In Germany, intellectual support for the Zionist idea came from Martin Buber who felt that one can detect in the most assimilated Jew the "immortal Jewish unitary drive – this will come into being only after the continuity of life in Palestine." Albert Einstein thought that the resistance to Jews could not be eradicated by any amount of well meant pressure.[6] But most Jews supported the Weimar Republic because it promised the rights that had been only grudgingly granted under the Kaiser. In the postwar world, nazism did not seem threatening. In 1928, the Nazi vote dropped from the 6.5 percent it had in 1924 to a mere 2.6 percent. But with the Depression, there was a movement on the part of rural Germans to Hitler. In 1930, the Nazis captured 18.3 percent of the vote. Jews observed this frightening phenomenon not from a single but from a plurality of perspectives.

1942

On the World's Battle Fronts

In 1942, the Japanese enjoyed the same lightning military successes that had characterized Germany's subjugation of the European continent in 1939 and 1940. On January 2, 1942, the Japanese occupied Manila when MacArthur's forces retreated to the Bataan peninsula. On the 11th of that same month, the Japanese invaded the Netherlands East Indies, and on February 15, Singapore was surrendered to the Japanese. The Allies lost a naval engagement in the Battle of the Java Sea, which raged from February 27 to March 1, and on March 7, the British evacuated Rangoon. Java was surrendered to the Japanese on March 9. On April 9, U.S. Forces under General Jonathan Wainwright retreated from Bataan to Corregidor. An April 18, in a desperate bid for good news, Colonel Jimmy Doolittle led a group of Army planes that bombed Tokyo. The Battle of the Coral Sea, May 4–8, ended with both sides claiming victory. The aircraft carrier *Lexington* was lost in the battle. On May 6, General Wainwright surrendered Corregidor to the Japanese. In the Battle of Midway, June 4–7, which in retrospect was seen as the turning point of the war in the Pacific, the Japanese invasion was soundly repulsed in the greatest sea battle in the war.

Meanwhile, in North Africa, General Erwin Rommel captured Tobruk on June 21. On June 25, General Dwight David Eisenhower was named commander of the U.S. Forces in the European theater. On the Russian front, Sevastapol fell to the Germans and Roumanians on July 1, after a twenty-five-day siege.

The U.S. Marines began their glorious movement across the Pacific when they landed on Guadalcanal in the Solomon Islands on August 7. On August 19, a daring raid on Dieppe on the French side of the Channel resulted in heavy losses. But in North Africa, General Montgomery defeated Rommel's *Afrika Korps* in the Battle of Alam Halfa in Egypt on August 31. Rommel, beaten in the Battle of Alamein, retreated to Tunisia on November 5, and on November 8, Allied Army, Navy, and Air Forces, under General Eisenhower, landed in North Africa. On November 11, the anniversary of the implementation of the armistice that had ended World War I, the Nazis occupied the hitherto unoccupied part of France. The British retook Tobruk on November 13, and from November 19 to 22, under General Zhukov, the Russians began a counteroffensive at Stalingrad. Thus was the somewhat bleak military situation against which Pius XII operated in 1942.

The Gradual Recognition of the Final Solution

Those concerned with the Nazi treatment of Jews only gradually understood the extent of the evil they faced. The phrase, "the final solution," seems to appear in Nazi documents only in the Spring of 1942, but it was at a conference held at Wannsee in Berlin on January 20 that the decision about the fate of the Jews was made. Reinhard Heydrick, head of the Reich's security agency, presented the assembled Nazi leaders, in and out of the government, with the plan for "the final solution of the Jewish question." It was aimed at 11 million Jews, including 330,000 living in England. There was to be a transfer of the Jewish population of Europe into Poland, using the Russian campaign as the ostensible reason. Emigration was no longer possible in 1942; now the Jews – men, women, and children – were to be expelled from their places of residence and relocated outside Germany. "Henceforth, the Holy See's activity definitely had to assume a new direction: Rather than facilitating emigration, which had become impossible, it was now necessary to oppose deportation, whose tragic end was already being suspected."[1] It was frustrating that little or nothing could be done in Germany itself. Orsenigo, the papal nuncio in Berlin, was in a dilemma. "He could satisfy neither his superiors in Rome nor the German bishops, and he had to at least keep up the appearance of correct relations with the officials at Wilhelmstrasse."[2] Appeals on behalf of some persons condemned to death were successful, but every effort on behalf of the Jews in Germany failed. The Nuremberg laws exempted Jews married to Christians, as well as their children if raised as Christians, but rumors were afloat already in 1942 that this would be changed and thousands hitherto protected would be in danger. But a year would go by before any arrests were made.

Poland

Poland was the first country to feel the full fury of the Third Reich. The Nazis invaded in 1939 in tandem with their ally of convenience, Soviet Russia. The bloody hand of the conqueror fell upon the Church, on priests and bishops, and on the Jews. Communication was difficult, the primate of Poland was outside the country, and demands multiplied that the Holy Father condemn the sacrileges being committed by the invaders. Polish exiles were especially insistent, but voices within the ravaged land made the same request. But there were other voices, other Poles, who begged the pope not to incite the satanic Nazis into further violence. Throughout the long years ahead, the pope was whiplashed between the desire to condemn eloquently and the prudence urged on him by those under the oppressor's heel. Letters sent to Archbishop Sapieha, to be distributed to the clergy, were judged too risky and retained. Thus even the pastoral voice of the pope failed to reach his priests, let alone the Polish people at large. Elements of this story have been told in our account of earlier years; more emerge in our accounts of this and the following years.

Rescue Operations

Rescue operations were helped when Spain opened her doors to refugee Jews.[3] "In 1942, Spain opened her borders to Jews. Moreover, some 120 Jewish refugees from central Europe who had escaped to Rome during the early years of the war, were helped by the Pope to reach Spain in 1943. Some 2600 others got to Spain, thanks to papal intervention and the ingenuity of a Capuchin monk."[4] Lapide remarks that other efforts stand in startling contrast to those of the Vatican: "Moreover, they stand in startling contrast to the unpardonable foot-dragging and hypocritical lip-service of those outside Hitler's reach, who certainly disposed of far greater means to rescue Jews whilst there was still time: The International Red Cross specifically and the Western democracies in general."[5]

The pope's Christmas message continued to resonate. "On January 18, 1942, the Primate of Belgium published a pastoral letter entitled 'The Papal Christmas Message,' based on the Popes's appeal for peace and justice of December 24, 1941. It was read out in all the Catholic churches of Belgium on February 1, 1942: 'the idea of force, stifling and falsifying the norms of justice; the notions of right and wrong are confused, and seem all but lost . . . the new order must be based on the unshakable rock of moral law which the Creator has put into the natural order of things; He has engraved it indelibly in the hearts of all men.'"[6]

Heroic Figures

In Holland, Catholics and Protestants alike passed a Christian judgment on the principles animating their country's conquerors. "Holland's Catholic bishops went as far as threatening denial of sacraments and Christian burial to Catholics who 'subscribed to this spirit hostile to Christianity,' yet neither their pastoral letters nor their open defiance of anti-Jewish enactments could stop the exclusion of Jews from public life and the mass deportation which began in 1942."[7] Pius XII was heartened by the words and deeds of brave bishops in the field, and he let them know it. "F. R. Bornewasser, the Bishop of Trier, who dedicated a sermon to the sanctity of life, heard from Pius on February 20, 1942: 'We rejoice . . . in your courage. We praise your courage and thank you that you have spoken up publicly in so manly a manner for the honor and the law of God. . . . We are grateful to the bishops whenever they . . . keep alive the conviction that the right to life and liberty is the equal due of all nations, and that Christian love always embraces all, including those belonging to alien races."[8] "Conrad Groeber, Archbishop of Freiburg, who had defended 'not only the Christian and Catholic values, but the ultimate moral bases of human life and human dignity,' was told by Pius XII in a letter dated March 1, 1942: 'We praise your zeal and encourage you to keep pursuing this line . . . in spite of possible reprisals by the other side. . . . Your own Fatherland will one day thank you for it."[9]

In the East

"The 'Final Solution' for Slovakia's 90,000 Jews began in March 1942, when 52,000 of them were deported 'to labor camps' within four months. On March 9, 1942, several days before the first transport was due to leave, Burzio reported to the Vatican: 'I have been assured that this atrocious plan is the handiwork of Tuka, working hand in hand with Mach. . . . Saturday I went to see the Prime Minister, who confirmed the plan, defending vehemently its legality, and he dared to tell me – he who makes such a show of his Catholicism – that he saw nothing inhuman or unChristian in it. . . . The deportation of 80,000 persons to Poland, at the mercy of the Nazis, is equivalent to condemning a great number of them to certain death."[10]

"In April two escapees from Auschwitz gave Monsignor Burzio a five-hour description of the fate awaiting their brethren in Auschwitz. But already three weeks before, on March 14, 1942, the Vatican submitted to the Slovak government a second protest. 'His Holiness Secretariat of State trusts that such painful and unjust measures against persons belonging to the Hebrew race cannot be approved by a government which is proud of its Catholic heritage. . . . The Holy See would . . . neglect its Divine Mandate if it would not deplore these enactments and measures which gravely hurt the natural human rights of persons, merely because of their race. . . . It is not correct to suppose that deported Jews are sent for labor service; the truth is that they are being annihilated."[11]

"On March 17, Mr. Solly Mayer, the President of the *Schweitzer Israelitischer Gemeinebund, Dr. G.* Riegner of the World Jewish Council and myself [Richard Lichtheim, head of the Jewish Agency Office in Geneva] were received by the papal Nuncio in Berne, Monsignor Fillipo Bernardini. In this audience we explained the position, especially in the Catholic countries. The Nuncio stated that he was aware of the unfortunate situation of the Jews and that he had already reported on previous occasions to Rome. But after hearing what we had told him, he was prepared to report again to the Vatican and to recommend certain steps in favor of persecuted Jews. The Nuncio, whose attitude was most friendly and sympathetic, then asked for a short memorandum which he promised to forward to Rome." The requested memorandum was submitted on March 18 and reached Rome a few days later.[12]

The German bishops did not of course remain silent and their pastoral letter caught the attention of *The New York Times*. "The German Catholic bishops issued a second pastoral letter on March 22, 1942. Both were formal protests against policies of the Nazi regime, and were read publicly in every Catholic pulpit through Germany. The second, read on Passion Sunday, protested vehemently against 'all violations of personal freedom,' against killing of insane persons and the proposal to kill incurables, against unjust seizure of individuals and their property." This appeared on June 7, 1942, and the following day, the *Times* editorialized as follows: "A courage no less exalted than that of the Christian martyrs in pagan Rome inspires the Passion Sunday letter of the

German Bishops read in all Catholic churches of the Reich. They go on to show with irrefutable logic that this assault on the church is only part of a broader attack on human rights, human freedom and the human spirit." (June 8, 1942)

The Holy See could help the victims of war in Italy with something approaching freedom, but helping the Jews in Germany was impossible. It was another thing in the countries that were occupied by Germany, although each had its particular aspects. The president of the Republic of Slovakia, Joseph Tiso, was a Catholic priest who had risen to his post after having been a leader of the national Slovak movement. It was anomalous for a priest to occupy such a post, but Giuseppe Burzio of the nunciature in Bratislava assured the pope that Tiso remained in office in order to save what he could. Nonetheless, an anti-Semitic code was promulgated in September of 1941. When Burzio informed the Holy See of this, he was instructed to protest in writing while the secretary of state scrutinized the text of the law. A note of protest was sent Karl Sidor who represented Slovakia at the Vatican. "On March 21, 1942, a pastoral letter was read, by episcopal orders, in all Slovak churches. The letter, which clearly speaks of the 'lamentable fate of thousands of innocent fellow citizens, due to no guilt of their own, as a result of their descent and nationality' was inspired by Rome."[13] The Jewish Agency in Berne was kept abreast of these efforts.

"On April 2, 1942, the Nuncio in Berne was able to reply to Lichtheim: . . . 'As I promised, I have informed the Secretariat of State of his Holiness of the situation of your co-religionaries in Central Europe. At this moment I have received news from H. E. Cardinal Maglione, according to which the Holy See has already made demarches with the Slovak authorities in an attempt to have measures, recently taken against non-Aryans, revoked."[14]

Nor were the Nazis unaware of what the Vatican was up to. The pope's influence was feared if German soldiers were allowed to visit Rome. In his diaries, Joseph Goebbels noted, "I proposed to the Fuehrer that he forbids the visits of German soldiers to the Pope. This series of visits has already become a public danger. . . . The present Pope is clever enough to use these things for obvious propaganda. (Goebbels dairies, page 16, April 5, 1942)."[15]

The Frustrations of Intervention

The papal nuncio in Slovakia sometimes had to give basic instructions in the faith and on morality to the officials with whom he dealt – for example, the prime minister Vojtekh Tuka, thought to be the author of the anti-Semitic laws. "In the Nuncio's report to Rome April 7, 1942, we read that Tuka had told him: 'I don't understand why you want to stop me from ridding Slovakia of the Jews, this pack of criminals and gangsters . . .' The Nuncio replied: 'It is not just to treat like criminals thousands of women and children like those included in the recent deportations. . . . Your Excellency is no doubt aware of the atrocious fate awaiting those deported Jews. . . . All the world knows of it. Admitting even that a state can abolish the norms of natural rights and the commandments of Christianity it cannot, in its own interests, ignore international opinion or the verdict of history. . . .' Two days later the Slovak President expressed his personal regrets to the Nuncio over 'the harsh words of the Minister' and as a gesture of goodwill canceled the deportation order for 4000 Slovak Jews."[16] "'It was then, under direct orders from Pius XII, that the Slovak Minister to the Holy See was summoned at once and requested to take immediate action with his Government, with a view to averting the implementation of these orders. At the same time the Nuncio in Bratislava was telegraphically informed of this demarche, and instructed to contact personally the President of Slovakia, appealing to his sacerdotal sentiments.' Richard Lichtheim confirms in a letter dated April 9, 1942: 'A telegram from Rome which has appeared in the press shows that the secretary of State Maglione has, on March 25, 1942, received the Slovak Minister to Rome, apparently in connection with this intervention.'"[17]

Jewish leaders wanted to make sure that the Vatican was aware of what was happening in Slovakia. Archbishop Bernardini, papal nuncio in Berne, sent a message that Aguda Israel (the international organization of orthodox Jews) wanted the pope informed of developments in Slovakia. And on March 13, Archbishop Rotta, the nuncio in Hungary, sent an appeal from the Jewish community in Bratislava, the note having been passed on to him by a Hungarian prelate. Cardinal Maglione said to Karl Sidor what Burzio the nuncio was saying to his government, concluding "With every hope that this information does not correspond to the truth, the Secretariat of State cannot believe that a country intending to be inspired by Catholic principles will take such grave measures which will produce such harmful consequences for so many families."[18]

"On April 8, 1942, Lichtheim reports to the Jewish Agency in Jerusalem: '. . . You will see that the Vatican, after receiving our memorandum, has intervened, and the object of our letter of today to the Nuncio [in Berne] is to induce the Vatican to watch events and intervene again. . . . It is, of course, too early to say if the Slovakian Government will be willing or in a position to follow the advice given by the Vatican, but there is now at least some hope, that the measures already taken, or to be taken in future, may be alleviated to some extent.'"[19]

When he was told that in Slovakia young Jewish women were being carried off and sent to German brothels in the east, on the pope's orders Maglione immediately called in Karl Sidor and "requested that he intervene as soon as possible with his government in order to stop such a horror."[20]

Under Vatican pressure, deportations had been stopped, but in late April they began again. At the pope's urging, the Slovak bishops published in the Church weekly *Katolicke Noviny* on April 26 an open letter in which the faithful were reminded that Jews are human beings and must be treated accordingly. In any observance of the law, the divine law must take precedence.[21] Blet tells us that the letter had been heavily censored before it could be published but retained the sentence, "The Jews are also people and consequently should be treated in a humane fashion." The Vatican was appalled at what was happening in a Catholic country. Maglione told Sidor that such actions as those against young Jewish women were a disgrace, especially in a Catholic country, and he insisted that his words be sent on to his government.

Despite all these efforts, a law authorizing Jewish deportation was passed, with no votes against. The deportation of half a million Jews to eastern Europe was part of a German plan, the Vatican was informed, that would involve France, Holland, Belgium, Hungary, and, of course, the Reich itself. The note from the Slovak government assured the Vatican that the Jews would be humanely treated. The Germans had told them so. The prime minister even argued canon law with the Vatican in defending the law against intermarriage. Cardinal Maglione repeated: "The Holy See would shirk its divine mandate if it did not deplore these arrangements and measures which gravely strike at people's natural rights from the simple fact that these people belong to the human race."[22] Such dogged diplomacy paid off. The Slovak ministers professed to be flattered by all this attention from the Holy See. The deportation of four thousand Jews, for which all preparations had been made, was suspended.

Jewish leaders were aware of these efforts, and were grateful for them, however mixed their results. "Benjamin Arditi, a former Israeli Knesset Member and one of the leading figures of Bulgarian Jewry at the time, mentions some of these interventions: 'After the concentration of the Jews of Sofia and those of the annexed regions of Thrace and

Macedonia, it transpired that the number of Jews deported was considerably smaller than those figuring on the deportation lists. . . . Many were never arrested, as a result of the intervention of foreign embassies in Sofia. A great share of these diplomatic interventions are to the credit of the papal Nuncio, who was also the Confessor of Queen Johanna and used his influence on behalf of the Jews. . . . On May 7, 1943, during the first meeting of Jewish representative with the Nuncio, he was requested to use his good offices with the Queen and the Catholic ambassadors, in order to urge the King and his Government to avert further deportations. He promised to do all he could and asked us to visit him on the morrow, after dusk. . . . The efforts of the Nuncio were crowned with success, though not completely. . . . Several hundred Jews from Thrace and Macedonia also owe their lives to the active intervention of the papal envoy. . . . Later, when deportations again threatened, he promised to ask for an urgent audience with the Queen and to insist that she obtain the King's cancellation of the deportation order.'"23

In Holland

Occupied Holland was under the heel of *Reichskommisar* Seyss-Inquart. The ploy of fomenting

The Terrible Truth

The Vatican did not for a minute believe the Slovak assurance that the families of Jews would remain united when they were resettled in Poland near Lublin. Richard Lichtheim, the Jewish Agency's man in Switzerland, passed this on to Jerusalem. In his letter of May 13, 1942, he drew attention to what the Vatican had tried unsuccessfully to do: "[as to] interventions of the Vatican, this as you know has been done, but the representations made by the Vatican have been of no avail." Lichtheim had been picking up persistent rumors of extermination of Jews in the Polish camps, and he asked for an urgent interview with the papal nuncio in Berne.[24] *"In June 1942, a Dr. Reifer of Czernovitz had written a letter in Latin to the Pope, which had arrived in Rome by means of the Nuncio's diplomatic pouch. The starvation, epidemics, cruel beatings and killings described in the letter were corroborated in another letter which the papal Nuncio in Berne sent a few weeks later on the strength of two eyewitness reports. Both letters conclude with a fervent appeal for papal help. These appeals, which were soon followed by reports from Cassulo in Bucharest and Roncalli in Istanbul, 'awoke the Vatican to the fate of the Jewish people as a whole, and to the necessity for action.'"*[25]

riots in which young Dutch men were supposed to harass Jews failed. When Seyss-Inquart continued the campaign against the Jews, the Catholic bishops of Holland, together with the Protestant bishops, sent a telegram of protest against the deportation of Dutch Jews.

> The Catholic bishops of Holland tried that gamble and failed. In July 1942, together with the Protestant churches, they sent a telegram of protest against the deportation of Dutch Jews. . . . The Germans retaliated by seizing and deporting all Catholic non-Aryans they could find, among them Edith Stein. There was thus some basis for the fear that a public protest, along with any good that could come if it, might make some things worse.[26]

The One and Only

Pius XII and his collaborators in the Vatican made constant use of the diplomatic apparatus of the Holy See, particularly of the papal nuncios located in key cities in the occupied countries. "During 1942, Dr. Alexander Shafran, the Chief Rabbi of Roumania, had several meetings with Cassulo 'who approached both Antonescus again on behalf of the Jews . . . but his request were deferred.' However, he kept on trying, as we learn from his diary: 'At this moment the Catholic Church is the one and only body which can intervene usefully in order to improve the lot of so many unhappy people,' he writes on July 3, and continues beseeching, imploring and petitioning even the German ambassador, von Killinger, and Captain Richter, Eichmann's local expert on Jewish affairs."[27]

Meanwhile, Hitler groused about these impertinent priests and looked forward to a time when he would settle accounts with them. On July 4, he told his inner court: "Once we stop paying the priests a billion a year, they will soon stop their impertinence, and instead of cursing us, they'll eat out of our hand. All attempts by the Church in matters of state must be ruthlessly rejected. After the war there will be an end of the concordat. I myself will take the pleasure of telling the Church all the cases where she broke the concordat."[28]

Meanwhile, in Holland as the first two trains carrying Jewish deportees left the country, the Catholic bishops on July 11, 1942, once again protested to the *Reichskommisar* "against the anti-Jewish measures which are in blatant contrast to the moral sentiments of the Dutch people, and in opposition to Divine Law."[29]

That July, in Roumania, the pursuit of Jews led the police to break into Church records in search of their prey, enacting "the forcible invasion of the central church archives by two police inspectors who demanded access to all records 'in order to copy the names of all converts together with the names of the priests who converted them.' The Nuncio's hurried intervention and his insistent clam of archival extraterritoriality saved the day – but three weeks later he was forced to submit the lists."[30]

Under the Occupation

As Eichmann's henchmen reached Paris and rounded up 12,884 stateless Jews, other French prelates followed the example set by the bishop of Toulouse. The bishop of Montauban, Monsignor P. M. Theas, instructed his priests to read the following urgent message: "My dear brethren, scenes of indescribable suffering and horror are abroad in our land . . . in Paris, by tens of thousands, Jews are being subjected to the most barbarous treatment. In our district we are witnessing heartrending spectacles of families being uprooted, of men and women being treated like beasts . . . I indignantly protest in the name of Christian conscience and proclaim that all men . . . are brothers, created by One God. The current anti-Semitic measures are a violation of human dignity and the sacred rights of the individual and family. May God comfort and strengthen those who are persecuted." The bishop of Montauban was later deported, but other clergymen rose to their pulpits to voice the indignation of the Church – Delay of Marseilles, Moussaran of Albi, and Remond of Nice. A joint declaration instituted by Cardinal Suhard of Paris, signed by all the cardinals and bishops of occupied France in July 1942, and submitted to Marshal Pétain, stated: "Profoundly shocked by the mass arrests and inhuman treatment meted out to the Jews, we cannot stifle the outcry of our conscience. In the name of humanity and Christian principles, we raise our protest in favor of the inalienable rights of the human being. . . . We ask you to comply with our appeal, so that justice and charity be respected."[31]

In Hungary, the premier urged the Nazis to reverse their decision to deport Budapest Jews, a policy against which the Spanish, Swiss, and Hungarian governments had protested.[32] Racial legislation had been enacted in Hungary despite the opposition of the bishops. Polish refugees had been expelled in 1941, but massive exportations of Jews did not take place until 1944 when the Germans took over the country. In the meantime, constant pressure was put upon the government, pleading with it to act according to common morality and Christian principles. The pope's representatives acted as soon as various situations were brought to their attention, sometimes reacting with great passion. The future John XXIII, the apostolic delegate in Istanbul, conferred with Chaim Barlas, the Jewish Agency's representative in Turkey. "Barlas describes this meeting with Roncalli: 'He rose in angry amazement and said in a whisper: "Good Lord! Is it possible? Lord in Heaven, help us!" And he rushed to his desk, opened the typewriter and wrote a long message on a cable form. Calling his attendant to have it delivered at once, he said : "Let us pray that this will save us.""[33] *"Us."* Pius XII and his nuncios had effectively identified themselves with the fate of the Jewish people, and Jewish representatives went to them with complete assurance that they would find allies in the desperate struggle to deny victims to the final solution.

In France, the whole hierarchy acted as one in condemning the racial policies of the occupying forces. Cardinal Suhard issued a condemnation in July which bore the signatures of all the cardinals and bishops of the "eldest daughter of the Church."

The Infamous Reichskommisar

The Dutch bishops, together with their Protestant counterparts, had vigorously opposed the Nazi racial policies administered by the *Reichskommisar* Seyss-Inquart. And the Dutch refused to shun their Jewish fellow citizens, now forced to wear the identifying star. From 1934, the Roman Catholic hierarchy had threatened with severe penalties anyone who joined the Dutch version of national socialism. This example has often been cited as one that should have been followed by the German hierarchy. "No religious community since Hitler's rise to power had more militantly opposed the rise of National Socialism in Holland than the Catholic Church . . . when the Dutch bishops spoke strong words [under the occupation] they must have felt themselves supported by the power and approval of the Holy See."[34] Indeed. Orsenigo, the nuncio in Berlin, was relaying to Rome what he heard from the Netherlands. It was his information, sadly untrue, that the bishops' protest had had the desired effect. But the heroism of the Dutch hierarchy would also serve as an object lesson in the tragic consequences of open confrontation. When their joint public protest with the Protestant bishops failed to deter Seyss-Inquart, they prepared another pastoral letter and intended to include their exchange of letters with the *Reichskommisar.* He warned them not to do this. The Synod of Reformed Churches agreed to the exclusion, but not the Catholic archbishop of Utrecht; he had it read in all the churches of his diocese on July 26, 1942. Here is a shortened form of the letter as it is found in Pinchas Lapide.

> Ours is a time of great tribulations of which two are foremost: the sad destiny of the Jews and the plight of those departed for forced labor . . . all of us must be aware of the terrible sufferings which both of them have to undergo, due to no guilt of their own, we have learned with deep pain of the new dispositions which impose upon innocent Jewish men, women and children, the deportation into foreign lands . . . the incredible suffering which these measures cause to more than 10,000 people is in absolute opposition to the Divine Precepts of Justice and Charity. These compel us to ask the authorities not to put into effect these orders . . . Beloved faithful, let us pray to God and for the intercession of Mary, Mother of mercy and compassion . . . that He may lend His strength to the people of Israel, so sorely tried in anguish and persecution.[35]

The response of Seyss-Inquart was immediate. "If the Catholic clergy does not bother to negotiate with us, we are compelled to consider all Catholics of Jewish blood as our worst enemies, and must consequently deport them to the East," Seyss-Inquart announced on August 3. There were 156 Jewish Catholics in Holland and Belgium. The angels of death descended. "German Jews were the principal object and, as is known, Edith Stein, who had become a Carmelite, was one of their number. It can be presumed that the 156 candidates for emigration to Brazil were likewise deported."[36] They were deported to Auschwitz, where death awaited them.

Solidarity of Catholics and Jews

The solidarity Catholics felt with the persecuted Jews is one of the most moving features of these dark days. Words could not stop the diabolical policy of the Nazis, of which Jews were the principal and most easily identified target. But prayers of anguish lifted to heaven where the God of Abraham and Isaac saw his people of both covenants caught in one of the great tragedies of history. Edith Stein, a Catholic of Jewish descent, offered her death for the Jewish people. Her canonization by John Paul II seals the solidarity of Catholics and Jews, manifest at dramatic moments in World War II, but subject since to assaults from the most surprising directions. In the *Bulletin* of the National Conference of Christians and Jews, note was taken of the reprisals against Catholics.

"Reprisals have been taken against the churches. Catholic priests are being treated harshly. State financial grants have been withdrawn, and Church property has been confiscated."[37]

The heroism of local hierarchies had its source in the souls of those who acted in the face of a menacing tyranny. But it is also clear that the papal nuncios and local hierarchies were being guided by Rome as well. Some historians guessed this, others found some evidence of it; now we know that, despite the difficulties of the German occupation, the Vatican diplomatic network functioned throughout. The nuncio represented the Church to the government, but he was as well the pope's man to his fellow Catholics, acting as a conduit through which information passed back and forth.

Cardinal Van Roey, the primate of Belgium, reported to Maglione in the Vatican. "At present, the treatment meted out to the Jews is really inhuman and arouses general indignation and compassion . . . I tried to obtain certain mitigations but, alas, to no avail." But the cardinal did not let the matter rest there. Later, in October, after 14,000 Jews had been deported, he addressed a clandestine meeting of *Action Catholique* in Brussels and said, "It is forbidden for Catholics to collaborate in the foundation of an oppressive government. It is obligatory for all Catholics to work against such a regime."[38]

The Nazi Reaction

The Nazis – and the American press – were aware of these exchanges. "On August 6, 1942, the press section of the Nazi Foreign Office in Berlin circulated the following 'strictly confidential' report to all missions abroad: 'According to reports from New York, the papal Nuncio in Vichy has lodged a protest, in the name of the Pope, against the anti-Jewish measures taken in France. The Nuncio has demanded of Marshal Pétain to stop, what he called, the cruel arrests of unprotected human beings. To Pétain's reply that he hoped the Pope would understand and approve his attitude, the Nuncio retorted: "Marshal Pétain, the Holy Father can neither understand this nor approve of it." Speaking of other protests, apparently timed to coincide with the Nuncio's appeal to Pétain, the *Christian Science Monitor* of August 6, 1942, wrote: "Leading Roman Catholic clergymen in France, apparently with support of the Pope, have made an appeal to the Vichy Government in an effort to alleviate the conditions of the Jews, and curtail an anti-Semitic program."'"[39]

Hitler himself professed to be amused by the efforts of the Church to thwart him. "Only when the book [Rosenberg's *The Myth of the Twentieth Century*] was mentioned in a pastoral letter, was it possible to get rid of the first 10,000 copies. . . . When, later on, the book was put on the Index, public demand for it continued to rise. And when the Catholic Church brought out all its combatant pamphlets against the concepts of Rosenberg . . . his editions climbed up to 170,000, and then even to 200,000 copies.'"[40] This remains the anguish and irony of opposing egregious falsehoods – the phenomenon was repeated with *The Deputy*. But the lesson to be drawn is not to let such calumny go unanswered. Lies are driven out by the truth.

A renewed protest by the bishops of Slovakia against deportations, made on August 13, brought about a six-month discontinuance of them. "By the end of 1942 some 55,000 Slovak Jews had been deported, but Eichmann and his minions could not get their hands on the rest. The reason is given by Mr. Gideon Hausner, the Attorney General in Israel's trial against Adolf Eichmann: 'Pressure was exerted through Church circles, and the Slovakian Government began to have doubts about continuing the deportations. Ludin, the German ambassador, reported that owing to the influence of the Church and the corruption of the Slovakian administration, the 35,000 Jews remaining in Slovakia had been issued with documents exempting them from deportation.'"[41]

La Bombe Saliège

Archbishop Saliège of Toulouse looms large among the forceful churchmen of these trying times. When the first deportations were made from France, he wrote a statement to be read by all his priests from their pulpits.

There exists a human morality which imposes duties and recognizes certain rights. Both come from God. They can be violated, but they must never be suppressed. Children, women and fathers, have been treated like animals. That the members of one family can be severed and shipped like cattle to unknown destinations is a sad spectacle reserved for our days. Why does the right of asylum no longer exist in our churches? Why have we surrendered? Lord, take pity on us! Our Lady of God, pray for France! In our diocese horrible scenes are taking place in the camps of Noé and Récébedou. Jews are men, Jews are women . . . they are a part of mankind. They are our brothers. A Christian cannot forget that. France, my beloved France, France which cherishes in the conscience of all its children the

*tradition of respect for the individual; France the generous and
chivalrous – France is not responsible for these horrors.*[42]
And he added at the bottom: "To be read out next Sunday without comment. August 22, 1942."

*When the prefect of Toulouse demanded that the pastoral letter be
withdrawn, Saliège refused "It is my duty to teach morals to the members
of my diocese, and when it is necessary, to teach them also to government
officials." The prefect cabled all districts in the Department to forbid its
reading. "Nevertheless it was read in some 400 churches, copied and
stenciled and soon dubbed the 'bombe Saliège.' The BBC repeated it,
and in matchboxes, tins and cigarette cases it found its way into the hideouts of the Maquis and the German prison camps. As the* Osservatore
Romano *puts it: 'Saliège became a national hero, a symbol of spiritual
resistance and courage.' It was on Pius XII's express orders that the*
Osservatore Romano *and Radio Vatican repeated Saliège's protest twice
and commented on it for four consecutive days. It was also Pius XII who
elevated Saliège to the Cardinalcy early in 1946. When Laval heard of
Saliège's appeal, he called the Nuncio's deputy, Monsignor Rocco, and
requested him to call to the attention of the Pope 'the French government's determination not to permit interferences of this type in French
internal affairs.' Laval also warned Rocco – on solid grounds – that 'in
the event of any attempt on the part of the clergy to shield deportable
Jews in Churches and cloisters, he would not hesitate to use the French
police to drag out the Jews.'"*[43] *Laval made clear to Valeri that the final
destination of those deported would be Poland, where the Germans, he
said, in grisly reference to the nuns, were thinking about creating "a type
of mother house."*[44]

The New York Times

The New York Times informed its readers on August 27, 1942, that when
the Vichy government began the deportation of Jews from unoccupied
France in the summer of 1942, Pope Pius XII intervened to save the
Jews, joined by what the *Times* called "a spirited protest against racial
and religious persecution" by Cardinal Suhard of Paris and Cardinal
Gerlier of Lyon. Readers were told that local bishops protested the government's action after the Vatican learned that the Germans had asked
for Jewish deportations to supplement farm and mine labor in Silesia
and Poland, a policy that was to be extended throughout Germany,
Austria, Poland, Czechoslovakia and the Baltic states, rounding up all
the Jews who had sought refuge since 1936. (*The New York Times,*

August 27, 1942.*)* On September 3, the *Times* reported on the way in which Jews were being helped and shielded from arrest and deportation. The Vichy government said the Germans made them do it. The *bombe Saliège* was reported in the issue of September 5, 1942.

In Holland, the bishops did not relent. "On August 23, 1942, after a rapid succession of transports had deported close to 40,000 Dutch Jews, the Catholic bishops again protested to Hitler's local satrap: 'Love of truth obliges us to protest energetically . . . our faithful have a right to know what is being done by their representatives . . . we appeal to you, in the name of humanity and Christian ideals . . . to stop forthwith all measures of deportation and internment.'"[45]

Across Europe, Jews tried desperately to escape their fate. "In the summer of 1942 when Nazi 'deportations to the East' were intensified, thousands of hapless Jewish refugees tried to swim, crawl or smuggle themselves across the German-Swiss border. Many were shot in the attempt, others were given away, but some made it. 'The [Swiss] authorities in Berne have now decided to stop this influx,' we read in a report of Richard Lichtheim, Head of the Jewish Agency in Geneva, dated August 28, 1942, 'and to send back a number of those who during the last weeks had arrived here. . . . You can easily imagine what it meant for those unfortunate people. They were not actually handed over to the Gestapo, but were led to the frontier and forced to cross it. Nobody knows what happened to them.'"[46]

The pope wrote to the Polish clergy on August 28, 1942, after all Vatican attempts to improve the lot of the Catholic Church in Poland had failed. The Holy Father offered moral encouragement, exhorting the clergy not to lose heart. The reply did not come until the end of October. Archbishop Sapieha thanked the pope but added that he dared not publish it as Pius had wished, "for this would bring about new persecutions."[47] The pope's concern encompassed the Jews in Poland as well. "On August 29, 1942, the Archbishop of Lwow, Metropolitan Andreas Szeptycki, wrote to the Pope: '. . . we foresee that the regime of terror will grow worse and turn against the Christian Poles and Ukrainians. The butchers, accustomed to massacre thousands of innocent Jews, are used to seeing blood flow in streams and they thirst for blood.' Thinking perhaps of the Poles complicit in these massacres, he went on to say: 'If persecution will take on the form of murder for religion's sake, this may be the salvation of our country. There is a tremendous need for blood voluntarily offered, to atone for the blood criminally shed.' And he concluded by asking papal advice. A reply from Pius, the contents of which we do not know, reached him on September

12, 1942. Two days later he replied, thanking the Pontiff for 'his wise counsels, and his true and sincere consolations.' On the next day, the Metropolitan sent an appeal to all his clergy in which he violently opposed all racial persecution."[48]

Interventions in Roumania met with some success. Deportations to Transnystria were renewed in the autumn of 1942, and the Council of Roumanian Jewry decided that the chief rabbi should appeal to Monsignor Cassulo. Cassulo went immediately to both Jon and Mihail Antonescu, but his request was refused. Cassulo asked them who had given them the authority to decide the fate of innocent human beings. He left in anger. In September he went to Rome for consultations, armed with extensive information on the treatment of Jews. On November 24, back at his post, he submitted a lengthy memorandum to the government, conveying the Vatican's condemnation of the way Jews were begin treated in Roumania. This was effective, as the Jewish leaders reported: Antonescu suspended the deportations.[49]

The Archbishop of Lyons

In September 1942 when Eichmann's men arrested six stateless Jewish families, the French agents – being French – conceded to the deportees the choice of taking their children with them or leaving them behind and gave them an hour to make up their minds. It was night, but they woke up Cardinal Gerlier, the Archbishop of Lyons, who also served as chairman of *Amitié Chrétienne*, a relief organization for Jewish refugees. At the hapless parents' request, the Cardinal took the nine children into his home, pledged himself for their safety – and promised in writing not to have them baptized. Four days later when the Prefect, on Eichmann's orders, came to the Cardinal's house to collect the children, they were gone. To the demand for their address, Gerlier replied, (and quoted himself in a subsequent report to the Vatican) "Monsieur le Préfet, I would not consider myself worthy to be the Archbishop of Lyons if I complied with your request. Good day."

As the arrests continued, Gerlier decided to protest publicly. He tried to do in his diocesan weekly, *Semaine religieuse*, but the censor stopped him. So he had the message typed out, mimeographed and distributed to all priests by the Catholic scouts of his city: "The deportations of Jews now in course cause such painful scenes that we must lift our voices in conscientious protest. We witness a dispersal of families in which nothing is spared, neither tender age, nor weakness nor the sick. . . . Who will stop the

Church from loudly confirming in this dark hour the irrefutable rights of men, and the sanctity of family ties, the availability of the rights of asylum, and that brotherly charity which Christ has taught us? . . . the honor of France demands that we never abandon these principles."

Laval soon implemented his threat. Three days after Gerlier's message, his right-hand man, Jesuit Elder Chaillet, was arrested and accused of hiding eighty Jewish children. Actually he had hidden over two hundred, in various public institutions and religious homes, with the active assistance of his Cardinal, who spirited them away as Chaillet went to jail. Chaillet alone, who was later released, is credited with the rescue of 1800 Jews. In the 1943 Bulletin of the U.S. National Conference of Christians and Jews, we read (pp. 24–26): 'As an outcome of the Church's defiance, Laval ordered the arrest of all Catholic priests who were found to have hidden Jewish children in their presbyteries. Within two months, more than 120 parish priests . . . were suddenly taken away from their homes to Metz, thence to be deported East "to unknown destinations." The first important Church-State conflict in France since the German occupation developed over the arrests of French clergymen because of their opposition to anti-Semitic decrees."[50]

Jewish leaders expressed gratitude for what the Vatican was doing for their fellow Jews on the occupied continent. "London's *Jewish Chronicle* wrote editorially on September 11, 1942: 'A word of sincere and earnest appreciation is due from Jews to the Vatican for its intervention in Berlin and Vichy on behalf of their tortured co-religionists in France. . . . It was a step urged, to their honor, by a number of Catholics, but for which we may be sure, the Holy Father himself, with his intense humanity and his clear sighted understanding of the true and deadly implications of the assaults on the Jewish people, needed no prompting.'"[51]

Nor were those responsible for the outrages against which the Church was working unmindful of their foe. Roberto Farinacci, editor of the Fascist *Regime Fascista* wrote in October 1942: "The Church's obstruction of the practical solution of the Jewish problem constitutes a crime against the New Europe."[52]

And *The Universe* in London, on October 9, 1942, gave contemporary witness to the activities of the Church under the direction of Pius XII. "From St. Peter's throne the late Pope himself uttered the strongest protests and declarations that anti-Semitism is an un-Christian policy.

His successor has repeated these warnings and quite recently sent his Nuncio to Vichy to protest in person against the anti-Jewish measures that have been decreed in France."[53]

A Concerted Campaign

Pinchas Lapide summarizes the concerted campaign on behalf of the Jews.

> Under the rigid discipline for which Pius XII was famous, these public utterances could hardly have been made without his prior approval. A hint at concerted Catholic action we find in the report of a further protest voiced by Cardinal Hinsley, as published by the London *Universe* on October 9, 1942: "Once again a public statement has been issued in which the Cardinal Archbishop of Westminster has associated himself with the heads of the Church of England and the Church of Scotland and the Free Church Federal Council . . . in the newly formed Council of Christians and Jews of which His Eminence has agreed to become joint president . . . for the specific purpose of endorsing the condemnation of anti-Semitism and as a mark of his strong protest against all persecution of the Jewish people. . . . On the question of the persecution of the Jews, whether in Germany or France or Poland or any other country, the head of the English hierarchy will, of course, go step by step in close accord with the heads of the Catholic hierarchies in the countries involved. . . . On the broad issue of denuding and assisting the Jewish people against the savage persecution which is being so widely inflicted upon them under Nazi direction, Cardinal Hinsley has ranged himself emphatically *with the heads of the Catholic Church in all countries*." It seems that repeated Church protests like these, against Nazidom and Jewish mass murder, sufficiently impressed the Hungarian Jewish historian Jeno Levai to entitle his latest book: *The Church Did Not Keep Silent* (Paris, 1966 [after *The Deputy*]) One last point; to make Pius' voice inaudible, all Mussolini or Hitler had to do was to outlaw the *Osservatore Romano* in Italy and to cut off the current from Radio Vatican – if necessary, in mid-broadcast. That both measures were planned by the Fascist government, Paul Duclos confirms in his book *The Vatican and the Second World War* (Paris, 1955).[54]

Nor was the work of the Church confined to its hierarchy and clergy, as a snarling report by a pro-Nazi journalist, Jacques Marcy, in September 1942 attests: "Every Catholic family shelters a Jew. Even the French authorities provide the Jews with false papers and passports.

Priests help them across the Swiss border." And *Au pilori*, a Paris Nazi journal, wrote on October 12, 1942: 'We demand the head of Gerlier, the raving Talmudist, traitor to his faith, his country and his race."[55] The reference is to Cardinal Gerlier, archbishop of Lyons.

Writing to Bishop Andreas Rohrbacher on October 15, 1942, Pius XII said that "in times of war it goes without saying that Catholic priests should afford every possible help to those suffering in body or soul." [56] On that same day the Fascist *Au Pilori* complained, "We are facing a proper declaration of war by several Princes of the Church . . . we have no illusions: the alliance between the upstarts in the Church and the Jewish community is now total and complete." Guenter Lewy bears him out: "In France the highest dignitaries of the Church repeatedly used their pulpits to denounce the deportations and to condemn the barbarous treatment of the Jews."[57]

The rescue of children went on in Poland as well, a country that had suffered more than any other from the Nazi war machine and the inhuman policies of the occupation. "In November 1942, Szeptychi threatened 'with Divine punishment' all individuals who 'shed innocent blood and make themselves outcasts of human society by their disregard for the sanctity of life.' He prohibited the rendering of sacraments to individuals who embraced the Nazi gospel of murder. After the Rohatin massacre, he wrote an indignant letter to Himmler, protesting the employment of Ukrainian police in such actions. But he did not content himself with interventions and pastoral letters. In his cathedral in Lwow he hid fifteen Jewish children and six adults, including Rabbi Dr. David Kahane, who, after the liberation of Poland, was appointed chief rabbi of the Polish Army. Twenty-eight others he disguised in monks' cowls in the monastery of St. Basileus. On orders of the Metropolitan, 156 Jews, most of them children, were hidden in convents of the Order of the Studiets in Eastern Galicia. Approximately 500 monks and nuns had knowledge of these facts, but in spite of the death penalty for sheltering Jews and financial rewards for all informers, none of the Metropolitan's wards fell into Nazi hands. His ringing appeals must have had some impact on a great many peasants and workmen, clerics and priests. By the end of 1943 650 Jewish children in Warsaw were hidden in various municipal, church and social institutions."[58]

Other Voices

Lapide draws attention as well to statements from Britain and America condemning the persecution of the Jews of Europe. The Catholic hierarchy in the United States, on November 14, 1942, issued a proclamation which denounced all racial persecutions and said: "We feel a deep sense of revulsion against the cruel indignities heaped upon the Jews in conquered countries, and upon defenseless peoples not of our faith." Cardinal Hinsley in Britain gave a written statement to the *Jewish Bulletin* in March 1942, in which he said that "The cruel treatment of the Jews at any time and in any land calls for the strongest condemnation. Whoever believes in God, Our Loving Father, revolts against the tyranny of governments which oppress His children of any race. To the Christian and Catholic, Jews and Gentiles alike are sons of the Eternal Father." And on July 8, over the BBC, the cardinal remarked: "to say the truth about the crimes committed in Poland: 700,000 Jews have been killed since the beginning of the war. Of this we have clear and repeated evidence. Their innocent blood cries out to Heaven for vengeance."[59]

From Belgium, Cardinal Roey reported to Rome on December 18, 1942: "The arrest and deportation of Jews, since I wrote you on August 4, has continued uninterruptedly. . . . These measures have been carried out with a brutality and cruelty which have profoundly revolted the Belgian population. I have intervened in many cases, but often in vain." Lapide opines: "The voice of the Pope, it seems, also contributed to the fact that Belgians from all walks of life, including the Dowager Queen Elizabeth, who rescued several hundred young Jews, took part in the great crusade against deportations."[60]

"A lonely Voice Crying Out in the Silence of a Continent."

As 1942 came to an end, Pius XII could take satisfaction in what his nuncios and cardinals and bishops were doing throughout occupied Europe. He was heartened when his bishops acted heroically and let them know it, recommending them as examples to others. Of course this was the sort of good news you would rather not get, given the fact that it was occasioned by one of the most cold-blooded campaigns in history, a final solution of the Jewish question that, it was becoming more and more obvious, meant the extermination of the Jews.

The Church and Catholics suffered as well, of course. But unlike some of the Jewish organizations, the Catholic Church had no rule against extending charity to non-Catholics. The pope's pleas – and this is reflected in the statements of the papal nuncios and the various cardinals and archbishops who issued statements – always reposed on a natural-law basis. The Christian must act on principles higher than those of the common natural morality, but that morality is included within Christian morality. It was those common principles to which Pius XII appealed again and again because the rights and duties they entail knew not Greek or Jew, Christian or pagan. If there ever was a time when the common condition of mankind was clear it was in 1942.

This note was sounded again in Pius XII's Christmas Message of 1942. "The Christmas message of 1942, which pleaded for 'the hundreds of thousands who, through no fault of their own, *only because of their nationality or descent*, are condemned to death,'" not only was withdrawn from publication by the Nazis, but the print shops which were caught reproducing it were closed down or otherwise punished. In this, as in other addresses, the Pope used the word *stirps* (race, descent) in a context which clearly referred to Jews. (*Stirps Iudaeorum* and *stirpe dei Giudei* were medieval clichés as old and well known as *deicide*.) However, to make his intention even clearer, the pope added: "The Church would be untrue to herself, would cease to be a mother, if she turned deaf ears to her children's anguished cries, which reach her from every part of the human family." *The New York Times*, to quote but one paper, clearly read the papal message and concluded its editorial[61] on December 25, 1942: "If a prominent personality who is obligated to the impartial consideration of nations in both camps, condemns the new form of Nation State as 'heresy'; when he accuses the expulsion and persecution of men, *for no other reason than their race* . . . then this impartial judgment amounts to the verdict of a supreme court . . . *this Christmas more than ever the Pope is a lonely voice crying out in the silence of a continent.*"[62]

The Plight of the Jews:
Juden Raus!

While Pius XI and his secretary of state, Cardinal Pacelli, discerned the nature of nazism early on and spoke with decisive clarity of its incompatibility with Christianity, such perception was rare. Nonetheless, historians have wondered if the Church did enough. We have seen the testimonial of Albert Einstein in 1940 and the gratitude expressed by the World Jewish Congress in 1939. In Germany itself, Christians and Jews reacted with fascination to the rise of Hitler. After Germany's humiliating defeat at the end of World War I, after the carnival of the 1920s and the failures of the Weimar Republic, the fanatic certainty of Adolf Hitler made many German pulses race.

It is easy in retrospect to see the whole tragedy of Nazi Germany laid out in advance in *Mein Kampf*. The brooding paranoia is there, the anti-Semitism is there, the mad sense of destiny that would turn Europe into a battlefield and Germany into a heap of ashes – how, we might ask, could anyone fail to see where Hitler would take his country? But many did fail to see it. Both Jews and Christians rallied to his side.

William L. Shirer tells us that industrial and financial leaders worked with Hitler on the chance that he would in fact succeed in taking over the German government.[1] He gives some names of persons, more names of companies and banks. But he makes no mention of the fact that many of the banks were in the control of Jewish directors. One he does mention, Baron Kurt von Schroeder, not identified as Jewish, was, Shirer tells us, "to play a pivotal role in the final maneuver which hoisted Hitler to Power."[2]

No doubt these powerful men saw Hitler as a means to their own ends rather than a Führer they would follow. What Shirer means by the "final maneuver" was the meeting arranged by Baron Kurt von Schroeder between Franz Van Papen and Hitler. The meeting took place on January 4, 1933, at Schroeder's home in Cologne. Shirer describes him here simply as "the Cologne banker who had contributed funds to the National Socialist Party."

> Hitler was accompanied by Hess, Himmler and Keppler, but he left his aides in the parlor and retired to Schroeder's study, where he was closeted for two hours with Papen and their host. . . .The banker maintained that what Papen suggested was the replacement of the Schleicher government by a Hitler-Papen government in which the two of them would be coequal.[3]

Hitler had no desire to share the chancellorship; he said that supporters of Papen could be part of his government but only if they agreed to certain changes. "These changes included elimination of Social Democrats, Communists and Jews from leading positions in Germany, and the restoration of order in public life." These words are from testimony Schroeder himself gave at Nuremberg.

On March 25, 1928, in a decree dissolving a missionary society called The Friends of Israel, Pius XI took the occasion to address a certain tendency in Italian Fascism. "Moved by Christian charity, the Holy See has always protected this people [the Jews] against unjust vexations, and just as it reprobates all rancor and conflicts among peoples, it particularly condemns unreservedly hatred against the people once chosen by God; the hatred that commonly goes by the name of anti-Semitism."[4] How could this comport with a story in *Osservatore Romano* on November 27, 1929, about a Jewish threat to the world? One answer is that there are Jews and Jews, and the opposition of non-Zionist Jews to Zionist Jews has been a feature of the contemporary history of the Jews as well.

"The essentials of Zionist doctrine on anti-Semitism were laid down well before the Holocaust: anti-Semitism was inevitable and could not be fought; the solution was the emigration of unwanted Jews to a Jewish state-in-the-making."[5]

Hitler and Zionism

The anti-Semitism of Adolf Hitler, whatever vague religious origins it may have had, became fixed as a racial matter when he encountered a Galician Hasid in the old city of Vienna. "Is this a Jew?" he asked himself. As opposed to what? He did not look on this apparition in black caftan and hair locks as a non-Christian. What his question came down to was, "Is this a German?" Can such a person be assimilated into the German people?

> And whatever doubts I may still have nourished were finally dispelled by the attitude of a portion of the Jews themselves. Among them there was a great movement, quite extensive in Vienna, which came out sharply in confirmation of the national character of the Jews: this was the Zionists.[6]

But for some Zionists, nazism offered a better instrument of their policy than czar or sultan or kaiser. And the British Mandate in Palestine offered a target for the emigration of German Jews. Thus the ancient cry of German anti-Semitism, *Juden Raus!* coincided with the aims of Zionism, whatever the theoretical chasm between Nazi and Zionist might be. The Nazis could use the Zionists; the Zionists could use the Nazis.

Baron von Mildenstein, head of the Jewish Department of the SS, had spent six months in Palestine and returned as a fervent supporter of Zionism. He learned Hebrew and collected Hebrew music. His favorable report on Palestine was run as a twelve-part series in Goebbels's *Der Angriff* in 1934. With his own soil beneath his feet, von Mildenstein said, the Jew is a new man, and Jews will be a new people. In May 1935, Reinhardt Heydrich urged his fellow SS members to divide Jews into two

Hitler knew that, however extensive the Zionist movement might seem in Vienna, it was a minority position among Jews. Alfred Rosenberg might dismiss the Zionist dream of a Jewish homeland as a ruse to establish a hideout for the International Jewish conspiracy, but Hitler's attitude seems almost benign by comparison. He proclaimed Palestine to be the proper place for the Jews and the only place where they could obtain their rights. But in Mein Kampf he had adopted the Rosenberg view. "For while the Zionists try to make the rest of the world believe that the national consciousness of the Jew finds its satisfaction in the creation of a Palestinian state, the Jews again slyly dupe the dumb goyim."[7] The Zionist dream could not be fulfilled because Jews were incapable of creating a state. None of these thoughts about Zionism led to any political connection with it on the part of the Nazis, however; they picketed the 1925 Zionist Congress which met in Vienna.

categories, the Zionists and those who sought to be assimilated into the German nation. His article ends on a tender note. "The time cannot be far distant when Palestine will again be able to accept its sons who have been lost to it for over a thousand years. Our good wishes together with our official good will go with them."

The infamous Nuremberg laws were passed in September 1935, and they were defended by the Nazis as being actually pro-Zionist. At the time the laws were passed, the only Jewish publication being printed was the *Rundsschau,* the organ of the Zionists. The *Rundsschau* printed the laws, along with a commentary by Alfred Berndt, editor-in-chief of the German News Bureau. All the Nuremberg laws meant, Berndt explained, was what had been said at the World Zionist Congress in Lucerne that same year. Zionists had affirmed that the Jews of the world were to be seen as a separate people no matter where they lived. Thus all Hitler had done was to meet "The demands of the International Zionist Congress by making the Jews who live in Germany a national minority."[8] A provision of the Nuremburg laws was that only two flags were permitted in the Third Reich, the swastika and the blue-and-white Zionist banner.

Zionists outside Germany reacted with dismay to these developments. Stephen Wise knew that "Hitlerism is Satan's nationalism," but he did not deny that there was a kinship between Hitler's desire to expel the Jews from Germany and Zionist hopes that Jews could emigrate to Palestine.

In treating the German Zionists in this way, the Nazis were perfectly well aware that most German Jews were non-Zionists and had no desire to consider themselves anything other than German citizens. The assimilated Jew did not hanker for Palestine. But assimilated or not, Zionist or not, there were German Jews who thought they could reach their own ends by entering into agreements with Adolf Hitler. In the financial stratosphere where such figures as Baron von Schroeder dwelt, to the ceaseless efforts to Zionists to achieve their goal, nazism appeared to be as much of an opportunity as a menace.

Many German Catholics were swept up in the Nazi frenzy, but they could not do so without the realization that the Church condemned the principles on which national socialism rested. In his Christmas message of 1930, Pius XI stated, "If there is in Christianity the idea of a mystery of blood, it is that, not of a race opposed to other races, but of the unity of all men in the heritage of sin, derived from our first father." The pope condemned not only racism but "egotistical, hardened nationalism." In January of the following year, Cardinal Bertram of Breslau declared: "In accordance with the open appeal of the Holy Father, the episcopate must speak up against the errors deriving from the false nationalism which recently has been propagated in all regions of our fatherland. . . . We Catholic Christians know no race religion."[9]

Mussolini in 1931 was all for Jews being further assimilated. He reprimanded the Italian Jewish journal *Israel* for protesting the growing number of mixed marriages with Gentiles. In *Non abbiamo bisogno*, Pius XI disputed Mussolini's contention that the state is the end of the individual. On February 12, 1933, the Fulda Conference of German bishops told the nation that national socialism put race before religion, rejecting the Old Testament and even the Mosaic Ten Commandments. German pastors were to tell their congregations that the Nazis had adopted the principles of Bismarck's *Kulturkampf*, and these are irreconcilable with Catholic teaching. Nazi banners were not to appear in Catholic churches, "lest people think that the Church has come to terms with National Socialism." For all that Cardinal Pacelli, secretary of state, was disappointed with the Fulda meeting, asking why the bishops had met the government halfway. If only they had waited a month or so. Why? Because a concordat was being negotiated with Germany.

The 1933 concordat is often depicted as doing what Cardinal Pacelli thought the Fulda Conference had done. It is objected that the Church, by entering into a concordat with Nazi Germany, lent prestige to a government whose principles they had publicly abhorred. In response, it should be said that diplomatic relations with country X do not amount to approval of the policies of that country's government. More positively, it has to be said that the purpose of the concordat was to insure the rights of the Church in Germany. It was in this connection that Pius XI said to some bishops a few months before the concordat was signed, "If it is a matter of saving souls, of averting even greater damage, we have the courage to negotiate even with the devil."[10] In this case doubtless he had, but the German concordat, like the fourteen others signed during the pontificate of Pius XI and overseen by Cardinal Pacelli, would prove to be one sure means of staying in contact with those subsequently subjugated by Nazi occupation. Gordon Zahn, whose *German Catholics and Hitler's Wars* displays a Torquemada relish in second-guessing the German hierarchy and faithful, exempts the concordat from his condemnations. "The opinion attributed to Pius XII – that the concordat, however personally distasteful it may have been to him, had spared the Church in Germany a far greater measure of hardship and persecution than that actually suffered by it during the Nazi years – was undoubtedly true."[11]

On January 28, 1935, the Bavarian Gestapo told the regular police that Zionist organizations, because their aim is emigration to Palestine, are not be treated with the same strictness as German-Jewish, that is, assimilationist, organizations.[12] Brenner asserts that the World Zionist

Organization, in its distribution of immigration certificates to Palestine, operated under quotas set by the British. German Jews received only 22 percent of the certificates issued during the 1930s. "Furthermore the WZO were not interested in the vast majority of Germany's Jews since these were not Zionists, did not speak Hebrew, were too old and, of course, did not have the 'right' trades. Either Jewish emigration had to be organized to other countries as well, or Germany would be stuck with the Jews neither it nor the Zionists wanted."[13] Such criticisms of the Zionists by non-Zionist Jews would grow sharper yet. But German Zionists were far from comfortable with their favored status under the Nazis. "It was very difficult for Zionists to operate," wrote Joachin Prinz. "It was morally disturbing to seem to be considered as the favored children of the Nazi government, particularly when it dissolved the anti-Zionist youth groups, and seemed in other ways to prefer the Zionists."[14] Nor should it be thought that Zionists escaped Nazi harassment. The *Rundsschau* was banned three times between 1933 and 1938; 1938 of course was the year of *Kristalnacht*, when Zionist headquarters were shut down. Zionists might have felt, as did Pope Pius XI, that they would negotiate with the devil himself, not for the devil's ends, but for their own.

It is of course unjust to see identity between the common Zionist and Nazi view of the "Jewish Problem." Zionists opposed mixed marriages and believed the Jews were an alien presence in Germany (and other countries) so that anti-Semitism was inevitable. Hitler agreed, so why not enlist him in the Zionist cause of emigration to Palestine? Was it even clear to Hitler himself at this time that his aim was not the emigration of the Jews but their extermination? Even when the horror began, it would be almost impossible to believe that a campaign of mass murder had become the policy of one of the most cultivated and Christian European nations.

Palestine

In the years 1933 to 1936, 164,267 Jewish immigrants came to Palestine, lifting the Jewish population there to 30 percent in 1935. The Arabs, of course, reacted to this influx of immigrants. There had been riots in earlier years, fomented by fanatics on both sides. The presence of the British in Palestine, under the Mandate, enabled the Mufti of Jerusalem to seek and get protection from Mussolini, but the Fascists never thought they got value for their money. In 1936, the Palestinian Arabs revolted because of the flood of Jewish immigrants. Guerrilla warfare began, the British dealt severely with both Arabs and Jews, and a British royal commission was appointed to look into the matter. The Zionists then sought a public commitment from the Nazis as to Palestine. The Jewish Agency, the highest body of the WZO in Palestine, with the German Immigrants Association, went to the German consul general on December 8, 1936. But he rejected their suggestion that he appear before the Peel Commission and state Germany's eagerness to have Jews emigrate to Palestine. But an upshot of this contact was that Feivel Polkes, a member of the military arm of the Jewish Agency, the Haganah, went to Berlin on February 26, 1937, to negotiate with the Security Service of the SS. Polkes was assigned Adolf Eichmann as his negotiating partner. "Eichmann had been a protégé of the pro-Zionist von Mildenstein and, like his mentor, had studied Hebrew, read Herzl and was the SD's specialist on Zionism."[15]

This is a scene that boggles the mind, a Jew from Palestine sitting down with the man who would be placed in charge of Hitler's Final Solution of the Jewish Problem and whose post-war trial in Jerusalem would prove to be a world sensation. Of course records were kept of their talks, What did the Nazis make of their visitor?

> Polkes is a national-Zionist. . . . He is against all Jews who are opposed to the erection of Jewish state in Palestine. As a Haganah man he fights against Communism and all aims of the Arab-British friendship. . . . He noted that the Haganah's goal is to reach, as soon as possible, a Jewish majority in Palestine. Therefore he worked, as the objective required, with or against the British Intelligence Service, the Sûreté Générale, with England and Italy. . . . He declared himself willing to work with Germany in the form of providing intelligence so long as this does not oppose his own political goals. Among other things he would support German policy in the Near east. He would try to find oil sources for the German Reich without affecting the British spheres of interest if the German monetary regulations were eased for Jewish emigrants to Palestine.[16]

On October 2, 1937, Adolf Eichmann arrived in Haifa and was met by Polkes, who gave him a tour. Remembering the visit years afterward, Eichmann told of how impressed he had been. "In the years that followed I often said to Jews with whom I had dealings that, had I been a Jew, I would have been a fanatical Zionist. I could not imagine being anything else. In fact, I would have been the most ardent Zionist imaginable."[17]

1943

The Progress of the War

The seemingly unending string of Axis victories came to an end in the new year. President Roosevelt and Prime Minister Churchill met at Casablanca from January 14 to 24. The British Air Force made a first daylight bombing raid on Berlin, bringing the war to the country that had put Adolf Hitler in office, though doubtless many innocent people were now to suffer for the dictator's follies. On February 2, the Germans, exhausted, surrendered at Stalingrad and in the far Pacific, the Japanese evacuated Guadalcanal after six months of resistance. Large portions of the Japanese fleet were destroyed in the Battle of Bismarck Sea, which was fought from March 2 through 4 off the New Guinea coast. On March 11, American forces landed on the Aleutian Islands, and on the same day Axis resistance ended in Tunisia. The Allies had won the battle for North Africa.

Sicily was invaded by Allied Forces under the general command of Dwight Eisenhower on July 9 and 10. Mussolini, who had strutted and fretted on the Italian stage for nearly a quarter of a century, resigned as premier on July 25 and was replaced by Marshal Badoglio.

On August 1, the oil fields at Ploesti in Roumania were bombed by American planes. The conquest of Sicily was completed on August 17, and the next move of the Allies was hotly debated. Italy, the Vatican, Pope Pius XII were, of course, unaware that there were those who thought the invasion of Italy an unnecessary diversion. But the ultimate decision was to invade, and Allied Forces crossed the Straits of Messina from Sicily to the Italian mainland.

Italy surrendered on September 6, but her travails were just begin-

ning. On September 10, the Germans first shelled, then seized Rome.
The Vatican was then surrounded by hostile forces whose ideology the
popes had been berating for a decade. The Italian Navy was turned over
to the Allies, and on October 1 the Fifth Army captured Naples.

On October 13, Italy declared war on Germany. The Germans were
then in the country of a foe, not an ally, however demoralized and ineffective. The situation in Rome altered accordingly.

In the Pacific, American troops landed on Bougainville in the
Solomon Islands on November 1. The Russians retook Kiev on Novem-
ber 6. American forces landed on Tarawa and Makin in the Gilbert
Islands on November 20.

The First Cairo Conference was held by Roosevelt, Churchill, and
Chiang Kai-shek from November 23 to 26. Roosevelt and Churchill
then went on to Yalta to meet with Stalin from November 28 to December 1. On Christmas Eve, Eisenhower was named Supreme Commander of Allied Expeditionary Forces and began to plan the invasion of
Europe which he will lead.

Relief Supplied by Pius XII

The Pontifical Commission of Assistance and the Vatican Relief
Commission supplied food, clothing, and medicine to thousands of
needy refugees, prisoners, and partisans, including 6,000 Jews in Rome
alone. Millions of dollars were spent during the remainder of the war on
these efforts, over a million during the first half of 1944 alone, getting
food and clothing to 90,000 needy persons who had been granted asylum, and cover, in religious houses, hospitals, clinics, and other institutions under the control of the Church. Pinchas Lapide estimates that if
one were to include all those who received a warm meal, shelter, first
aid, or an overcoat at the five Vatican refugee camps in Italy, where the
only qualification for help was need and hunger, the number of Jews
assisted would surely exceed 35,000.[1]

As the year 1943 opened, Cassulo, the nuncio, on papal orders,
sought to visit the Jewish camps in Roumania. He was turned down
twice by Antonescu and then asked to postpone the tour for several
weeks. The obvious implication was that the government wanted to
make the camps, if not Potemkin villages, at least somewhat less horrendous to the archepiscopal eye. Cassulo had been entrusted by the
pope with a considerable sum of money to be distributed to the refugees
during these visits.

Throughout the tour of Kishinev-Terraspol-Odessa-Czernowitz, he made copious notes, met hundreds of Jews, received some twenty-five memoranda, and on his return to the capital had a two hour conversation with Radu Lecca, Roumania's Commissioner for Jewish Affairs. Cassulo must have been most eloquent, for at the end of their talk, we learn, the inveterate anti-Semite Lecca promised to grant, sight unseen, ten requests. Submitted on the next day, these included the removal of all deportees from German-controlled territory, the return home of all widows, the authorization of various forms of relief work, and the dispatch to Palestine of 400 Jewish orphans.[2]

Meanwhile Pius XII's 1942 Christmas letter provided ammunition for the churchmen on the front lines. In Brussels, Cardinal Van Roey issued a pastoral letter in January that was based on the pope's Christmas message. Stressed was this statement: "Let all those magnanimous and honest in spirit solemnly vow not to rest until all nations and peoples on earth return to the immutable realm of Divine Law. This vow humanity owes to the hundreds of thousands of persons who, without any fault of their own, only because of their nationality and descent, are condemned to death or exposed to progressive extinction." A pastoral letter of Cardinal Van Roey's, which stressed that "blood cannot be the source of a superior life, for all races are equal at heart" was reproduced on Pius's orders in *Osservatore Romano* and broadcast in its entirety over Vatican Radio. This broadcast, like many similar ones, was jammed by German and Italian transmitters.[4]

If there was anger at the papal "interference" in occupied countries, the same was true in Rome, especially after the Nazis took over after Mussolini's resignation. "The Nazis were displeased with the courageous attitude of Pius XII and with certain of his interventions. They assigned to him a senior German officer whose mission would be to give the Pope suitable 'advice' as required by the circumstances. Pius XII received this emissary in his private office and listened to him without saying a word. When he had finished speaking, the Pope stood up and said to him, 'Tell your chiefs that the Pope is not afraid of concentration camps.'"[3] In Munich he had faced down hooligans of the Left; his personal courage was even more evident when he dealt with the Nazis.

We have already seen how Cardinal Van Roey, in a clandestine meeting with Action Catholique, characterized the occupation government as unjust, thereby seeming to authorize rebellion against it. In

February 1943, when there were massive round-ups throughout Holland, the Church told Catholics they should practice civil disobedience rather than participate in the hunting down of Jews.[5]

If the efforts of Pius XII and the Church in the occupied countries was unrelenting, the forces of evil went tirelessly about their task. In Slovakia, because of Church pressure, the government became uneasy about deportations, and in 1942, 35,000 Jews had been issued certificates which exempted them from deportation. This infuriated the German ambassador, Ludin, and on February 7, Mach growled, "We must resume the battle. . . . Once spring is here, I assure you that the Jewish transports will move again."[6] Seyss-Inquart had called the defenseless converted Jews in Holland the greatest enemy of the Reich. German officials regularly spoke of their pursuit of innocent Jews as a war, and of particular operations as battles. It was of course a war, but spiritual, not military. The Slovak bishops, spurred on by Burzio, the papal nuncio, protested the treatment of Jews again on February 17.[7]

"We are filled with the deepest compassion for the numberless persons called upon to bear such great and bitter sufferings," says the pastoral letter which was read simultaneously in all Dutch Catholic churches on February 21, 1943. "We would fail in our duty if we did not publicly raise our voice against the injustice to which such a large part of our people is being subjected. In this *we are following the path indicated by our Holy Father, the Pope,* who in his latest Christmas message declared: *The Church would be untrue to herself . . . if she turned a deaf ear to her children's anguished cries which reach her from every class of the human family . . . the Church cannot renounce her right to proclaim to her sons and to the whole world the immutable laws, in order to save them from very perversion, obfuscation, corruption, false interpretation and error.* The churches have denounced before the increasing lack of justice; the persecution and execution of our Jewish fellow citizens. . . . In the midst of all the injustice and anguish, our sympathy goes out in a very special manner . . . to the Jews, and to our brethren in the Catholic faith who are of Jewish descent." The letter concludes with the words: "And should the refusal of collaboration require sacrifices from you, then be strong and steadfast in the awareness that you are doing your duty before God and your fellow men." The Dutch underground paper *Vrij Nederland,* which reprinted the six page pastoral letter, added editorially: "One of the many miracles of these years is the discovery made by so many: *the Church is the conscience of the Nation.*"[8]

Atque in Germania

In Germany, Bishop August von Galen of Münster, who had spoken out forcefully from his pulpit on "the fundamental rights of man," received a grateful letter from Pius XII on February 24. "Both your pastoral messages have our unqualified consent, because they defend so courageously the rights of the Church, the family and individual man. It is always a comfort to us when we learn of a frank and courageous word spoken by a German bishop."[9]

Archbishop Orsenigo, papal nuncio to Berlin, in what was probably the most difficult and frustrating Vatican diplomatic post, made appeals and remonstrances again and again. In one instance, in March 1943, he handed a summary note to Ribbentrop's deputy Weizsäcker. The deputy shoved the note back into the nuncio's pocket unread. Had he read it, he would have found a detailed account of the crimes committed against the Polish church. There were at the time a thousand Polish priests in Dachau, and the Vatican knew that many of them had already been executed. The Germans refused to allow that Orsenigo was now the Vatican official to whom Polish bishops reported; first, they wanted Church recognition of the new borders of the Reich, a concession they never received.

Recounting this episode prompts Lapide to make the following remark.

> It is difficult to gainsay the statement of Monsignor Nowowiejsky, one of the six bishops who spent the war in a German concentration camp, "If the Pope could no nothing against the Nazi criminals who habitually broke their promises and ignored every diplomatic obligation; if he failed to save his own priests from death, what would Hitler have conceded to him on behalf of others?" In fact, some 3000 Catholic priests monks and nuns had been murdered by the Nazis – in spite of numerous energetic interventions and protests by the Pope and his Nuncii in Germany, France, Belgium, Poland, Austria and elsewhere.[10]

Meanwhile, Eichmann was busy in France. In spring 1943, his deputy, Brunner, arrived in Paris, and the Nazis extended their operations to all of Vichy France, including, in September, the so-called Italian zone, Mussolini having resigned.[11]

In Berlin, after an exchange of notes and several conversations, the Berlin Foreign Ministry, on March 5, informed the Portuguese ambassador that Germany, having taken into account Portuguese public opinion, would now allow Portuguese Jews to return to Portugal.[12]

In Slovakia

The Slovak bishops received a reply to the February 17 protest on March 3, in which Prime Minister Tuka remarked that "The Slovak clergy, with some exceptions, has rarely demonstrated such zeal for the interests of its own nation, as it evinces now for the interests of the Jews, and in many cases also for those not baptized." The bishops responded with a pastoral letter dated March 8 which was read in all the churches on March 21; they proclaimed, "Aware of our responsibility before God . . . we firmly raise our voice in warning against the measures with which here . . . masses of our faithful and other fellow citizens are wronged in their personal liberty. . . . To every citizen applies our constitutional law: All inhabitants, without distinction of origin, nationality or religion, are guaranteed their life, their liberty and their property."[13]

Despite the fact that Lecca broke his promise to the "interfering" Roumanian bishops, "72 Jewish children arrived in Athlit, Palestine, after a trip through Roumania, Bulgaria and Turkey, according to a German report to von Killinger dated March 11, 1943. Some 200 children were to follow from Hungary and Roumania later on. Theodore Lavi stresses, 'Monsignor Cassulo also played an important role in the rescue of orphans from Transnystria.'"[14]

> On April 7, 1943, when the Slovak Interior Minister Mach threatened to comply with the reiterated demands of Wisliceny, Eichmann's aide, for "further trainloads of laborers," the Nuncio expressed the Vatican's stern disapproval, following it up on May 5, 1943 with a fourth note of protest. "The Holy See has entertained the firm hope that the Slovak Government, interpreting also the sentiments of its own people, Catholic almost in its entirety, would never proceed with the forcible removal of persons belonging to the so-called Jewish race. It is therefore with great pain that the Holy See learned of the continued transfers of such a character from the territory of the Republic. This pain is aggravated further now that it appears, according to reports from various parts, that the Slovak Government intends to proceed with the total removal of the Jewish residents of Slovakia, not even sparing women and children. . . . [T]he Holy See would fail in its Divine Mandate if it would not deplore these measures . . . which gravely hurt men in their natural human rights, merely for the reason of their belonging to a determined race. The pain of the Holy See is even more profound, considering that such measures are carried out in a nation of profound Catholic traditions, and by a government which declares itself to be their follower and custodian," we

read in the long and detailed papal protest. The transports, which Mach had already prepared were not dispatched."[15]

Pius XII Guides His Bishops

On April 30, Pius XII wrote to Archbishop Von Preysing of Berlin with whom he often consulted. Von Preysing had nixed the notion that the shadowy Von Papen might be received as German ambassador to the Holy See and, asked about a possible bishop, described him as weak with respect to the Nazis. The man's name was scratched from the list. In the April 30 letter, Pius stated his general policy. "We give to the pastors who are working on the local level the duty of determining if and to what degree the danger of reprisals and of various forms of oppression occasioned by episcopal declarations – as well as perhaps other circumstances caused by the length and mentality of the war – seem to advise caution, *ad majora mala vitanda* despite alleged reasons urging the contrary."[16] In that same letter, he explained that "our endeavors for greater humaneness apply with equal concern to all victims of war, to those suffering materially or emotionally from the tribulations of warfare." The pope went on to tell Von Preysing that such prudential considerations impose limits on his own declarations. "For the non-Aryan Catholics as well as for Jews, the Holy See has done whatever was in its power, with charitable, financial and moral assistance. To say nothing of the substantial sums which we spent in American money for the fares of emigrants." Such sums were gladly spent, and Jewish organizations had been warm in thanks for the Holy See's rescue operations. "As for what is being done against non-Aryans in the German territories, we have said a word in our Christmas radio message."

The moral principle the Holy Father invoked in the letter to Von Preysing, that one should act so as to avoid a greater evil (*ad majora mala vitanda*), should not be taken to mean that a little evil can be done lest a greater evil come about. The Pauline principle is absolute: Evil may never be done in order to attain a good. The evils of which the pope speaks are those being done by others and the question that arises is: Would a ringing condemnation of the evil being done prompt the evil doers to yet more awful deeds. There is, of course, no simple rule of thumb in such matters, but when one is dealing with Nazis, experience had shown that further excesses were always possible. The pope and his bishops each had to apply these general considerations to particular acts done in circumstances which were of unprecedented seriousness. Prudence is one of the cardinal virtues, and it is virtuous action the pope is holding himself and his bishops too. But their actions would differ accordingly. Thus to the bishop of Trier, who had made a courageous statement, the pope wrote, "We believe that reprisals, even if they are violent and even if they extend not only to the bishop but perhaps to others as well, cannot cancel out the good that the bishop's words, like your own, bring about among Catholics and certainly among others as well."[17]

Prime Minister Kallay of Hungary met with Pius in April 1943 at which, "He [the pope] condemned the system and methods of the Germans which independently of the war were inhuman and brutal, especially toward the Jews . . . the Roman Church could never cooperate with Governments which followed methods like Germany's or Russia's and built up their systems on those methods." Pius added that he had never seen any trace of anti-Semitism in the German people when he was nuncio there.

The courage of the Dutch bishops continued to display itself. "By May 1943 some 60,000 Dutch Jews had already been deported, and further mass arrests were being prepared by the Nazis. 'These deportations are not only a national calamity, but they are a crying shame and an outrage to Divine and human laws. As pastors of your souls we cannot remain silent. . . . we must speak up in the name of justice,' the bishops said in another pastoral letter dated May 15, 1943.'"[18]

The papal nuncio had expressed the Holy See's condemnation of deportations to the Slovak Interior Minister Mach on April 7, when Mach was about to accede to the demands of Wisliceny, Eichmann's aide, to ship four trainloads of "laborers."

Angelo Roncalli was the apostolic delegate in Istanbul. When Barlas, head of the Jewish Agency's Rescue Committee in Turkey sought Roncalli's intervention against deportations, the response was immediate. "So will it be, and if God helps me, we shall get it done!" "A year later, when Eichmann had reactivated the deportations, and the Vatican's fourth protest had stopped them, Roncalli in Istanbul wrote to Barlas of the Jewish Agency on May 22, 1943: 'I am very happy to be able to inform you that according to reports received from Bratislava, the deportations of Jews have been suspended for the time being, as a result of the intervention of the Holy See.'"[19]

"Confirmation of this good news came from Amin el Husseini, the Mufti of Jerusalem, [who] protested violently to Ribbentrop 'against the arrival in Palestine of 4000 Jewish children accompanied by 500 adults,' asking the German Foreign Minister 'to do his utmost to prevent further emigrations from Bulgaria, Roumania and Hungary.'"

Whatever was being done on behalf of Jews fell woefully short of what was wanted. The *Jewish Comment* of May 14, 1943, reflected the mood at the World Jewish Congress held in Bermuda. Speaking of the U.S. and British statesmen the article said: "The truth is that what stands in the way of aid to the Jews in Europe . . . is not that such a program is dangerous, but simply lack of will to go to any trouble on their behalf."[20]

In Holland things got worse:

> On May 21, 1943, when it became clear that all Jews of mixed marriages were confronted with the choice between sterilization or deportation, the Catholic and Protestant churches submitted a joint letter of protest to the Nazi regent: "After the many events in the years of occupation which have forced the Christian churches of the Netherlands to complain to Your Excellency – especially in the matter of our Jewish citizens – something so frightful is now being perpetrated, that we cannot but address a word to you in the name of our Lord . . . sterilization is a physical and spiritual mutilation, directly at variance with God's Commandment that we shall not dishonor, hate, wound or kill our neighbors. It is the last consequence of an anti-Christian racial doctrine which destroys nations, and of a self-exaltation without bounds. . . . It is the duty of Your Excellency to stop this shameful practice of sterilization."[21]

Excommunicate Hitler?

Don Luigi Sturzo, the founder of the Christian Democratic movement in Italy, in war-time exile in the United States, was asked by Dr. A. Kubovny, once secretary general of the World Jewish Congress, why the Church didn't excommunicate Hitler and Mussolini. In answering on May 30, 1943, Sturzo recalled the cases of Napoleon and Elizabeth I of England, cases where excommunication had little effect. "I fear that in response to a threat of excommunication, Hitler will kill the greatest possible number of Jews. And nobody will be able to stop him from doing so." He added that he was certain "that Pius XII has made every possible effort, both through diplomatic and personal channels, in order to exert influence on Hitler and his staff."

Apparently Pius did consider excommunication. "I have repeatedly considered excommunicating Nazism," he told an Italian Field Chaplain, Don Pizzo Scavizzi, "in order to castigate before the civilized world the bestiality of Judaeocide. But after many tears and prayers, I have concluded that a protest would not only fail to help the persecuted, it might well worsen the lot of the Jews." Scavizzi quoted the pope: "Perhaps my solemn protest would have gained me the praise of the civilized world, but I would have brought on to the poor Jews a still more implacable persecution than the one they now suffer. I love the Jews. Was it not from among them, the chosen people, that the Saviour was to be born? And did not the Virgin Mary, the Apostles and the first sons of the Church belong to this people?"[22] Pius thought that he might be praised for such an action throughout the civilized world, but in the world under the domination of Nazi Germany the result would be very different. Of course the pope would not excommunicate nazism as such – he had already condemned it and said it was incompatible with Christian principles. What he might have done is excommunicate any Catholic who belonged to the Nazi party.

Of course the Vatican was the main source of information about what was happening in occupied Europe. German atrocities were regularly broadcast to the world. Guenter Lewy, author of *The Catholic Church and Nazi Germany*, said "the Vatican Radio and *Osservatore Romano* told the story to the world." And yet the very ones for whom the pope spoke begged him to stop such broadcasts because of the reprisals they brought.[23]

To his cardinals, Pius said on June 2, 1943, "Every word spoken by us with this end [to help the Jews] in view, to the competent authorities, and every reference made in public by us, have to be most seriously pondered and weighed in the interests of those who are suffering, in order not to render, unwittingly, their situation even graver and more unbearable." He felt that he found himself "sometimes before doors which no key can open."

Encore Saliège

Archbishop Saliège of Toulouse had proved himself a worthy churchmen in most difficult conditions, defying the Nazi anti-Semitic laws and policies. This could not be borne by the Germans. A dramatic scene resulted.

On June 9, 1943, two German plainclothesmen knocked at a door on Rue Perchepinte. Upon entering the studio they asked:

"Are you M. Saliège?"

"I am," he said, rising from his chair.

Quietly he called his old housekeeper, Sister Henriette, took his hat and overcoat and said:

"I am ready."

As they turned to the door, the nun cried out, "Are you mad? You want to arrest a sick old man of seventy-five? He can't even walk without a cane. If he leaves this house, you are responsible for his life."

The two men briefly consulted, said, "We shall come back tomorrow," and never returned.[24]

Spain and Portugal were to prove to be hospitable to Jewish refugees. In the case of Spain, this is particularly gratifying. Hitler kept trying to lure Franco into the war on his side, but the Caudillo procrastinated: His country had had enough of war in 1936. Meanwhile, in quiet defiance of German racial theories, he opened the door to refugee Jews. As did Portugal under the leadership of another dictator, Salazar. The Nazis took notice of all this. "The Spanish ambassador here, Palencia, has publicly manifested his friendship for Jews, in connection with the Spanish Jews of Bulgaria, by legally adopting both children of the Jew Leon Arie who has been executed," said a report from the German embassy in Sofia to Berlin, June 16, 1943. "Papal influence, which was traditionally strong in Spain, also resulted in the following cable, received by the representative of the World Jewish Congress in Buenos Aires on July 26, 1943: 'Spanish Embassy communicated readiness Spain admit Spanish Jews and permit transit all Jews.' Spain was governed by Franco, had some kind of alliance with Hitler and was Catholic."[25]

Goebbels confided to his diary, on April 11, 1942. "The Pope has appealed to the Spanish bishops . . . to see to it that Spain stays out of the war. He supports his arguments with humanitarian phrases. In reality he hereby gives expression to his enmity for the Axis." He added on July 27, 1943, "Undoubtedly the Vatican is standing behind the revolt against Mussolini."

When Mussolini resigned and Marshal Badoglio took over the Italian government, Hitler met with his generals. "In a conference with his generals on the evening of July 25, 1943, only a few hours after Mussolini's dismissal, Hitler brushed aside Yodl's argument that they ought to wait for exact reports. 'I'll go right into the Vatican! Do you think the Vatican embarrasses me? We'll take that over right away. It's all the same to me. That rabble is in there. We'll get that bunch of swine out of there. Later we can make apologies.' Subsequently, under pressure from Ribbentrop and Goebbels, Hitler agreed to spare the Vatican, but for some days he still played with the idea of an immediate coup."[26]

Mystici Corporis

In the Europe of German occupation, even Pius XII's encyclical on the Mystical Body of Christ was studied for political implications. The Germans saw the document as aimed against them. Reich Security regularly forbade disseminating papal radio messages, finding them deeply subversive of the Nazi cause. So too the encyclical *Mystici Corporis* unnerved the Nazis. In Brussels, Cardinal Van Roey was informed in a letter from the German commander in chief that he must not make known the papal text, in part or in full. Lapide too cites sentences in the encyclical that signal the pope's judgment of the Nazis, e.g., "for we must recognize as brothers of Christ, according to the flesh, summoned with us to eternal Salvation, those not yet one with us in the Body of Christ."[27]

Sheltering Jews

In the so-called Italian Zone of Vichy France, which had come under the German racial laws, they were so regularly subverted that Ribbentrop complained to Mussolini about it. No problem. Il Duce appointed Guido Lospinoso to take care of the matter. Lospinoso ended by cooperating with monks who were sheltering Jewish refugees. The Vatican had set the example.

> After the 8th of September 1943, close on five thousand Jews found refuge in convents, parish churches, religious institutions and even inside the Vatican as well as various (some 180) extra-territorial Church buildings in Rome. . . . The same occurred in virtually all other places, big and small, of Central and Northern Italy where there were Jews. . . .
>
> The Vatican State's neutrality was substantially respected (during the war). Somewhat less complete was the respect accorded to those buildings which belonged to the Holy See and which, under the terms of the Lateran Pacts enjoyed so called extraterritorial rights. In effect, these were the buildings most used by Roman prelates – under the indulgent eye of the Holy See which, in fact, authorized the practice while officially ignoring it, for the purpose of sheltering political and Jewish refugees. The most notorious case of a breach of the convention was the search of the Abbey of St Paolo fuori le muri, conducted by the Fascist police under the German occupation.
>
> Renzo de Felice, the foremost historian of Italian Jewry under Fascism summarizes: ". . . Pius XII's fundamental principle was: to save lives, that is to say, to give concrete aid to persecuted Jews without, however, permitting himself to adopt dangerous positions which were liable to exasperate the Nazis and end up unleashing their bestiality. . . . The highly noteworthy and ever increasing help accorded, apart from individual Catholics, by almost all Catholic institutions and very numerous priests, to Jews hunted by the Germans after September 8, 1943, fully tallies with this line of the

Holy See. This aid, moreover, had already been afforded for many years in such Nazi occupied countries as France, Roumania, Belgium and Hungary, and had, apart from the plane of mere material assistance, found expression, at least since 1941, in several official Vatican demarches."[28]

The Vatican Surrounded

On September 13, 1943, the Governor of Vatican City received a phone call from the Military Commander of Rome informing him at 4 P.M. on the same day German sentries would be posted at the Vatican-Italian boundary line. At the appointed hour, Nazi paratroopers appeared in full battle dress, with helmets and machine guns and took up "protective patrol." This was the beginning of a period of unparalleled difficulty for Pius XII who became in effect a prisoner of the Nazis. But worse was to come a few days later: Berlin Radio warned of "severe measures unless the Pope accepts the policies of Hitler and Italian Fascism." In addition, incoming and outgoing postal facilities were cut off from Vatican City; telephone trunk lines passing into Rome were tapped, crude attempts were made to bribe and intimidate Vatican employees."[29]

An interesting sidelight on the attitude of Lwow's Metropolitan, and Pius' likely influence on him, is given by a Nazi agent of the German Foreign Office, Mr Frederic, who toured all of occupied Europe in order to feel the pulse of public opinion for his superiors. In his secret report to Berlin of September 9, 1943, he discusses his meetings with Szeptychi, who frankly told him of his disgust at the inhuman treatment of the Jews by the Nazis, whom he bluntly blamed for killing 100,000 in Lwow alone, and several million in the Ukraine. Mr Frederic tried to counter the Metropolitan's charges with the usual Nazi argument, but the latter remained adamant in his condemnation of Judaeocide. To his description Frederic added: "On this issue the Metropolitan made the same statements and even used the same phrasing as the French, Belgian and Dutch bishops, as if all of them were receiving the same instructions from the Vatican."[30]

Nazis in Italy

On September 26, 1943, the Jewish community was ordered by Kappler, the Gestapo chief, to hand over 50 kilos of gold within 36 hours – or 300 hostages would be taken. When it transpired that such an amount could not be raised, Chief Rabbi Zolli went to see

Nogara, head of the Vatican treasury, who, upon the Pope's approval, gave him a loan of some 15 kilos of gold. . . .

On September 27 the Chief Rabbi was informed by General Kappler that he was to deliver to the German authorities by noon of the following day one million lire in cash and fifty kilograms of gold. If he failed to comply, the Nazis would order "the dispersal of the entire community." What happened on the same day is described in recently published Jewish documentation:

As soon as the Vatican found out about this, it discreetly informed the leaders of the Jewish community that, if the required quantity of gold could not be collected within the stipulated time, it would furnish whatever was missing.[31]

The ransom was paid to the Gestapo on September 28 without using the papal loan.

Lapide summarizes:

Papal caution and circumspection saved close to 90 percent of Roman Jewry; would papal clamor have saved more – or, conversely, would it have endangered those Jews then in precarious hiding? One of the Jews who lived through the Roman round-up of October 1943, and safely reached Spain a few weeks later, thanks to Pius XII's personal intervention, has a cogent reply: "None of them wanted the Pope to speak out openly. We were all fugitives, and we did not want to be pointed out as such. The Gestapo would only have increased and intensified its inquisition. If the Pope had protested, all the attention would have been turned on Rome. It was much better that the Pope kept silent. We all felt the same, and today we still believe that," said A. Wolfsson in March 1963.[32]

"On October 15, 1942 the Pope reminded the German Bishop Andreas Rohrbacher that 'in times of war it goes without saying that Catholic priests and bishops should afford every possible help to all those suffering in body and soul.'"[33]

When on October 16 the round-up of Roman Jews began in earnest, three German police companies managed to arrest only 1259 people, of whom 1007 were shipped off to Auschwitz. At that time there were some 9600 Jews in Rome, of whom approximately 1500 were refugees from Nazi occupied countries; 8500 – that is to say more that 85 percent – were hidden by Christian clerics, monks, nuns and other Catholics. The then Chief Rabbi, Israel Zolli reports: "The Holy Father sent by hand a letter to the bishops instructing them to lift the enclosure from convents and monaster-

ies, so that they could become refuges for the Jews. . . . No hero in
history has commanded such an army; an army of priests works in
cities and small towns to provide bread for the persecuted and
passports for the fugitives. Nuns go into canteens to give hospital-
ity to women refugees. Superiors of convents go out into the night
to meet German soldiers who look for victims. . . . Pius XII is followed by all with the fervor of that charity that fears no death.

When Zolli accepted baptism in 1945 and adopted Pius' Christian name
of Eugene, most Roman Jews were convinced that his conversion was
an act of gratitude for wartime succor to Jewish refugees, and repeated
denials notwithstanding, many are still of this opinion. Thus Rabbi
Barry Dov Schwartz wrote in the summer issue 1964 of *Conservative
Judaism*: "Many Jews were persuaded to convert after the war, as a sign
of gratitude, to that institution which had saved their lives. We may pre-
sume that such was the case with Rabbi Israel Zolli, the Chief Rabbi of
Rome."[34]

> Unable to get any action out of shilly-shallying or from the
> well-meaning Red Cross President, Pius XII took two other semi-
> official steps with the German authorities:
> First, he caused Bishop Hudal, Rector of the German Church
> in Rome, to send a last minute appeal to the German General
> Stahel which, under the circumstances, was a masterpiece of
> diplomatic subtlety: "I have just been informed by a high Vatican
> office in the immediate circle of the Holy Father, that the arrests
> of Jews of Italian nationality have begun this morning," writes the
> ranking German prelate to the senior German commander on
> October 16, 1943. "In the interests of the good relations which
> have existed until now between the Vatican and the High German
> Military Command . . . I would be very grateful if you would give
> an order to stop these arrests in Rome and its vicinity right away;
> I fear that otherwise the Pope will have to take an open stand
> against these arrests which will supply ammunition to the anti-
> German propaganda of our enemies."
> At the same time the Pope sent Father Pancrace Pfeiffer, the
> Superior General of the Salvatorians (who is credited with having
> personally saved many hundreds of Jews, thanks to his excellent
> relations with his fellow-Germans), to intercede personally in a
> semiofficial capacity with German Generals Stahel and Kappler.
> 'Pius XII gave carte blanche to Father Pancrace . . . he could serve
> as an intermediary between the Holy See, in the name of the Pope,
> and the German headquarters, without any official mandate, but
> with no less weight of authority. The German Command accepted

Father Pancrace, for General Stahel highly valued Pfeiffer's absolute sincerity.[35]

The historian of Italian Jewry under Fascism relates: "These two demarches produced the desired results. On October 17 Bishop Hudal was informed by the German Military Commander of Rome that Himmler, upon learning of the stand taken by the Vatican, had issued instructions to stop the arrests." Lest Himmler be suspected of sudden softheartedness, the Center of Contemporary Jewish Documentation adds: "These orders of Himmler were in all likelihood dictated merely by calculations of a practical nature, and not by diplomatic considerations. If the *razzia* did not go on during the following days, this was due to the Providential Circumstance that the forces of Kappler and Dannecker (Eichmann's aide) were physically unable to carry out further arrests of Jews, since the latter had meanwhile repaired to chance refuges all over Rome."

As a result of the *razzia* of October 16, several thousand Jews, both Romans and refugees from Central Europe, roamed the streets of Rome, afraid to return to their blacklisted homes, unable to get new lodgings in the heavily policed city, and thus liable to be picked up as vagrants or spies at any moment. To get these fugitives under a roof and out of harm's way seems to have been the purpose of the Pope's next move.

Pius had an editorial published in the *Osservatore Romano* which contained the following key passage: "After the Pope has in vain endeavored, as is well known, to avert the outbreak of the war . . . he has used all possible means at his disposal in order to alleviate the sufferings which in any manner resulted from the heinous world conflagration. With the aggravation of so much misery, the activities of universal and paternal succor have multiplied; they know no limitations, neither of nationality, religion, nor race. This manifold and ceaseless activity of the Pope has, of late, grown still further in depth, due to the increased suffering of so many unfortunate people."

These words in 1943 had only one clear meaning to the tens of thousands of Romans – many of whom sheltered Jews in their homes – who avidly read Italy's only non-Fascist newspaper, on, but even more between, the lines: The Pope wants all Catholics to do all they possibly can to hide and save Jews from the clutches of the Germans.[36]

In the meantime (immediately after October 16) throughout the city, priests, nuns and other religious, often at great personal risk, smuggled Jews to places of sanctuary in churches, monasteries and other hide outs. . . . . More than 180 places of refuge were made available in Rome and secret asylum was extended to more than 5000 fugitive Jews during the Nazi occupation of Rome.[37]

These three papal interventions, meek and cautious as they were, enjoyed partial success: "Altogether 1259 people were seized in the round-up. After the release of some half-Jews and Jews in mixed marriages (thanks to Father Pfeiffer and others) a total of 1007 Jews were shipped off on October 18, 1943 to Auschwitz." At the Pope's request, two more Jews were released from the deportation train by General Kappler, minutes before it left Rome. However, Gunter Lewy reports; "About seven thousand Roman Jews – this is seven out of eight – were able to elude their hunters by going into hiding. More than four thousand, with the knowledge and approval of the Pope, found refuge in the numerous monasteries and houses of religious in Rome, and a few dozen more were sheltered in the Vatican itself."[38]

As the year wore down, the Nazi policies were drawing criticism not only from Churchmen but from diplomats as well. "The Secretary of the Spanish Embassy Diez visited me today and asked to stop forthwith the arrest of Spanish Jews in France. . . . The Spanish Government had now finally decided to take over into Spain all Spanish Jews from the territories occupied by Germany. (Aide-memoire of Von Thadden in the Nazi Foreign Minster, dated December 22, 1943.)"[39]

Lapide to the Rescue

Pinchas Lapide, whose book *The Last Three Popes and the Jews* is a gold mine of information and a model of evenhanded commentary, is not only the historian of rescue efforts, but had the privilege of taking part in a memorable way. He served with the British 8th Army, which fought in Italy, and was with a unit that liberated a refugee camp. The inmates were Jews who had been on a ship that would not be permitted to land and eventually was hailed by an Italian patrol boat and taken to a camp on Rhodes.

But one did not have to be far from Rome to benefit from Pius XII's policy toward refugees. "No less than 3000 Jews found refuge at one time at the Pope's summer residence at Castel Gandolfo; sixty lived for nine months at the Jesuit Gregorian University, and half a dozen slept in the cellar of the pontifical Biblical Institute whose rector was Agostino Bea – now dubbed the 'father of the Jewish Schema' [of Vatican II]. The Palatine Guards, which in 1942 possessed a strength of 30 men, had grown by December 1943 to 4000 holders of the precious Palatine laissez-passers, some 400 of whom at least were Jews, of whom approximately 240 were accommodated within the Vatican precincts."[40]

And in Belgium, Cardinal Van Roey was successful in helping some Jews, personally and financially.[41] "In the NCCJ Bulletin of 1943 we read: 'Details of the round-up of Jews in France were published in the *Schweitzer Kirchenzeitung*, journal of the Catholic Church in Switzerland, with the comment that the abuse of the Jews continued 'despite protest by cardinals, archbishops and other Roman Catholic leaders.'"[42]

One of the unintended consequences of Pius XII's coming so magnificently to the aid of persecuted Jews was that many of them chose to become Catholics, notable among them Chief Rabbi of Rome, Israel Zolli. Jews and Catholics will of course interpret conversion to Catholicism differently. Some Jews understood these conversions as acts of gratitude, but this seems inadequate as an explanation and irrelevant as a motivation. Why not say that in Pius XII many saw the embodiment of Christian charity and were drawn to what he represented? Zolli took the baptismal name Eugene as if to signal that it was Pius who had opened his eyes to the truth of Christianity.

The Plight of the Jews: Eretz Israel

The Nazis' treatment of the Jews was evil enough when it seemed to mean only transportation. For the Jewish family that was uprooted, its property stolen, its future in an unknown land obscure, this was devastating enough. But when in 1942 the depths of the Nazi evil became known and what the "Final Solution" consisted of was unmistakable, it became all the more urgent to help Jews escape the clutches of the Eichmann death machine.

Not everyone felt this urgency. The governments of the Allied Powers, chiefly the United States and Britain, were reluctant to offer the wholesale resettlement of Jews, let alone save all those of Bulgaria, say. Roosevelt aide Harry Hopkins said brutally, "If we do that, then the Jews of the world will be wanting us to make similar offers in Poland and Germany. Hitler might take us up on such an offer and there simply are not enough ships and means of transportation in the world to handle them."[1] What about Palestine? The British foresaw trouble with the Arabs if Jews began to flood into the Mandate. Who will say that such cautions and concerns were imaginary?

The rescue of their fellow Jews was seen by Zionists through the lens of a Jewish homeland. Accordingly, a Jewish legion was created, to fight alongside the British; it earned gratitude by its military record and thus British support for a Jewish state in the post-war world. Anti-Zionists described the Zionist aim in tendentious terms, saying that Zionists "were inclined to leave the front-line fighting as such, if unconnected to Palestine, to the Jews of the Diaspora."[2] The fighting they envisaged was in Palestine, not on the continent, on behalf of the Jews beset upon by Hitler. Was this merely deciding to do what could be done or failing to do what might also have been done? "During 1940 and 1941 the Jewish Agency Executive rarely discussed the Jews of occupied Europe and, aside from their half-hearted efforts at illegal immigration, the agency did nothing for them."[3]

The British discouraged sending relief packages to the occupied countries on the ground that it was Germany's duty to feed the peoples they had conquered. Such aid was argued to be a contribution to the German war effort. "The WJC-AJC apparatus not only stopped sending food, but it pressured the non-Zionist Jewish relief agencies to stop as well, and almost all did except the Aguda."[4] A dispute broke out among various Jewish groups on this issue and interpretations of the motives behind conflicting policies cut to the bone.

These disputes took place before it became clear to the world that the aim of Hitler was to exterminate the Jews of Europe, not to relocate them. In 1941 and 1942, the Russians said that systematic killing of the Jews was going on in the Ukraine. Considering the source, this was dismissed by many, including the World Zionist Organization, which regarded it as Bolshevik propaganda. But corroboration for such reports came from others. "In February 1942 Bertrand Jacobsen, the former representative of the Joint Distribution Committee in Hungary, held a press conference on his return to the USA and relayed information from Hungarian officers about the massacre of 250,000 Jews in the Ukraine." Seven hundred thousand Jews were said to have been killed in Poland. A report on the scope and methods of extermination were sent on August 15, 1942, to Jerusalem. The reply he received on September 28 expressed skepticism. "Just as one has to learn by experience to accept incredible tales as indisputable facts, so one has to learn by experience to distinguish between reality – however harsh it may be – and imagination which has become distorted by justifiable fear."[5] Were such doubts sinister? Walter Lacquer, in *The Terrible Secret*, is remarkably understanding in his account of how the Final Solution was only gradually believed and, when believed, dealt with prudently.[6]

It should be remembered that the Jews in Palestine viewed with trepidation that possibility that Rommel's *Afrika Korps* might move into Egypt. Their situation was far from being as dangerous as that of Jews under German domination, but Palestine was anything but an unthreatened paradise. This was the point of Moshe Shertok's letter to General Claude Auchincleck, commander of the British 8th Army on April 17, 1942. "The destruction of the Jewish race is a fundamental tenet of the

Nazi doctrine. The authoritative reports recently published show that this policy is being carried out with a ruthlessness which defies description. . . . An even swifter destruction, it must be feared, would overtake the Jews of Palestine."[7] When the true fate of their fellow Jews in Europe sank in, the Jews of Palestine were horrified. "However, there was no change in political focus among the Zionists. A Jewish state after the war remained their priority, and the Holocaust was not going to jeopardize this."[8] Dov Joseph, in the political department of the Jewish Agency, discouraged publication of reports that millions of Jews were being slaughtered in Europe because "we will justifiably be asked where the millions of Jews are, for whom we claim that we shall need to provide a home in Eretz Israel after war's end."[9] No *special* rescue efforts were undertaken.

This apparently heartless decision was due to the belief that nothing could be done to save Europe's Jews, and money sent to Europe for escape, resistance, or rescue would be wasted. But rescue efforts did of course continue, under Yitzshak Gruenbaum, if only "to be able to say after the war that everything possible had been done."[10] This cynical view was attributed to Gruenbaum by Yehuda Bauer, but Gruenbaum was much criticized at the time in Palestine. He defended himself at a meeting of the Zionist Executive on February 18, 1943, complaining that his associates had let him take all the blame. He himself reprinted his remarks in his book, published in Hebrew, *In the Days of the Holocaust and Destruction.* Brenner quotes Gruenbaum's defense against criticism at great length. He saw the main complaint to be this: Do not put Eretz Israel in priority in this difficult time when European Jewry is being destroyed. He has been called an anti-Semite because he does not give priority to rescue operations. "I think it is necessary to say here: Zionism is over everything. . . . Zionism is above all – it is necessary to sound this whenever a Holocaust diverts us from our war of liberation in Zionism."[11]

There were criticisms as well of the rescue operations that were undertaken. The Zionist Rescue Committee was interested in rescuing Jews as such, not individuals as such, but fellow Jews without qualification. Gruenbaum complained that his son had not been rescued, and seemed not to understand the non-discrimination practiced in actual rescues.[12] But who will blame him for wanting his son out of the clutches of the Nazis?

Bribes were offered in exchange for Slovak Jews. Rabbi Michael Dov-Ber Weissmandel contacted Dieter Wisliceny, Eichmann's representative, in March 1942, on behalf of world Jewry, and offered $50,000 dollars in exchange for the lives of the Jews of Slovakia. The money was taken and the Jews were safe – until 1944 when they were captured after a failed partisan revolt.[13] Weissmandel was an outstanding Jewish figure during the Holocaust. His postwar book, *From the Depths*, is described by Brenner as "one of the most powerful indictments of Zionism and the Jewish establishment."[14] The dispute turned on the use of money in Europe, which Weissmandel wished to turn to a number of purposes beyond bribery, though he wanted to see whether any senior SS or Nazi officials could be bought. He wanted to mobilize Slovak partisans. He wanted the rail lines into Auschwitz bombed. He was a fighter.

Wisliceny was approached again by Weissmandel in November 1942. How much money would it take to save the Jews of Europe? His answer came in early 1943. The sum was $2 million. When he sought the money from the Joint Distribution Committee in Zurich, he was told that it was against American law to send money into enemy countries. Insult was added to injury. Solly Mayer, a Zionist and representative of the Joint Committee in Zurich, said, "the letters that you have gathered from the Slovakian refugees in Poland are exaggerated tales for this is the way of the '*Ost-Juden*' who are always demanding money."[15] Brenner's judgment is severe. "Zionism had come full turn: instead of Zionism being the hope of the Jews, their blood was to be the political salvation of Zionism."[16]

Representatives of the Allies addressed the issue in a disheartening way. At the Casablanca Conference, President Roosevelt expressed his views on what Jews should be rescued. "The President stated that his plan would further eliminate the specific and understandable complaints which the Germans bore toward the Jews in Germany, namely that while they represented a small part of the population, over fifty per cent of the lawyers, doctors, schoolteachers, college professors, etc. in Germany were Jews."[17]

Thus there grew up the charge that Jewish leaders had remained silent during a time when the Jewish people confronted one of the most horrendous threats in their long and tragic history. "It is no accident that this legend has grown up," Bernard Wasserstein replied. "On the contrary, this is an accusation first voiced during and immediately after the war by a specific group: the Revisionist Zionists and their various off-shoots. . . . This was their rallying cry which they used in their attempts to mobilize Jewish youth in a misguided and morally tainted campaign of invective and terror."[18]

An example of Zionist singleness of purpose was David Ben

Gurion's words about saving Jewish children in Germany. "If I knew that it would be possible to save all the children in Germany by bringing them over to England, and only half of them by transporting them to Eretz Israel, then I would opt for the second alternative. For we must weigh not only the life of these children, but also the history of the People of Israel."[19] Of course this is only a hypothetical, but it does underscore the Zionist priority. By the same token, Ben-Gurion insisted that the refugee problem must never be discussed independently of the Palestinian homeland. It was not a matter of getting the Jews out of Europe to somewhere, anywhere – their destination had to be Palestine or . . . "If we allow a separation between the refugee problem and the Palestinian problem, we are risking the existence of Zionism."[20]

1944

On the Battle Fronts

On January 22, American and British troops landed at Anzio, below Rome, and established a beachhead. The troops that had crossed the Straits of Messina half a year before had been slogging their way up the peninsula. Anzio was to take the pressure off them and open a way to Rome.

The Soviet Army entered Estonia on February 2 and launched an attack on Latvia. In the Pacific, U.S. Marines captured Roi-Namur in the Marshalls and took Kwajalein Island five days later. Hideki Tojo was named chief of the Japanese Army General Staff and became military dictator of Japan.

On March 20, the Nazis invaded Hungary because of the threat to the Balkans, and in London General Charles de Gaulle became head of the French Provisional Government on April 5. In the Pacific, MacArthur led the American landing in Netherlands, New Guinea, on April 22, and on May 9 the Russians retook Sevastopol.

In Italy, the Germans yielded the entire coastline from Anzio south to Terracina on May 25.

June 4. American and British troops entered an undamaged Rome.

June 6. D-Day. Eisenhower began the invasion of Hitler's Fortress Europe with landings on Normandy beaches.

The German response to the Normandy invasion was to attack England with the unnerving V-1 rockets, beginning on June 13. On June 14, General de Gaulle visited the Normandy coast, setting foot on his native land for the first time in four years. The following day, June 15, U.S. superfortresses raided Japan for the first time. The Battle of the

Philippine Sea was fought on June 19. Cherbourg fell to the Allies on June 27. American forces in the Pacific took Saipan in the Marianas on July 8 after a bloody twenty-five-day struggle . The Red Army crossed into Latvia and Lithuania on the 11th, and the British on July 18 broke through the German lines at Caen.

July 20: Hitler was slightly wounded by a bomb attempt on his life in his headquarters at Rastenburg on the Eastern front.

The Marines established beachheads on Guam on July 21; in France, the Americans broke through west of St.-Lô on July 26. Guam was conquered August 10.

In Italy, the Nazis abandoned an undamaged Florence on August 11, as the Allies closed in. American armor reached the Seine River north and south of Paris.

August 23: Paris was liberated, and on August 27, General Eisenhower entered Paris.

Although nearly a year of war remained, the end was clearly in sight. Brussels was liberated on September 3. Russia signed an armistice with Finland on September 4, but declared war on Bulgaria the following day. But on September 9 an armistice between the two countries was signed. Roosevelt and Churchill met in Quebec on September 10. On September 24, the Russian Army advanced into Czechoslovakia. from Poland. On October 3, the Warsaw Resistance Army surrendered to the Russians after a two-month struggle.

In the Pacific, the Americans landed at Leyte in the Phillippines; the Battle of Leyte Gulf raged from the 23rd to the 26th of October, with heavy Japanese losses. On October 24th American planes, flying from Saipan, bomb Tokyo.

A German counteroffensive, the Battle of the Bulge, began on December 16.

A Nazi Ploy

On January 6, 1944 – the feast of the Epiphany – Cardinal Maglione, secretary of state, received Weizsäcker the German ambassador to the Holy See. The ambassador referred to the alliance between the Americans and British with Soviet Russia. "If Germany, a bulwark against Bolshevism, should fall, all Europe will become Communist." The cardinal replied, "What a misfortune that Germany, with its antireligious policy, has stirred up such serious concerns."[1]

Rescue in Roumania

Refugees were now at the mercy of the vagaries of war. Jews who had been deported to Transnystria were now threatened by the retreating German troops. "Till 1944 Romania had escaped German military control, and the SS squads were not free to execute a policy of deportation to occupied Poland. But Transnystria was always a center of concern for both the Jewish community and the nuncio, especially now that a deteriorating military situation brought about the fear that, in withdrawing, the Romanians would allow the Jews to fall into the hands of the German forces already present in the area."[2] Chief Rabbi Herzog of Palestine appealed to Monsignor Roncalli in Istanbul for help. Roncalli cabled the Vatican on February 28, 1944. "Chief Rabbi of Jerusalem came personally to Apostolic Delegation thanking officially Holy Father and Vatican for many forms charity afforded to Jews these years; implores papal interest for 55,000 Jews concentrated in Transnystria, gravely endangered during possible retreat German troops."[3]

The necessity to act with circumspection and caution in his dealings with Nazi Germany was dictated by the fear of reprisals against the innocent. There were several occasions when Pius XII seems almost to long for personal danger, much as the Archbishop of Toulouse, the magnificent Saliège, had risen immediately from his chair at the prospect of arrest. Facing down the pistol-waving Red in Munich had taught Pius that he was possessed of personal courage, and when threatened he assured the Nazis that he had no fear of firearms or of concentration camp; he was ready for either. "On May 13, 1940, Pius said to Dino Alfieri, who begged him to be more careful in his pronouncements: 'We were not afraid of guns pointed at us once; we shall fear them even less the second time. . . . We ought to speak words of fire against the atrocities in Poland, and the only thing which restrains us, is the knowledge that words would make the fate of these wretches worse.'"[4] That courage seemed about to be tested in early February, 1944. "On February 1, 1944, the German Ambassador, Weizsäcker, informed the Pope of Hitler's 'invitation' to come to Germany. On the next day the pontifical guards, for the first time, exchanged their medieval halberds, for modern submachine guns; and three days later, while the foreign ambassadors who had been given asylum within the Vatican burned their secret files, the Pope told the College of Cardinals: 'Whatever may happen, we shall not abandon the Holy See, and certainly not our beloved Rome.' To Weizsaecker, Pius said officially a few hours later, that 'he would not leave Rome, come what may.' From February 5, nobody tried to make him leave."[5]

The saga of Jews in Roumania and in Hungary continued with a marked increase in cooperation on the part of Jewish organizations with the Holy See and its representatives. Pius XII sent the sum of 1,350,000 lei by means of the Roumanian Foreign Ministry to the Jewish Council, which received it in February 4, 1944. The money was intended for the assistance of Jews in Transnystria. Pius's intervention at this crucial juncture was crucial. The Roumanians were happy to pass on the money and sent with it an unctuous letter drawing attention to the role they were playing. This special manifestation of papal interest had its effect. With it as background, Cassulo, the nuncio, stepped up diplomatic pressures as well.

On March 23, Monsignor Roncalli could reply to Chaim Barlas, the representative of the Jewish Agency in Istanbul, that he had referred Chief Rabbi Herzog's request for intervention to the Holy Father on behalf of those deported to Transnystria, and the Vatican had at once replied that the nuncio in Bucharest would deal with the matter. He added that a favorable solution might be expected. On March 25, Barlas replied: "Excellency, I was very much touched by your kind reception as well as by your sentiments of profound humanity for our people in these fatal days. It is with great satisfaction that I have learned of your kindness in calling on the Holy See, as well as the Nuncios of Budapest and Bucharest, asking them to use their influence in these matters, according to our discussion. I have taken the liberty of informing the Jewish Agency as well as Chief Rabbi Herzog accordingly."[7]

That Pius XII dug deep to help the Jews is confirmed by the story that he spent his personal Pacelli fortune in this effort. "When on March 16, the nuncio hinted in a report to the Vatican that money was running low, the Pope sent another remittance, in time for Passover 1944. In this connection it is germane to quote Father Leiber, Pius' private secretary and personal confidant: 'The Pope sided very unequivocally with the Jews at the time. He spent his entire private fortune on their behalf . . . Pius spent what he inherited himself, as a Pacelli, from his family."[6]

Particularly at issue was the emigration of orphan children to Palestine, some four thousand of them. The government had fixed the age limit at twelve. Safran asked Cassulo to intervene, and the nuncio spoke to the foreign minister on January 26, asking that he raise the age to sixteen. The Vatican was also helpful in the matter of the ships that would take Jews to Palestine. The Roumanian government had no reason to oppose the emigration of Jews, so the War Refugee Board rented a Turkish ship, the *Tari*, which would make several trips evacuating the Roumanian Jews from Constantia on the Black Sea. The operation was to be carried out in the name of the International Red Cross, which insisted that a safe conduct be obtained from the Germans! On April 21, the board sought the Vatican's intervention on behalf of the *Tari* and its 1,500 passengers. The ship set sail without a safe conduct and with the tacit permission of the Roumanian government. The papal nuncio was able to inform the Vatican on July 11 that the first shipload of emigrés had arrived in Istanbul.[8]

"Dr. Shafran [the Chief Rabbi of Roumania] wrote to Cassulo on April 7, 1944: 'In these hard times our thoughts turn more than ever with respectful gratitude to the Sovereign Pontiff, who has done so much for Jews in general, and to your Excellency who has acted so superbly on behalf of the Jews in Roumania and Transnystria. In our worst hours of trial, the generous aid and noble support of the Holy See, by means of your invaluable assistance, has been decisive. It is not easy to find the proper words to express the relief and solace which the magnanimous gesture of the Supreme Pontiff has given us, in offering a large subsidy in order to alleviate the sufferings of the deported Jews. Roumanian Jewry will never forget these facts of historical importance."[9]

The satisfaction all these men felt in cooperating on so urgent a matter is palpable. Cassulo and Roncalli, and the Holy Father for whom they acted, earned the gratitude and respect of the Jewish leaders who turned to them, perhaps reluctantly at first, but with the growing certainty that the Catholic Church would respond with alacrity. In the present instance, as Dr. Shafran's letter makes clear, the cooperation involved not just Jews in Roumania but those in Hungary as well.

Cassulo had informed the Vatican in December of 1941 of the state of mind in which Jews had turned to the Church for help when they were being treated under the pretext that they were Communist sympathizers. "Having no one in authority who is capable of supporting them, they address the Holy Father's representative, convinced as they are that he is the only person in authority who can help them. And so I find myself in a very delicate and troubling situation. On the one hand, I believe that I have to show interest in so many poor families; on the other hand, I must do so with tact and discretion toward the government so that I am not meddling in the country's affairs."[10] In the end, it was the former not the latter that took precedence.

The Jews of Hungary

Roumanian Jews had special reason to be concerned about the

Hungarian Jews. In August 1940, the northern part of Transylvania was ceded by Roumania to Hungary. There were 150,000 Jews in that area, and many of them had been sent to Auschwitz in May and June 1944. Rabbi Safran appealed to Archbishop Cassulo, and the nuncio reported to the Vatican on July 11, "It appears that for some time now they are finding themselves in a very difficult situation" and in a later report spoke of "exceptional coercive measures" being used. He forwarded to the pope a letter from six Jews whose parents were in Transylvania: "For some time now we have had no news concerning our parents since all our efforts to learn something about their fate have come to naught." Dr. Ernest Grossman, representing the Jews of northern Transylvania, asked the Holy See to get permission from the German authorities to send these Jewish families to Palestine by way of the Danube. Grossman wrote, "I am anxious to stress that the emigration of the Jews from Europe agrees with the views of the German authorities. Since I know what the Catholic Church has done up to the present for the Israelites of all countries, I am convinced that in this matter also we will have its full cooperation, all the more so because this pertains to a deeply humanitarian work for which six thousand souls will thank God."[11]

On January 29, 1944, Archbishop Cicognani, apostolic delegate to the United States, transmitted to the Vatican a request from the World Jewish Congress to use its influence with the Hungarian government on behalf of a plan to provide funds from the United States to relieve Hungarian Jews. On March 23, the Wehrmacht rolled into Hungary and seized control of the country. The Vatican would be besieged by requests for help coming from Rabbi Isaac] of Jerusalem, the Chief Rabbi of London via Archbishop Godfrey, d'Arcy Osborne on behalf of the British government.

Pius XII, on behalf of Hungarian Jews, cabled Prime Minister Horthy, asking him "to use all possible influence in order to stop the pains and torments which innumerable persons must undergo for the sole reason of their nationality or their race." These exchanges on March 19 between Pius XII and Horthy were transmitted in clear language and by means of the Budapest Post Office, and became known to the Germans who exercised surveillance and censorship. Ribbentrop told his representative in Budapest "to inform the Hungarian government that it was not opportune to cede to various foreign pressures in favor of Hungarian Jews."

On March 29, 1944 – and thus before the Germans finally invaded and took over the country – the Hungarian cabinet decreed that all Jews must wear a yellow star. Catholics and Protestants claimed exemption for their converts – some 62,000 in all, arguing that the Star of David was an emblem of Jewish religion, not race. Thus, Cardinal Seredi argued in protesting the decree, it would amount to a renunciation of faith if worn by Christians. On April 4, Prime Minister Sztojay exempted "members of the Christian clergy, wives, widows and children of war veterans, Jews in mixed marriages, Jewish widows of Christians."[12] On April 21, 1944, the president of the United States asked the Holy See whether his country could transmit financial aid to Polish Jewish refugees in Rome and to the Jewish children's aid society in Rome.[13] In its reply on April 25, the Vatican agreed, adding that "it will continue as it did in the past, to work in favor of all victims of the persecution."

The request about the stars was turned down, and on April 17, Hitler summoned Regent Horthy to Germany and gave him a tongue-lashing because of the laxity of the Hungarian government in settling the Jewish question. The Führer wanted swift and effective action.

> It came quickly. Hungary was divided into five zones, and ghettos were set up in each of them. Round-ups were followed at once by deportations and, by May 1, daily death trains rolled on Eichmann's schedule to Auschwitz. As the appalling news of the atrocities spread, the papal Nuncio, Monsignor Angelo Rotta, returned to the counterattack. On April 27 he insisted on and obtained another audience with the Deputy Foreign Minister in which he informed him of the profound regrets of the Holy Father concerning the development of the situation, "which seems to prove that Hungary, a Christian nation . . . has embarked upon a road contrary to the teaching of the gospel." Half a dozen oral protests later, Rotta was the first foreign envoy to submit a formal note of protest: ". . . The Nunciature has every reason to believe that [the Government] even wants to go as far as the deportation of hundreds of thousands of persons. Everybody knows what these deportations signify in practice. The Apostolic Nunciature considers it its duty to protest. . . . Animated by a sentiment of justice and of Christian charity, the Nunciature once more appeals to the Royal Hungarian Government not to exceed, in its campaign against the Jews, the limits imposed by natural right and Divine Law . . . and to abstain from any action against which the Holy See would have to protest energetically. . . . The Nunciature hopes that the Government in its wisdom will benevolently accept this appeal which echoes the distress of the Holy Father . . ." This note Rotta had delivered to the Hungarian Head of Government, together with a personal letter in which he wrote: "The holy Father is deeply pained and I do hope that as Supreme Shepherd of the

Church, guardian of the rights of all his sons and defender of truth and justice, he will not have to raise his voice in protest . . ."[14]

The pressure on the Hungarian government was salted with reminders of the country's religious traditions. Papal Nuncio Rotta, in a note to the prime minister, reminded him that to persecute anyone for the sole reason of that person's race violated natural law. One notices in the protests of all the nuncios the recurrence of locutions first used by Pius XII. Rotta even held out the threat of a public papal condemnation. "I hope that in his position as supreme pastor of the church, as the one who safeguards the rights of all his children, and as the defender of truth and justice, he [the Holy Father] will not be obliged to speak out in protest."[15] "Two days later, on May 17, Arnothy-Jungerth, the Hungarian Deputy Foreign Minister, told Cabinet Ministers that the Nuncio had shown him a letter from Pius XII in which the Pope enjoined Rotta to redouble his interventions on behalf of the victims of persecution. In this letter, the Pope termed the manner in which Jews were treated as 'unworthy of Hungary, the country of the Holy Virgin and of St. Stephen.'"[16] The official reply to the nuncio came on May 27. It denied that any mass removal of Jews from Hungary had taken place or was planned. There was only "the dispatch of a certain number of Jews to Germany as workers." "In another note, dated June 5, the Nuncio categorically refuted the Government's arguments: '. . . Since old men of 70, and even of 80, elderly women, children and sick people are deported, for what kind of work does one wish to utilize these human beings? . . . We are told that Jews are enabled to take their families with them. . . . Since Hungarian workers, leaving for work in Germany, cannot take their families with them, it is indeed surprising that this great favor is granted only to Jews.'"[17]

In June Cardinal Spellman, archbishop of New York, made a broadcast to Hungary in which he echoed Pius XI and Pius XII as well as Holy Scripture. "Abraham is our Patriarch, our ancestor. Anti-Semitism is not compatible with this sublime reality. Spiritually, we are Semites. No man can love God and hate his brother." Asked why he had done it, Cardinal Spellman replied, "I made the broadcast at the request of Pope Pius XII to protest the bloody persecution of Hungarian Jews."[18]

Despite President Roosevelt's offer of financial help to European Jews, there was disappointment in his policy toward making immigration to Palestine easier. Recalling these days in 1944, a writer in the *Jerusalem Post* on June 2, 1965, wrote "Efforts of the U.S. Congress in 1944 to help Jewish refugees from the Nazi holocaust to find a refuge in Palestine were blocked by the State Department with the connivance of President Roosevelt, who took a pro-Jewish position in public, while in private he endorsed the State Department manouevres."[19]

The Liberation of Rome

On June 4, 1944, Allied troops entered Rome and liberated the city. The *Bulletin* of the Jewish Brigade Group which fought with the British 8th Army and in which Pinchas Lapide served had this moving statement.

> To the everlasting glory of the people of Rome and the Roman Catholic Church we can state that the fate of the Jews was allevi-ated by their truly Christian offers of assistance and shelter. Even now, many still remain in the religious homes and houses which opened their doors to protect them from deportation to certain death.

And *Davar*, the Hebrew daily of Israel's Federation of Labor, quoted a survivor: "If we have been rescued, if Jews are still alive in Rome, come with us and thank the Pope in the Vatican."

Such heartfelt contemporary witness can never be expunged by a hostile revisionism.

The Committee on Army and Navy Religious Activities of the American Jewish Welfare Board wrote to Pius XII on July 21, 1944:

> Your Holiness,
> . . . . We have received reports from our military chaplains in Italy of the aid and protection to Italian Jews by the Vatican, priests, and church institutions during the Nazi occupation of the country. We are deeply moved by this extraordinary display of Christian love – the more so as we know the risk incurred by those who afforded shelter to Jews. . . . From the bottom of our hearts we send you the assurances of undying gratitude. . . .'[20]

A camp near Cosenza was liberated. On October 29, 1944, the camp elders went to Rome and presented to the pope a letter:

> Your Holiness.
> Now that the victorious Allied troops have broken our chains and liberated us from captivity and danger, may we, the Jewish internees of Ferramonti, be permitted to express our deepest and devoted thanks for the comfort and help which Your Holiness deigned to grant us with fatherly concern and infinite kindness throughout our years of internment and persecution. While our

brothers were hunted, imprisoned and threatened with death in almost every country in Europe, because they belonged to the Jewish people, Your Holiness has not only sent us large and generous gifts through the Apostolic Nuncio Msgr. Borgnongini-Duca, on 22 May 1941 and 27 May 1943, but also has shown Your lively fatherly interest in our physical, spiritual and moral well-being. In doing so Your Holiness has as the first and highest authority upon earth fearlessly raised his universally respected voice, in the face of our powerful enemies, in order to defend openly our rights to the dignity of man. You have thus restored confidence in those among us who were on the verge of despair, and strengthened in all of us the faith in the triumph of those ideals. . . . When we were threatened with deportation to Poland in 1942, Your Holiness extended his fatherly hand to protect us, and stopped the transfer of the Jews interned in Italy, thereby saving us from almost certain death. With deep confidence and hope that the work of Your Holiness may be crowned with further success, we beg to express our heartfelt thanks while we pray to the Almighty: May Your Holiness reign for many years on this Holy See and exert your beneficent influence over the destiny of the nations. The President and community of Jewish internees of the former camp at Ferramonti-Tarsia.

October 1944   [signed] Jan Hermann
                                      Dr. Max Pereles[21]

Dr. Weizmann demanded that the Allies publish a declaration that they were prepared to accept refugees, to provide shelter, warn Hungarian railroad employees, write Stalin and ask that he warn Hungary. Bomb railway tracks. "Mr. Eden's reply : 'One should consider it – as for the bombing, the Air Ministry should be contacted,' but they procrastinated and in the end nothing was done."[22]

"The Nuncio did not content himself with diplomatic interventions. On June 8 he went to see Cardinal Seredi and asked him 'why the Hungarian bishops did not intervene more energetically with their Government.' Seredi, in his reply, claimed that 'a pastoral letter would be of no use either; it would only harm the Church and her faithful.'"[23]

Rescuing Hungarian Jews

"Lord Moyne, the British Deputy Minister of State in Cairo, told Yoel Brand in June 1944, when he brought him Eichmann's 'Europe Plan' – to deliver a million Jews in exchange for 10,000 trucks: 'What shall we do with a million Jews?' he asked. 'Where

shall I put them?' By the end of July most of the Hungarian Jews were dead."[24]

Throughout 1944, the Holy See was occupied with the fate of the Jews in Hungary. Here is the telegram that Pius XII sent to Nicolas Horthy on June 25, in French.

> From many sides We receive requests to use every means so that in this noble and chivalrous country there not be an increase and intensification of the sufferings, already too heavy, that are endured by a large number of unfortunate people due to their nationality or race. Since Our heart, that of a Father, cannot remain insensitive to these urgent requests, and by reason of Our ministry of charity which extends to all, We personally address Your Royal Highness, appealing to your noble sentiments and being fully confident that you wish to do all in your power in order that so many unfortunate people be spared further afflictions and sorrows.

The reply from Regent Horthy, not a Catholic, came on July 1:

> It was with deepest understanding and thanks that I just received the message sent by wire from Your Holiness, and I ask you to be indeed assured that I am doing everything possible, especially by asserting the Christian requirements of humanitarian principles. May I be permitted to again ask Your Holiness to look with favor upon the Hungarian people in their hour of trial.[25]

Between the two notes, President Roosevelt sent, on June 26, a sharp note to Budapest. On the 27th, Cassulo informed Cardinal Seredi that the pope wanted him to convene a consistory of Hungarian bishops to take action "in defense of Christian principles." The nuncio officially informed the primate of Hungary that Pius XII's desire was "that the Hungarian episcopate should publicly take a stand on behalf of their compatriots who were unjustly hit by racist decrees."

On January 29, a pastoral letter was prepared, which included the following: "We would be neglecting our moral and episcopal duties, were we not to guard against justice being wronged and against our Hungarian fellow citizens and our Catholic faithful being made to suffer merely on account of their origin. . . . Pray and work for all our Hungarian fellow citizens, without exception." The letter was to be read on a Sunday when a special collection would be taken up for the refugees. The pope added his appeal to that of the Hungarian bishops, sending it to Cardinal Seredi.[26]

Horthy, within twenty-four hours of receiving the pope's cable, convened the Royal Council, told its members of the papal intervention, and commanded that the deportations be stopped immediately. Eichmann tried to circumvent this order but without success.

On July 1, the nuncio went to see the prime minister and told him that the deportations were an abomination that dishonored Hungary. Sztojay promised some relaxation if Rotta would persuade the hierarchy not to circulate the pastoral they had prepared on June 29. The nuncio emphatically refused, telling Sztojay that "it was the right and duty of the Church to raise her voice in all matters contrary to Christian morality." In the event, the primate altered the letter. "The Prince Cardinal of Hungary . . . informs the faithful that he has repeatedly appealed to the Hungarian authorities in the matter of the legislation concerning the Jews, particularly the converted ones, and that he continues his negotiations in this respect."

But the pressure on the Hungarian government continued. Ribbentrop was asked to put a stop to the deportations, and telegrams arrived in Budapest from the King of Sweden as well as the pope. The nuncio was calling several times a day. "We must state openly that as far as aid to the Jews is concerned, priests and clergymen . . . unfortunately are in the first rank." Outstanding in the field of this "intervention" was the Nuncio; he was aided by a group of young priests and nuns who distributed safe-conducts and pontifical letters of protection at the average rate of 500 a day. Jeno Levai: "Over 15,000 of such protection letters were issued, not to speak of thousands of false ones in circulation."

The Hungarian Government was deluged with telegrams from the king of Sweden and the pope. The nuncio was calling several times a day. Horthy ordered an immediate stop to the deportations. On July 11, the nuncio also called on Veesenmayer, Hitler's top diplomat in Hungary, and begged him to use his influence to stop the deportations. And, on August 21, he called together in his office the diplomats of neutral countries and secured their signatures for the following statement, which was delivered to Horthy that same day. "The diplomatic representatives of the Holy See, of Portugal, of Sweden, Spain, Switzerland, have learned with painful amazement that preparations are on foot to deport all of Hungary's Jews. . . . Fully aware of the significance of these deportations which will constitute a mortal blow to the prestige of Hungary and the good name of its people . . . we hereby protest energetically against these acts which are both unjust in their motivation and inhuman in their execution."[27]

Preparations for evacuations stopped, the curfew was relaxed, Jewish stores reopened.

Lapide quoted the SS chief in Hungary as saying after the war that once the oil fields in Roumania were lost, the remnant of Hungarian Jews was not worth straining relations with Horthy over.[28]

On July 15, the apostolic delegate in London was able to write to the representative of the World Jewish Congress. "At this moment I have a telegram from the Holy See. The Holy Father has appealed personally to the Regent of Hungary on behalf of your people, and has been assured that the Regent will do all possible to help. Hereupon the deportations ceased – until August 19, when the Germans made preparations to transfer the Jews of Budapest to camps 'outside the city'."[29] Mr. Sharett, in the meanwhile, had met with Anthony Eden, the British foreign minister, telling him, "This remote chance of saving a remnant is not to be missed. We realize our proposals are unorthodox and unprecedented, but they are warranted by a tragedy which is without parallel."[30]

Jewish Assessment

Roumania surrendered to the Red Army on August 24, 1944. How are the efforts of Pius XII and his representatives in the field to be assessed? What were the views of the Jews for whom and with whom they worked at the time? Lapide reminds us that only 16 percent of the population of Roumania was Catholic, and half of those Greek, not Roman, Catholic. Thus, the nuncio's authority cannot be grounded in any quantitative consideration. There were 250,000 Jews to welcome the liberation of their country – the greatest number to survive in any Nazi-occupied country. What share the papal nuncio had in this survival we hear from the lips of Chief Rabbi Dr. Shafran (who, understandably and justifiably, highlights his own role in these activities):

> Our prime concern in those days was the vast problem of saving the remnants, the widows and orphans and the deportees of Transnystria. Nuncio Andrea Cassulo brought every problem we asked him about to the Government. I also asked him to arrange a visit to Transnystria and to inspect for himself the conditions obtaining there, in that vale of tears. I also convinced him to request the Vatican that they try to soften the heart of Mihail Antonescu when he visited Rome with Queen Elena. Cassulo also tried to soften the harsh approach of the German envoy to Bucharest, Manfred von Killinger. This Righteous One of the Nations [Cassulo] neither rested nor kept silent until he had wrested from Antonescu's hand a promise of the Jews' return to the homeland. It sometimes happened that Cassulo appeared before

them twice in one day on some burning issue. . . . [On one occasion] he returned and showed me "the paper" – a copy of some permit – tears flowed from his eyes, and he thanked me because I had given him the opportunity of doing a good deed.[31]

Should this efficacious activity have been accompanied by rhetorical flourishes? Would crying out the moral judgment on the deportation policy that it surely deserved have helped things along? We have a contemporary discussion of this question between Chief Rabbi Herzog of Jerusalem and Monsignor Hughes, the papal delegate to Egypt and Palestine, when they met in Cairo on September 5, 1944. Saul Friedlander gives the complete transcript of the meeting.[32]

> In the course of the conversation, Herzog expresses a hope that anyone might have had. "I suggest that the Pope should publicly address himself to the Hungarian people and demand that they put obstacles in the way of deportations; that he publicly declare that anyone who sabotages the deportations has the blessing of the Church, whilst those who helped the Germans would be excommunicated."
>
> Hughes replied that he would pass on to the pope what Rabbi Herzog had said, but added, "I believe that he will fear that public appeal to the Hungarian people might spur the Germans to liquidate the rest of the Jews." The chief rabbi saw the point, but added that he would be grateful if the pope would keep his suggestion in mind. Hughes: "You may rest absolutely assured that the Holy Father does everything possible, but does not desire publicity. He intervenes at the most appropriate moment in the most suitable place."

The chief rabbi went on to give advice as to what the pope should be doing in Poland and Hungary, urging Catholics to give shelter to Jews, as he knew was done in Slovakia. Monsignor Hughes went on to give particular instances of the way in which Jews were being helped. Friedlander seems to find this a diversion from the enunciation of a sweeping policy. That policy had been stated over and over again by Pius XII and his predecessor. Everyone in the world, and certainly Catholics, knew what the Church made of the persecution of Jews and others by the Nazis. Lapide takes the Cairo exchange as persuading Herzog about the efficaciousness of following his advice of raising a clamor. Furthermore, Lapide sees Herzog's request as unique. "To the best of my knowledge, the only responsible Jewish leader who ever suggested a public papal protest in order to save Jews was the late Chief Rabbi Herzog who, after hearing the arguments against such a move, acquiesced."[33]

At the end of their discussion, Chief Rabbi Herzog handed a letter to Monsignor Hughes. "In these critical moments, the eyes of the people of Israel, and of all humanity longing for liberty, are turned on the Pope. All our suggestions are in his hands, so that he may, in his wisdom, make use of them at a time and in a manner that seem to him opportune. The eyes of the people of Israel and of humanity which yearn for freedom are in these fateful moments directed to the Pope."[34]

On September 27, just weeks after the liberation of Roumania, the chief rabbi said: "For two long years, when the deportations of Roumanian Jewry were already decided and about to be carried out, the high moral authority of the Nuncio saved us. . . . With what deep satisfaction did he inform me that they might leave for the Holy Land!"

Cassulo was honored by Israel as Righteous of All Nations and was invited to Jerusalem for the planting of a tree on the Mount of Remembrance. What could be more precious than the statements of those who lived through the horror and

Many Jews needed no persuasion on the wisdom of the course Pius XII pursued. "On the other hand, there are on record several statements by Jewish leaders similar in tenor to the words of Dr. Marcus Melchior, the Chief Rabbi of Denmark, who himself was rescued, together with virtually his entire Jewish community, thanks to silent unpublicized endeavors: 'I believe it is an error to think that Pius XII could have any influence whatsoever on the brain of a madman. If the Pope had spoken out, Hitler would have probably massacred more than six million Jews and perhaps ten times ten million Catholics, if he had had the power to do so.'"[35]

attributed the success of the papal efforts precisely to what would later become an accusation. The response to Chief Rabbi Herzog was not: If the pope should follow your advice, Catholics or non-Jews would be harmed. It was: To follow your advice would threaten the liquidation of the Jews. Herzog saw that point. Others still have to comprehend it.

On October 15, Horthy was arrested when the Nazis got wind of his intention to withdraw Hungarian connection with the Axis. The Nazis put a puppet leader in place, Szálasi, leader of the rabidly anti-Semitic Arrow Cross Party. On the 18th, Archbishop Rotta went to Baron Gabor Kemeny, the new foreign minister, and protested the measures being taken against the Jews. A short time later, several hundred ill and handicapped Jews were escorted into the building that housed the Jewish Council. On October 20, 22,000 Jews were rounded up as the police pounded on doors marked with a star. Since no trains were available, they were forced into an infamous death march. When Rotta heard of this, he at once organized a relief convoy, supplying the commander of it with 2000 pontifical safe conducts, all blank and signed by Rotta, along with a letter which read: "The Apostolic Nuncio hereby certifies that Mr. Sando Gyorgy is charged by the Apostolic Nunciature to locate on the roads and in camps persons of Jewish origin who enjoy its diplomatic protection and to collect these." Two thousand Jews were saved by this maneuver by the papal nuncio.[36]

On October 21, Rotta spoke to Szálasi, now styled Führer of the Nation, for over two hours, and extracted a promise that Jews would be neither deported nor exterminated but would work in Hungary itself. On November 9, the papal nuncio presented Baron Kemeny a memorandum asking for specific alleviations for women, children, and the old, as well as human treatment for those working in concentration camps.[37]

Still the atrocities committed by the Arrow Cross mounted daily. On November 17, the nuncio convened the diplomatic corps in his office, and all heads of mission signed this protest: "In spite of solemn promises made by His Excellency F. Szálasi himself . . . we learn from absolutely trustworthy sources that the deportation of all Jews has again been decided. . . . The entire world is witness to these inhuman acts . . . the atrocities which accompany these removals permit us to foresee the end of this tragic exodus. In the face of such horrors, the representatives of the neutral Powers cannot sidestep the obligation, dictated by humanitarian sentiments and Christian charity, to express their most profound distress."[38]

Throughout November, the nuncio, working with the Red Cross, distributed hundreds of blank safe-conducts. When a Hungarian Red Cross worker objected that the issue of forged or blank documents violated the Geneva Convention, Rotta said to him, "My son, you need have no qualms of conscience, for the rescue of innocent people is a virtuous deed. Continue your work for the glory of God." It is estimated that the papal nuncio issued some twenty thousand passports which got thousands of Jews out of Hungary before the end of 1944.

"'I asked the Pope what I should do,' Angelo Rotta related in 1964. 'The seat of the Nunciature had been bombed and half destroyed; communications with the Vatican were extremely difficult and our life was in constant danger. His answer was: If it is still possible to do some charity, remain!' During the final nightmare of November 1944–February 1945 when Budapest Jews were at the mercy of the Hungarian Arrow Cross, the Nuncio hid some two hundred within his palace and urged local clerics to do likewise. . . . Jeno Levai concludes: 'During the autumn and winter of 1944 there was practically no Catholic church institution in Budapest where persecuted Jews did not find refuge.'"[39]

On November 16, Monsignor Bernadini, nuncio in Berne, explained to the German Embassy in Berne the attitude of the Holy See toward the persecution of Jews in Hungary: "The Holy See has always endeavored with all means at its disposal to mitigate the pains and sufferings of those who are subjected to persecution due to their nationality or race . . . therefore the Holy See has repeatedly intervened with the Hungarian Government on behalf of persons of Jewish extraction . . . the Holy Father has personally cabled Horthy demanding of him to exert all his influence so that so many unfortunate people be spared further misery and pains. . . . The Holy Father himself . . . has again manifested his personal interest in people persecuted owing to their religion, origin or for political reasons."[40]

As Jeno Levai, in his conclusion to his *Hungarian Jews and the Papacy* sums up the not-so-silent protests of Pius: "Until 1929 Cardinal Pacelli was Nuncio in Berlin, then he became Secretary of State at the Vatican. In these capacities he obviously played a decisive part in the dispatch of the sixty notes in which the Vatican protested to Hitler against the persecution of the Jews up to the outbreak of war – quite apart from the papal encyclical of 1937 beginning with the words 'Mit brennender Sorge.'"

Public protests about the treatment of the Jews of a kind often retrospectively desired were made by Churchill and Roosevelt. Churchill said that punishing Germany for its butcheries and terrorism had now become the main purpose of the war. Roosevelt announced that the American people would hold the perpetrators of crimes accountable. And so we did. But what was the contemporary result and assessment of these undoubtedly moving announcements? The secretary general of the World Jewish Congress said on November 28, 1944: "Unfortunately, the Germans, convinced that their march toward world domination could not be halted by any power on earth, not only refused to be deterred by these warnings; they even accelerated the pace of the massacres and brought their technique to ghastly perfection."[41]

Dr. Robert M. W. Kempner, the U.S. deputy chief prosecutor at the Nuremberg War Crimes Trial in 1945: "Pius XII knew that the public threats of Roosevelt and Churchill, voiced in 1942 and 1943, of the punishment awaiting the murderers of Jews, failed to produce any of the desired results."

The World Jewish Congress, holding a war emergency conference at Atlantic City, sent a telegram to the Holy See on December 1, 1944, expressing cordial thanks for the protection it had given "under difficult conditions to the persecuted Jews in German dominated Hungary."[42]

The Plight of the Jews: Home to Palestine

American Jews are perhaps the most numerous and affluent Jews in the world, and since the founding of the state of Israel are perhaps the most faithful and generous supporters of the Jewish state. A Jewish state was the dream of Theodor Herzl and has been the guiding star of Zionism from its beginnings in the nineteenth century in the wake of the Dreyfus Affair. American Jews, like other Americans, are immigrants. How did Zionism appear to them? What did American Jews do for the Jews of Europe during World War II? Since the upshot of the war was the founding of Israel, since American Jews are the staunchest supporters of Israel, and since a Jewish state was the goal of the Zionist movement, it may seem that American Jews are Zionists. That claim could possibly be made now, but has it always been so?

Jews in Europe

We have already seen the difference that obtained between Jews in the west of Europe and the more numerous Jews in the east, in Russia and Poland chiefly. The French Revolution and the Enlightenment out of which it sprang enabled Jews to regard themselves differently from their earlier views of themselves in ghettoized European cities. Jews were acknowledged to have the same rights as any other citizen; they were Frenchmen among the French, not a strange and alien nation within a nation to which they did not quite belong. In response to this attractive new status, a Jewish Enlightenment grew up that was the complement of the Enlightenment *tout court*. The Haskalah had some of the effects of the Enlightenment it mimicked.

The rise of the modern state and the political theory on which it was based had as its background the religious wars which had rent Europe after the Reformation. Christians wanted their polity to reflect their religious beliefs, and since Christianity was now divided *grosso modo* into Catholics and Protestants, there was an enmity between Protestant and Catholic polities which expressed itself in warfare. The modern state was in many respects the daughter of necessity. European states would not be able to live together if religious differences were a perpetual possibility of animosity. More seriously, a nation which included believers of different kinds must either treat some of them as something less than citizens or dissolve in civil war. Philosophers sought some common denominator on the basis of which citizens could live together in harmony despite the differences of their religious beliefs. The doctrine of natural rights was born.

Philosophers argue about the relationship between the doctrine of natural rights and the traditional doctrine of natural law. Whatever their seeming similarities, natural rights took human beings one at a time, almost in isolation, and discussed the rights one had prior to involvement in society. The state was a construct meant to protect the rights men brought to the state when, so to speak, they joined it.

From the point of view of natural rights, religious beliefs looked to be an add-on, something further, that did not trump rights but presupposed them. Thus began the privatization of religious belief and the seeming irrelevance of religion to public life. So it was that Jews and Christians, Protestants and Catholics, could be seen first as human beings with rights. The liberation of the Jews was grounded in this.

The price paid by the Jews of the Haskalah was a gradual redefinition of Judaism. Reform Judaism sought to rethink the ancient covenant in modern terms. A split appeared between being Jewish and being French, say. Theodor Herzl thought that the Dreyfus Affair showed this to be an illusion. Zionism returned to the notion of Jews as a nation within a nation, but it did not wish to stop there. As long as Jews lived in a country into which they could never be fully assimilated, there would be a persistence of the "Jewish Question." The answer, for Zionism, was to move the Jewish nation to a Jewish state and thus dispense once and for all with any need to assimilate to an alien nation.

Jews in Eastern Europe were largely unaffected by the Haskalah and the assimilationism which drove Reform Judaism. Their separate status from others in the country where they lived remained unchanged. The pogroms in Russia and Poland that followed on the assassination of Czar Alexander II caused a vast movement of Jews out of Russia and

Poland and into Western Europe. It was the flood of immigrants into Herzl's Vienna that brought about an anti-Semitic reaction.

Jews in the United States

There have been Jews in America since colonial times. In 1645, twenty-three Sephardic (Iberian) Jews arrived in New Amsterdam from Brazil. But if the Jews formed part of the country from the beginning, in 1825 there were only 6,000 Jewish Americans, most of whom lived on the East Coast. It has been said of American Jewry at the

There had even been an American species of Zionism before Theodor Herzl, offspring of the Hibbat Zion ("love of Zion") that immigrants in the 1880s and 1890s had brought with them in their spiritual luggage. The first Zionist Conference was held in New York on July 4 and 5, 1898. Participants were largely Russian Jews, although the leaders were German Jews. But American Jews who had come from Germany vehemently opposed Zionism, as indeed the majority of Jews in Europe did. There grew up an enmity between Reform Judaism and Zionism.

beginning of the nineteenth century that it was small, English speaking, and Americanized. The 1830s brought a wave of German-speaking Jewish immigrants from Bavaria, the German part of Poland, Bohemia, and Hungary. The number grew from 15,000 in the 1840s to 50,000 in 1850 to 150,000 before the Civil War. By 1880 there were a quarter million Jews in the United States, scattered about the country in more than a thousand communities. German Jews arrived under the influence of the Haskalah. They were all but indistinguishable from other German immigrants; indeed, they seemed more German than Jewish. They adopted Reform Judaism.

Abraham Geiger, a man of great influence, held that morality was the essence of Judaism. It was an ethical monotheism. The diaspora, or dispersion, of the Jews was not to be considered a punishment for sin but rather part of God's plan to spread ethical monotheism. The Americanization of the German Jewish immigrant and Reform Judaism were two sides of the same coin. In 1873, Isaac Mayer Wise consolidated Reform Jews into the Union of American Hebrew Congregations. Hebrew Union College, founded in 1875, would be the training ground of Reform rabbis. The Central Conference of American Rabbis, formed in 1889, was a Reform group.

American Jews, as the nineteenth century ended, were thus a homogeneous people assimilated into the American mainstream. But they were soon to be joined by Jews fleeing Eastern Europe because of the pogroms that followed the assassination of Czar Alexander II. Between 1881 and 1914, 2 million Jews arrived in the United States, bringing the total Jewish population to 3 million. In 1925, new laws stopped Jewish immigration.

The portrait of American Jewry could then be taken. As many as five-sixths of American Jews were now from Eastern Europe, and they looked askance at the Reform Jews who had preceded them. They regarded Reform as sham Judaism; their name for German Jews was *Yahudim*. The earlier arrivals considered the newcomers primitive, medieval, clannish, Asiatic, unrefined, radical. Reform Jews called Russian Jew "kikes." But with time, they grew closer together, a phenomenon due to the eventual prospering of the Russian Jews.

The American Jewish Com-mittee was formed in 1906, and in 1914 the American Jewish Joint Distribution Committee was formed to provide relief for Jews abroad. In post-war Ameri-ca, East European Jews succumbed to the blandishments of their new country. They rose into the middle class. They began to join Reform temples. By 1930, half the members of Reform temples were East European by origin. Despite this change, the Jews from Eastern Europe provided most of the American support for Zionism.

American Jews and Zionism

American Reform Jews reacted to Zionism's reassertion of Jews as a nation within a nation, much as the assimilated Jews of Europe had. Before the controversy, Rabbi Gustav Posnanski declared in 1841 that "this country is our Palestine, this city our Jerusalem, this house of God our temple." In 1885, Reform Jews rejected a national definition of Judaism, and in 1896 they explicitly repudiated Theodor Herzl's conception of a Jewish State. Up until the First World War, Reform rabbis saw Zionists as a nuisance and fantastic. It was a deviation from the mission of Jews as they understood it, namely, to spread ethical monotheism throughout the world. Zionism was, in a phrase, reactionary self-ghettoization. Anti-Zionism was at its zenith, and the Balfour Declaration had the effect of increasing opposition to Zionism, an opposition that did not begin to fade until 1922. During the 1930s resistance to the Zionist idea became less strong. The Zionist Rabbis Stephen Wise and Abba Hillel Silver built up support for Zionism among American Jews until, in 1935, the rabbinate became officially neutral on the subject. In 1939, the United Jewish Appeal combined Zionist and non-Zionist relief efforts. With the outbreak of war, Zionist stock rose among American Jews. This brought about the formation of the American Council for Judaism on November 23, 1942. The new organization had as its specific purpose to oppose Zionism in the name of Reform Judaism.

The timing was unpropitious. The day after the formation of the AJC, on November 24, the State Department confirmed that there was indeed a mass extermination of European Jews by the Nazis. Rabbi Stephen Wise, who had known about the extermination program since the previous August but remained silent, was designated to announce the finding. "Not only did news of the atrocities undermine the liberal assumptions of Reform anti-Zionists, but it also rendered them vulnerable to Zionist charges of lack of sensitivity to suffering Jews."[1] Thomas A. Kolsky, the historian of the wartime battle between American anti-Zionists and Zionists, in his even-handed account, enables his reader to enter sympathetically into the rival viewpoints.

It would not do here to rehearse the complicated story Kolsky tells, one that could be made a good deal more complicated by going into the divisions among Zionists and the need to distinguish non-Zionists from anti-Zionists. The question we must ask is this. What, against the background of this struggle, did American Jews, Zionist or not, do for the suffering Jews in Europe? That suffering created sympathy for the Zionist and antipathy to the anti-Zionist, and in the end, with the creation of Israel, it seems true to say that some form of Zionism dominates American Judaism. Thomas Kolsky himself asks our question, and gives his answer to it.

> One aspect of the confrontation between the American Zionists and the Council is most troubling. Neither of the two antagonists made serious efforts to rescue Jews during the Holocaust. That was an inexcusable failure. Rather than suspend their ideological war and join in a common endeavor to save Jewish lives during a time of crisis, both groups were preoccupied with plans for the postwar period. The American Council for Judaism issued impressive statements about the virtues of emancipation and free immigration after the war as the best way to solve the problem of Jewish suffering. The Zionists, who campaigned steadfastly during the war to convert Americans to their program, assigned a much higher priority to promoting support for Jewish statehood than to rescuing Jews.[2]

Jewish Criticism of American Jews

Lenni Brenner, a thoroughgoing anti-Zionist, is not gentle with the conduct of American Jews during World War II. But he is far more severe with Zionists in Palestine. He writes that the Jewish Agency Executives rarely discussed the Jews of occupied Europe during 1940 and 1941, and that apart from weak support for illegal immigration [legally there were quotas] "the Agency did nothing for them."[3] "Nor were their colleagues in neutral America much more helpful, despite the fact that Goldman had arrived there for the duration in 1940 and both Ben-Gurion and Weizmann went there for several extended visits in 1940 and 1941." He goes on to say that the American Zionist leadership campaigned against those Jews who were trying to aid the stricken. American Jews were told by the State Department that sending parcels to Poland was not in the interest of the Allies, and Dr. Stephen Wise said, "We must stop for the good of England."[4] Zionist relief agencies complied, and non-Zionist Jewish relief agencies were also persuaded to stop sending food to the Jews in Europe – except the Aguda, who continued to send packages.

Brenner gives a less-benign account of the time lag between August 1942, when Rabbi Stephen Wise learned that European Jews were being exterminated, and late November, when he announced it. The first reports, of slaughter in the Ukraine, came from the Russians, in October 1941 and January of 1942. In February 1942, Bertrand Jacobson, who had represented the Joint Distribution Committee in Hungary, revealed that Hungarian officers had told him of the massacre of 250,000 Jews in the Ukraine. Yitzhak Gruenbaum, head of the Jewish Agency's Rescue Committee refused to believe it. On August 15, Richard Lichtheim sent a report of massacres to Jerusalem from his post in Switzerland, but the reaction was skeptical. On August 8, the Geneva office of the World Jewish Council obtained detailed accounts of a gassing program. Wise was sent the information immediately and was sent another copy on August 28, when he learned that the State Department was withholding the information. "They then asked him not to release the news to the public pending verification; he agreed and said nothing until November 24 – 88 days later – when the State Department finally confirmed the report. Only then did Wise make a public announcement of a Nazi plan to exterminate all the Jews in their grasp."[5] An equally severe account of Wise's behavior on this matter is given by Walter Laqueur, who ends by citing this remark: "The fault was not of a few men or groups but of American Jewry which had put horny shell over its soul 'to protect it against pain and pity. We have become so dulled that we have even lost our capacity for madness.'"[6]

Pinchas Lapide quotes Nahum Goldmann, one of the main objects of criticism. "If there is room for accusations, they should be directed against the Jews of the free world for their conduct during the years of horror. All of us – leaders and members of the community – failed the test; as one of those who dealt with the rescue and defense of Jewish rights in the holocaust period, I stand here this evening and confess: we all failed."[7]

1945

The War Ends

On January 9, MacArthur's forces landed on Luzon in the Philippines. Warsaw fell to the Russians on January 17. On February 3, American troops entered Manila. At Yalta, a dying Roosevelt met with Churchill and Stalin from February 4 to 11 with terrible consequences for Eastern Europe that would last nearly half a century. On March 7, American troops crossed the Remagen bridge into Germany, and Cologne fell to the Allies. It was no *Blitzkrieg* but a carefully drafted and well-executed plan to move inexorably toward Berlin. On March 9, 100,000 were killed in a bombing raid on Tokyo.

President Franklin Delano Roosevelt, who had been elected to the highest office a historic four times, died and was succeeded by his vice president, Harry Truman.

Vienna fell to the Russians on April 13, and the Red Army began the race for Berlin. On April 25, American and Russian forces met at the Elbe. The war against the Axis was effectively won.

Mussolini and his mistress were assassinated near Lake Como on April 28 and their bodies strung up in a gas station for viewing.

On April 30, in his Berlin bunker, under the rubble of the city he had led to ruin, Adolf Hitler and his mistress Eva Braun committed suicide.

American soldiers released 30,000 prisoners from the concentration camp at Dachau near Munich.

May 8, 1945. Victory in Europe or V-E Day, as it was dubbed.

August 6. The first atomic bomb is dropped, on Hiroshima, on August 6. A second was dropped on Nagasaki on August 9.

August 14, 1945, Japan surrenders. V-J Day.

The Sheltering Continues

The war had been over in Rome ever since its liberation by the American Army. Nonetheless, at the beginning of 1945, Pius XII looked out at a world ravaged by continued war, where battles still were being fought. Camps of refugees had been liberated in Italy, but in Poland, in Germany, elsewhere, the victims of Adolf Hitler's racial and political theories continued to be pinned up. Worse, the Final Solution, the extermination of captured Jews, was accelerated as it lost what mad point it had – a Thousand Year Reich populated by Aryans alone, all Jews wiped from the face of the earth. Now the Third Reich was doomed, but the gassing and burning went on with methodic madness.

Even as Berlin was being bombarded in April 1945, in the cellar of the Reich chancellory, orders were issued. "Above all, I enjoin the government and people of Germany to uphold the racial laws to the limit and to resist mercilessly that poisoner of all nations, international Jewry."[1]

In Poland, the sheltering of Jews continued. A priest in Kampinos, urged his people to aid the Jewish inmates of forced labor in the vicinity of the parish. In Pruzany, nuns saved sixty by clothing them in the habits of their order, and a priest in Vilna saved eleven Jews by concealing them in his church and even devised a well-disguised synagogue within the church. Ursuline nuns in Warsaw, Franciscan nuns in Laski, the Sisters of the Order of Our Immaculate Lady in Szymanow and Niepokalanov, sisters in the city hospitals of Warsaw and Ortwork – they all risked their lives daily for years by sheltering, feeding, and clothing Jews until 1945.[2] Tragically, in the summer and autumn of 1945, Polish militiamen burned synagogues and perpetrated pogroms, murdering hundreds of Jews who had escaped Hitler's Holocaust.[3] Of the some 2,000 Polish priests who were in Dachau alone, 816 were still alive in April 1945. Poles and Jews were alike victims of Hitler's racial policies. Lapide plaintively asks, "Did it need the tortures of hell in order to bring priests and Jews into that simple touching brotherhood of man which Jesus never tired of teaching?"[4] Some 3,000 Catholic priests, monks, and nuns were murdered by the Nazis. And as Bishop Nowowiejsky, who spent the war in a concentration camp wrote, "If the Pope could do nothing against the Nazi criminals who habitually broke their promises and ignored every diplomatic obligation; if he failed to save his own priests from death, what would Hitler have conceded him on behalf of others?"[5]

As we have seen, the statements of Pius XII which graduates of the Hochhuth Correspondence School of Imaginary History find too timid, brought swift reprisals, and the pope was begged by Polish bishops to say no more.

In the autumn of 1945, Harry Greenstein from Baltimore, a close friend of Chief Rabbi Herzog of Jerusalem, told Pius XII how grateful Jews were for all he had done for them. "My only regret," the pope replied, "is not to have been able to save a greater number of Jews."[6]

As the End Drew Near

Various feelers were put out concerning peace negotiations by Weizsäcker, the German ambassador to the Vatican, but it became clear that the Allies would accept nothing less than unconditional surrender. They had no intention of negotiating a peace with the Nazis. This policy put at risk those held in German concentration camps. In Poland, as the Russians approached, the prisoners were not immediately massacred but moved to other camps. Papée, the Polish ambassador to the Holy See, warned that the occupants of camps in Poland were doomed to extermination. "Oswiecim [the Germans called it Auschwitz] was the principal object of his misgiving, with sixteen thousand men and thirty-nine thousand women being in danger of death. According to Papée the camp commandant, like those of other camps, was prepared to kill all the detainees within a very short period of time, and he was only waiting for a written order before starting the executions."[7] The apostolic delegate in Washington reported that Jewish representatives were urging that the pope appeal to the Germans, government and people "as the only way to save the lives of Jews and, in particular, the forty-five thousand Christians of Polish, French, and Czech nationality interned at Oswiecsim and in imminent danger of death." Archbishop Cicognani also mentioned in his cable the camp at Birkenau-Näuss and the labor camps in Lithuania.[8]

The Vatican no longer relied on what the German government said, since the SS units and Gestapo were thought to be under special orders. Orsenigo had been obliged to move to Eichstat, and his ability to exert any influence, never great, had waned. The Holy See was whiplashed between alarming predictions of what might be done to internees – all of them perfectly credible, given the Nazi record – and the fear of inciting the Gestapo into apocalyptic excesses as the fortunes of war had now turned against them – in a war that could be ended only by unconditional surrender. In Berlin, there was the mad hope that the rockets now being launched against England would put the Germans once more in the ascendancy. As the end drew near, Weizsäcker continued his ridiculous efforts to portray the Nazis as the shield against communism and the savior of Christianity. Monsignor Tardini greeted this claim sardonically. Of course he knew that communism like nazism – "the double face of materialism" – was a threat to Christian civilization, but he doubted that Roosevelt and Churchill would be moved to negotiate with the Nazis. "Who would believe that Nazism was misunderstood and that it wanted all Europe to be free, Tardini asked. As to the Jews, how often did the Holy See speak out against acts of cruelty, all to no avail? Regarding the church, Nazism had prohibited Catholic schools, destroyed Catholic organizations, closed convents, hunted down religious, and prosecuted, imprisoned, and executed so many priests."[9]

In the end, it was the United States and Britain who delivered Poland – the ostensible excuse for war in 1939, when it had been invaded by Germany from the west and Russia from the east; Poland, which had known great acts of treachery and great acts of heroism under the German occupation – this Poland was delivered over to the Communists by the terms of the Yalta Conference. It was ludicrous of Germany to suppose that its own crimes against the natural law and its anti-religious policies could be overlooked because communism was no better. There is little doubt that communism was as bad as Nazism, but then one could make an equally plausible argument that Soviet Russia was an acceptable partner in destroying nazism. But this did not justify the post-war settlement that, in the words of Winston Churchill, whose hands were not clean in the matter, an Iron Curtain came down between the West and an Eastern Europe colonized by the Soviet Union.

What Did Pius XII Do for the Jews?

Perhaps no student of what Pius XII did on behalf of the Jews during the war years has been so exhaustive, fair, and careful as Pinchas

Lapide. Throughout his long book, he notes the numbers rescued in this instance or that. Thus when he arrives at a total, it is based on all of the data he gathered. His book remains one of the best source books on the question. He amassed an arsenal of facts to support his own view which, on balance, is favorable to Pius XII. And no wonder.

> . . . we may add, in the light of the previous chapters, that the Catholic Church, under the pontificate of Pius XII was instrumental in saving at least 700,000, but probably as many as 860,000 Jews from certain death at Nazi hands. (The total number of Jews who survived Hitler in ex-Nazi-occupied Europe, excluding Russia, thanks, in part at least, to Christian help, is approximately 945,000. To these must be added the 85,000-odd whom Christians helped escape during the war to Turkey, Spain, Portugal, Andorra and Latin America. Of the resultant total, exceeding one million Jewish survivors, I deducted all reasonable claims of rescue made by the Protestant Churches – mainly in France, Italy, Hungary, Finland, Denmark and Norway; the Eastern Churches – mainly in Roumania, Bulgaria and Greece – as well as those saved by Communists, self-declared agnostics and other non-Christian Gentiles. The final number of Jewish lives in whose rescue the Catholic Church has been instrumental is thus at least 700,000 souls, but in all probability is closer to the maximum of 860,000.)[10]

Eight hundred and sixty thousand Jews saved from certain death by the Catholic Church under the pontificate of Pope Pius XII.

Others did not show any such concern. "It is against this background of genocidal indifference and callousness, that the Catholic effort within Nazi-stricken Europe must be evaluated. On one hand, statesmen, diplomats and generals who refused to save Jews, to avoid 'embarrassment' or 'complications'; on the other hand, peasants, priests, housewives, nuns and workers who, unarmed, defied the mightiest juggernaut in modern times, in order to save some 800,000 Jews."[11]

When Monsignor Hughes informed Chief Rabbi Herzog what the Catholic Church had done and was doing for Jews, Herzog replied: "I thank the Pope and the Church from the bottom of my heart for all the help they have afforded."

Moshe Sharett, on April, 22, 1945, reported to the Jewish Agency of his meeting with Pope Pius XII. "I told him that my first duty was to thank him, and through him, the Catholic Church, on behalf of the Jewish public, for all they had done in the various countries to rescue Jews, to save children, and Jews in general. We are deeply grateful to the Catholic Church for what she did in those countries to help save our brothers."

On September 21, 1945, the general secretary of the World Jewish Council, Dr. Leon Kubowitzky, presented a sum of money to the pope "in recognition of the work of the Holy See in rescuing Jews from Fascist and Nazi persecutions."

"The Catholic Church and the papacy have given proof that they have saved as many Jews as they could," said Raffaele Cantoni, president of Italy's wartime Jewish Welfare Committee.[12]

"We Jews are a grateful people," Pinchas Lapide has written, adding that "no pope in history has ever been thanked more heartily by Jews for having saved or helped their brethren in distress."[13]

5

The Defamation of Pius XII

The Deputy

"I was 14 in 1945, and the total collapse of Germany was a great emotional shake-up for me. I considered it my responsibility to study the shameful history of the Third Reich. Again and again I came to think, 'What would you yourself have done if you were old enough to act?'" So reminisced Rolf Hochhuth. Eventually, when he decided to turn his dramatic imagination loose on this hypothetical question, a number of obvious avenues were open to him. Since the Third Reich had been established in Germany, he might have asked how a German old enough to act at various stages of the Nazi rise to power might have acted. He might have written a play about heroic Germans who did in fact act during the years of the Nazi hegemony and paid for it with their lives or freedom. Alternatively, he might have written about someone who had succumbed to the lure of the Nazi message – surely a play about the gradual and willing seduction of a hitherto sensible German to the Nazi lorelei would not have been lacking in dramatic interest.

Rolf Hochhuth took none of these paths, nor other similar ones open to a reasonably active imagination. He came to believe that by exterminating, or very nearly exterminating, the Jews of Europe, the Germans had brought upon themselves the greatest guilt and shame of the twentieth century, perhaps of Western history. He came to believe in the collective guilt of the German people. But Hochhuth himself was a German. He joined the Nazi *Jungvolk* in 1941 at the age of ten. He describes this experience dismissively in terms of playing cowboys and

Indians and being able to have fights without parental supervision. Perhaps – along with daily doses of Nazi ideology. With the crushing defeat of Germany, and given his view of collective guilt, an enormous burden of shame descended upon young Rolf Hochhuth.

But collective guilt is stratified. German society was hierarchical, and guilt is distributed over that hierarchy, descending from the people at the top and, by a kind of cadenza, reaching ordinary folk. A trickle-down theory of collective guilt. (Hochhuth seemed unaware of Pius XII's condemnation of the conception of collective guilt, with particular reference to Germany.[1]) There was some relief to be had from that consideration. The German nation as a whole, not just Hochhuth, bore the burden of guilt. The next step was to involve non-Germans in this collective guilt. "But we were not alone. In a sense the whole civilized world shares guilt by association with that deed."[2] One can feel Hochhuth's burden of personal guilt beginning to lift. But his effort at exculpation had not ended.

It was not by accident that Hochhuth used the notion of hierarchy when he wished the collective guilt of the German nation on the whole civilized world. One of the things that set his mind going, he tells us, was a book by Gerald Reitlinger called *The Final Solution*. He was struck by the account of what Catholics had done for Jews persecuted by the Nazis. Now Rolf Hochhuth himself was a Protestant, and one obvious way in which Catholics differ from Protestants is that Catholics have a hierarchy. Just like the Reich. But if there is a hierarchy, there is a dictator on top, who bears maximum responsibility within the Church. Did Rolf, as a Protestant, perhaps resent being told what Catholics had done for Jews during the dark days of nazism? He says he looked into the matter. Not to tell the story of Protestants who had acted heroically under Nazism but to brood about Catholicism. Catholics were led by a single man, like the Führer in the Reich. Catholics would have responded to any command of the pope, the way good Nazis did, or else. Now his earlier hypothetical question could be replaced by another: *What should the pope have done to stop the Nazis?* Research might have made him aware of at least some of the things recounted in this book. He wrote to Reitlinger, who told him, "I do not think this need have happened if there had been a better Pope." Surely this is a fatuous statement. Was Reitlinger referring to Pius XI, perhaps, who was pope when Hitler came to power and made it as clear as could be, to the German people and the world, that nazism was the polar opposite of Christianity? Who knows? Such a remark held out the promise of relief from guilt and shame that Hochhuth craved.

When Pius XII died in 1958, Hochhuth listened with growing resentment to the way the late pontiff was praised and thanked for his wartime record. About being a Protestant, one of his characters says, "One cannot always bear it." The time had come to act. Pius XII had to be exposed as a pope who could have stopped the Holocaust but didn't. Any attempt to prove this historically confronts enormous obstacles – the truth of the matter, for instance – as a tribe of scriveners have shown by their failures to undo the actual record of what Pius XII did for the Jews. Aristotle said of history and poetry "that the one describes the thing that has been, and the other a kind of thing that might be." Since history could not provide him with the Pius XII he wanted, Hochhuth invented one of his own, keeping the same name, of course, in order to damage the innocent.

In 1963 *The Deputy,* a sprawling incoherent play that would have taken seven hours to be acted in its entirety, burst upon the world. Rolf Hochhuth had found the answer for his own and everyone else's guilt. His preposterous thesis was that Pius XII was responsible for the extermination of the Jews.

This was vilification on a truly Goebbels scale. The Nazis had been the first to slander and defame Pius XII, calling him "the deputy of the Jew God." It was in the atmosphere of such propaganda that Hochhuth had been raised. Obviously it was contagious. In *The Deputy* he presented a Pius who was the deputy of the Jew-hating Nazis.

That a troubled, guilt-ridden, ex-Nazi youth and resentful Protestant should have dreamt up such nonsense is one thing. That *The Deputy* was taken seriously as either drama or history represents one of the great mysteries of the post-war world, a harbinger of impending cultural collapse. The play became a world-wide sensation, enjoying a success that must have made its author financially independent. Its specious history has been refuted again and again. And yet it is as alleged history that it has been received, discussed, and continues to exercise a nefarious influence on the reputation of Pope Pius XII.

The Nazi theory was that if you tell a lie big enough you can get away with it. Doubtless this means that if the lie is sufficiently outrageous, refutation of this point or that will not affect it. There were people who were ready to think that Pope Pius XII, a noble and saintly man who deserved the posthumous praise that brought a snarl from Rolf Hochhuth, had been – a Nazi. There were people who wanted to believe the big lie that Pius XII was somehow responsible for the Holocaust. He was someone on whom, like Christ whose Vicar on Earth he was, the guilt of all could be loaded. A scapegoat.

One sympathetic reviewer of the play, John Simon, said that Hochhuth "has put forward all conceivable reasons for the pope's silence: the safety of Catholics, business and financial considerations, ecclesiastical politics (danger of schism), European politics (Hitler as bulwark against Stalin and communism), a kind of aristocratic hauteur and lack of human warmth, failure of nerve."[3] *All* conceivable reasons? Apart from the non-historicity of those that Simon mentions, one familiar with the facts recalled in Chapter 4 of this book will note the glaring admission of the primary reason Pius XII actually did have not to thunder denunciations – *lest more Jews be killed.*

Pinchas Lapide, having expressed his gratitude for what Pius did for the Jews, added: "Were I a Catholic, perhaps I should have expected the Pope, as the avowed representative of Christ on earth, to speak out for justice and against murder – irrespective of the consequences."[4] This echo of Hochhuth from Lapide is surprising, since he himself has documented how Pius condemned the injustice and murders the Nazis were committing. He must have in mind a condemnation which would have tried all the tropes of rhetoric, permitted the pope to luxuriate in the sound of his own voice, and then what? Irrespective of the consequences? Even if savage reprisals resulted? The consequences Pius XII sought to avoid while making the essential judgment on nazism again and again – a reiterated judgment which no one failed to get – were reprisals on those for whom he spoke. Catholic morality is not of the kamikaze type, particularly when the moral condemnation would result in the death of those one is determined to rescue. Morally, "whatever the consequences" refers to consequences to the agent for doing what he ought to do, not consequences for others, a consideration for whom could alter the object of the action, that is, the moral nature of *what* one is doing.

The reader of Lapide's book will know that Pius XII himself found obliquity and nuance painfully necessary, and accepted that necessity reluctantly. To suggest that the way he condemned nazism by word – waiving for the moment the *deeds* which, by Lapide's count, saved 860,000 Jews from certain death – shows that he was worried for the safety of Catholics alone, or money, or schism, or adopting the risible suggestion made by Weizsäcker that Nazi Germany was saving Europe from communism – to suggest any of these things requires an ignorance of the facts that is culpable in anyone commenting publicly on these matters.

But what about the supposed silence of Pope Pius XII on the fate of the Jews under Hitler?

SHHHHHHH?

An Audible Silence

Cromwell, the agent of Henry VIII, complained that the silence of Thomas More was heard all over England, and More really had remained silent. The alleged silence of Pius XII cannot be real silence because it was both heard and reported all over the world. As Robert Kempner, deputy chief U.S. prosecutor in the Nuremberg war-crimes trial wrote in his prologue to Jeno Levai's *Hungarian Jews and the Papacy,* "The archives of the Vatican, of the diocesan authorities and of Ribbentrop's Foreign Ministry contain a whole series of protests -- direct and indirect, diplomatic and public, secret and open." The pope's words, not his silence, and his words were understood by those who heard them – were praised or resented, but understood. The voice of Pius XII went out over Vatican Radio, and of course he would be held primarily responsible for all the station's broadcasts.

> Some of the most courageous broadcasts aired by Radio Vaticana at this time were those that unveiled the horrors of the Nazi Holocaust. On January 20, 1940, an American Jesuit became the first announcer in world radio to report the imprisonment of Jewish and Polish prisoners in "sealed ghettos." From that point on, Vatican Radio continued to feature stories on concentration camps and other Nazi torture chambers. From 1940 to 1946, Vatican Radio also ran an information Office, transmitting almost 1.25 million shortwave messages to locate prisoners of war and other missing persons.[5]

As Pius XII said, speaking to his cardinals in June 1943, after having expressed his great sorrow for the persecuted: "Every word we have directed to the competent authorities and every intimation we have made public we had to weigh carefully in the interests of those suffering so that we should not against our will make their situation more complicated and intolerable."

The savage reprisals taken by Seyss-Inquart after the Dutch bishops' pastoral was read out in all the Catholic churches on the Ninth Sunday after Pentecost in 1942 is a dramatic instance of the risk taken. As a result of the pastoral, all Catholics of Jewish descent were rounded up and put on trains for the death camp. It was not a matter of thinking a protest would be ineffective, that is, not have the desired effect; but the grounded expectation that it would have the opposite effect.

Did this mean that the messages and allocutions and broadcasts were so timid and obscure that no one knew what he was talking about? Consider the following sample of contemporaneous reporting of papal statements.

Reporting the "Silence"

Anyone who glanced at the newspaper headlines in the major cities of the world would have found extensive stories on the "silence" of Pius XII. Those who read smaller print would have found in the **October 28, 1939,** edition of *The New York Times*, a story in which it was reported "that a powerful attack on totalitarianism and the evils which he considers it has brought on the world, was made by Pope Pius XII in his first encyclical . . ." And there was more: "It is Germany that stands condemned above any country or any movement in this encyclical – the Germany of Hitler and National Socialism."

On **January 9, 1939**, while still secretary of state to Pius XI, Cardinal Pacelli sent a circular to all the archbishops of the world telling them to prepare for the reception of 200,000 emigrants from Germany. The following day, he appealed to the cardinals of the United States and Canada to find suitable posts for Jewish scientists and professors expelled from Germany.

Had he become mute when he was elected pope? It seems not.

POPE DECRIES WAR, DICTATORS, RACISM ran the head over the continuation of the story on Pius's first encyclical.

And from Berlin, in the same issue: "It is known to what extent the opinions of the National Socialist State on the problems treated in the encyclical differ from those of the Vatican."

The silence of Pius XII was audible in Berlin as well as New York.

JEWS RIGHTS DEFENDED. So ran the subhead of a story that appeared in *The New York Times* on **March 14, 1940**. The story recounts the famous visit of Ribbentrop to the Vatican, in the course of which visit, the *Times* reports, the Pope Pius "also came to the defense of the Jews in Germany and Poland." That seems clear enough.

On **January 23, 1940**, *Izvestia* accused the pope of being the tool of Great Britain and France. Far off in Russia, they must have heard something.

The Tablet of London, on **April 5, 1941**, reported on a broadcast in which Vatican Radio warned the French of the base folly of supporting

Nazi Germany. "Alsace, Austria, Sudeten, Germany, provide object lessons of what is intended everywhere where Germany rules, so that there will be no independent source of moral judgment, lest by it the wickedness of Hitler should be judged." No equivocation there. Everyone knew who Hitler was.

POPE IS SAID TO PLEAD FOR JEWS LISTED FOR REMOVAL FROM FRANCE. This is a headline in *The New York Times*, **August 6, 1942,** over a story in which we read that "The church pleas were reportedly made after the Vatican had learned that the Germans asked for a roundup in both zones of German, Austrian, Polish, Czech, Baltic and Jewish refugees who sought safety in France in 1936."

VICHY SEIZES JEWS; POPE PIUS IGNORED – That is how *The New York Times* headlined a story on **August 27, 1942.** In order to be ignored, the pope must have said something.

POPE SAID TO HELP IN RANSOMING JEWS – This was a headline one would have seen in *The New York Times* of **October 17, 1943**.

Even in London attentive ears picked up the silence of Pius XII. The *Times* of London of **October 11, 1942**, explained to its readers why the pope hadn't endorsed the Allied cause. "To be disappointed by the absence of a formal benediction of the cause of the United Nations would be to ignore the character of the Church of Rome as a spiritual body and as a political corporation. Because the Church refrains from making a pronouncement which would necessarily engage her political form as well as her spiritual essence, it does not follow that the occupant of the throne of Peter, or his highest counselors, are deaf to the appeal of Christians and of others who unite with them in condemnation of armed wickedness. A study of the words which Pope Pius XII has addressed since his accession in encyclicals and allocutions to the Catholics of various nations leaves no room for doubt. He condemns the worship of force and its concrete manifestation in the suppression of national liberties and in the persecution of the Jewish race."

October 24, 1942. *The Tablet*: "We read in the *Jewish Chronicle*: 'Under the direction of Goebbels, the Nazi Party Department for Public Enlightenment has issued a special pamphlet condemning the recent intervention of the Vatican against the persecution of the Jews in Nazi-occupied countries. The pamphlet is being translated into many languages, and altogether 10,000,000 copies will be distributed free in Europe and Latin America. The pamphlet says that since the twelfth century eighteen popes have identified themselves with the anti-Jewish policy now pursued by Nazi Germany, and that only the present Pope has found it necessary to make interventions on behalf of Jews. Finally, the pamphlet alleges that the action of the present pro-Jewish Pope has produced a feeling of lack of confidence in him in the Catholic world. 'The extreme Nazi organs in Germany have been expressing great dissatisfaction at concessions made to the Vatican during the past two months which have enabled about 300 Jews to leave Nazi-occupied countries, including the ghettoes of Poland, and go to Spain and Portugal. The Vatican appears to have obtained Spanish and Portuguese visas for these Jews.'"

The Tablet on **April 3, 1943**, cites *La Bourse Egyptienne*, Cairo, a statement of Monsign Hughes, apostolic delegate: "I have just received from Cardinal Maglione, Secretary of State to His Holiness, the assurance that the Holy See has worked and is still working for the protection of Jewish communities in the occupied countries, and that, despite the want of success of so many precious endeavors, the Holy Father does not cease to do everything that is possible. Only recently the Vatican has been strongly criticized by certain sections of the Central European Press for its defense of persecuted Jews, and for its articles in the *Osservatore Romano*." Even in Cairo the pope who is said to have kept silent was heard.

The Tablet on **July 3 1943**, headlined a story THE JEWS AND THE NATURAL LAW. "The seven Bishops of Slovakia met new measures against the Jews in their country by issuing a joint pastoral letter on March 8 defining the rights of Jews under the natural law. The following are excerpts from the text as broadcast in full in German by the Vatican wireless on June 21. 'We believe,' said the announcer, 'that our listeners will welcome hearing it.' The pastoral begins: 'The only way to make up your mind about any question is according to the Natural Law and Divine Revelation.'"

The Tablet heard things in America as well, as is clear from a story in its issue of **December 25, 1943**, which draws on the *Baltimore Synagogue Bulletin* in which Rabbi Morris Lazaron said. "We can well imagine the anxiety in the hearts of our Catholic fellow-citizens in these days when the head of their Church again becomes a prisoner of the Vatican." He goes on to quote the pope's condemnations of anti-Semitism, and the action taken by bishops and priests throughout occupied Europe to protect Jews driven like animals; from their homes.

"They have shielded and healed them at the risk of their own lives, and indeed many priests have been jailed and not a few killed in their effort. But it is more than a mere reciprocal gesture which prompts our prayers for His Holiness. . . . We can place ourselves in the position of our Catholic friends."

On **June 2, 1945,** when retrospection was possible, Pius XII said to the College of Cardinals: "Would it have been possible in those days [of *Mit brennender Sorge* in 1937], by opportune political action, to check once and for all the outbreak of brutal violence, and to put the German people in a position to shake off the tentacles that were strangling them? Would it have been possible thus to save Europe and the world from this immense innundation of blood? No one will dare to give an unequivocal answer. But in any case no one can accuse the Church of not having denounced and exposed in time the true nature of the National-Socialist movement and the danger to which it exposed Christian civilization.

"Continuing the work of Our predecessor, We Ourselves have during the war, and especially in our broadcast addresses, constantly opposed the demands and the perennial laws of humanity and of the Christian faith to the ruinous and inexorable application of National-Socialist teachings, which even went so far as to use the most exquisite scientific methods to torture or eliminate people who were often innocent. This was for Us the most opportune, and, We might say, the only efficacious way of proclaiming before the world, the immutable principles of the moral law, and of confirming, in the midst of so much error and violence, the minds and hearts of German Catholics in the higher ideals of truth and justice. And Our solicitude was not without its effect."

The Grumbling Begins

Already in 1955, there were those who, like Hochhuth later, apparently began to resent all this gratitude to Pius XII. Sadly, it began with Jews. In 1955, two Israeli papers [*Hakol* and *Ma'ariv*], while still acknowledging that the Church under Pius had saved great numbers of Jews, wondered whether the pope had sufficiently, etc. etc. Why hadn't he published an encyclical on the matter? Perhaps they thought that, unlike *Mit brennender Sorge,* another encyclical would have changed the course of human history. And so it began.

After the orgy that followed the appearance of *The Deputy* in 1963, the gloves came off. In 1965 Guenter Lewy published, *The Catholic*

Church and Nazi Germany. The review in *The Tablet* on January 16, 1965, said,

> It is not, I think, an unfair summary of Mr Guenter Lewy's deductions from his mass of quotations to say that, in his view, the Church should, and could, have stopped Hitler; that its authoritarian character made it easier for Catholics to "go along" with the Nazism; that an anti-Semitic tradition in the Church inhibited German Catholics, and possibly the Holy See, from the requisite strength of protest against Nazi racialism; and finally, that the Church's professed ability to work with all forms of government is an opportunism which enables it "to be on the winning side," that it aims at preserving itself as an institution at all costs, even to the extent of failing in its moral mission.
>
> Catholicism is singled out because Mr. Guenter Lewy holds it to be a guardian of human morality, a task in which, he considers, it has failed miserably.

But some Jews had not forgotten the wartime solidarity with Catholics and the results of Pius XII's efforts. "We Jews are a grateful people," Pinchas Lapide has said, and proceeded to chronicle the basis for gratitude to Pius XII. Perhaps he wrote his own magnificent book to counter the carping criticisms that were being voiced by his fellow Jews. In the midst of those dark times, Pius XII had remarked on the difficulty of being heard. He also expressed what nowadays would be called "a preferential option for the Jews."

The Tablet, London, **June 12, 1943**, reported the pope's address to the College of Cardinals on June 2:

> When the ferment of violent passions was not yet set free, and when the sense of brotherly confidence was still to be found among the nations, the voice of the Supreme Pastor could reach all the faithful freely and directly, through the voices of their Bishops, without being obscured, garbled or "interpreted." The evidence of the facts, no less than the clarity of the language, was sufficient to defeat and render vain all attempts at altering or disguising the words of the Vicar of Christ. If that were so even now, even today, all honest men of goodwill would have the means and the opportunity of ascertaining that the Pope has, for all peoples without distinction and without exception, wishes only for peace and not for affliction.

Thus it was that Pius XII explained the pride of place he gave to the Jewish victims of the Nazis. "Do not be astonished, beloved brethren and sons, if We lend Our ear with particularly profound sympathy to the voices of those who turn to Us imploringly, their hearts full of fear. They are those who, because of their nationality and descent, are pursued by mounting misfortune and increasing suffering. Sometimes, through no fault of theirs, they are subjected to measures which threaten them with extermination."

The New York Times, on **June 3, 1943**, reporting on the same allocution, quoted: ". . . our high mission obliges us to defend and save the spiritual heritage of our saints and our wise predecessors and to denounce with truth, but in love, the errors that are at the root of so much evil, so that man may awaken and return to the road of salvation." Pius strove for a delicate balance between condemnation and persuasion. It had not been his intention, Pius said, to formulate indictments. Rather, "Our voice was that of the watchful sentinel; on the eve of this great conflict it was the sob wrenched from the paternal heart which was torn by the vision of the imminent catastrophe."

"Do not expect from us now that we give you here the details of all we have attempted to realize in order to lighten the sufferings and protect their indestructible religious rights, while we attempted to better their moral and juridical status."

BERLIN BROADCAST ATTACKS VATICAN. "The Vatican, the prelates, all the hierarchy of the Church, from the Pope down to the parish priests, have this choice: either with Fascists and Catholic Italy or against it." *Facts on File*, **September 20, 1943**.

On **December 25, 1941**, *The New York Times* said of Pope Pius XII's Christmas message: *"The Voice of Pius XII Is a Lonely Voice in the Silence and Darkness Enveloping Europe this Christmas."*

That was the voice that so many Jews heard and appreciated, among them one of the world's great scientists, who fled to America.

> Being a lover of freedom, when the Nazi revolution came in Germany I looked to the Universities to defend it, knowing that they had already boasted of their devotion to the cause of truth; but no, the Universities immediately were silenced. Then I looked to the great editors of the newspapers, whose flaring editorials in days gone by had proclaimed their love of freedom; but they, like the Universities, were silenced in a few short weeks. Then I looked to the individual writers. . . . they too were mute. Only the Church stood squarely across the path of Hitler's campaign for suppressing truth. I had never had any special interest in the Church before,

but now I feel a great affection and admiration . . . I am forced, thus, to confess that what I once despised I now praise unreservedly.

Thus Albert Einstein, late in 1940 in *Time.*

It is, accordingly, demonstrable nonsense to say that Pope Pius XII remained silent about the fate of the Jews. What he said was widely reported, was welcomed by many, and was resented by Nazis and Fascists.

This being the case, the accusation is altered. It was not what he said, but what he did not say, that opens the pope to the posthumous censure of revisionists. It is suggested that if Pius had written an encyclical in which he had laid out in grisly detail what the Nazis were doing to Jews and other innocents who fell into their power, the impact would have been so great that . . . well, the exact effect is left vague. Since the facts about the treatment of the Jews were condemned early and late by Pius XII, and this was known to anyone who listened to the radio or read the papers, something more than the mere facts were envisaged as the essence of this possible encyclical.

Excommunication of Hitler and Goebbels and Mussolini? Inciting the Catholic people of totalitarian regimes to rise up and overthrow their dictators? Even in retrospect, it is difficult to compose the encyclical which would have changed the course of human history.

Rolf Hochhuth doubtless would have wanted something more theatrical, with the pope as Führer holding a kind of Nuremberg Rally in St. Peter's Square, haranguing the faithful and whipping them up into a righteous rage. For that sort of performance, they could go down and listen to Mussolini from his balcony overlooking the Piazza Venezia. In fiction, great moments provide a peripety which turns the action toward a satisfying resolution. But fiction, like revisionist history, has to exclude most of the real circumstances of action in order to get a clean and controllable narrative sequence.

So it is that many have *imagined* papal words which would have turned the course of history. Reflection on the effects of *Mit brennender Sorge* of 1937, aimed unequivocally and linguistically at the Nazi regime, should have moderated such imaginings. The encyclical unnerved the Gestapo, who tried to stop its being printed and circulated. It galvanized many of the faithful. It made it absolutely clear the Christian condemnation of the Nazi ideology. But it did not change the course of history.

Surely it is naive to think that another such encyclical from Pius XII, when Hitler was far more entrenched than he had been in 1937, when he was about to plunge the world into war, would have been the one thing needed to stop the persecution of the Jews by tumbling Hitler from power.

But it is one thing to speculate about what Pius XII might have done and to ponder various counterfactuals. After all, his were prudential decisions, applications of moral principles, and in so acting Pius, like of all us, was fallible. No one was more conscious of this than he himself. But another and sinister note has been added to such second-guessing. The motives of Pius XII, against everything we know of the man, have been questioned. He is portrayed as the willing and approving facilitator of Nazi policies.

This is calumny. This is defamation.

Deeds, Not Words

To speak is a human act but for all that we distinguish between saying things and doing things. "What you are speaks so loudly that I cannot hear what you say." In Chapter 4, we have gathered together chronologically the things Pius XII did along with what he said during the course of the war years. We saw that he himself lamented that he had not been able to do more for the Jews, who had suffered so terribly under Hitler. But we also saw what the effect of his manner of acting was.

Eight hundred and sixty thousand Jews were saved from certain death at the hand of the Nazis. We are told that only 2 million European Jews survived the Nazi years, many by emigrating or escaping. This means that Pius XII and the Catholic Church were responsible for nearly half the survivors of the Holocaust.

He thought he could have done more. Perhaps he could have.

But no one else, no other group, no other organization, came anywhere close to the actual record of Pius XII in rescuing Jews during the Hitler years.

The record of non-European Jews in rescuing fellow Jews from Hitler was spotty.

Some Zionists were far more intent on securing a Jewish homeland in the post-war world and subordinated rescue efforts to that end.

If Pius XII had said anything like what David Ben-Gurion said about the Jews in Europe, one might understand the animus against him. But of course he did not. Jewish organizations turned to the pope for help in the increasing confidence that they would get it, immediately, without discussion, out of sense of natural justice as well as Christian charity.

There is something worse than absurd about poring over the words of the pope, parsing them in such a way that they mean the opposite of what they say, writing posthumous speeches for him, when all along there is the overwhelming fact of what he achieved: **860,000 Jews rescued from certain death under the Nazis because of the efforts and leadership of Pope Pius XII**.

Voices should fall silent. Heads should bow. God should be thanked for this saintly and effective pope.

A Literary Genre

Hochhuth opened the door to what soon became an Olympic event – throwing mud at Pius XII. The very titles of the books forewarned the reader that yet another attack was under way: Guenter Lewy's *The Catholic Church and Nazi Germany* (1964), Saul Friedlander's *Pius XII and the Third Reich* (1966), Carlo Falconi's *The Silence of Pius XII* (1965). These books were just the beginning. In striking contrast to all these, Pinchas Lapide's *The Last Three Popes and the Jews*, which appeared in 1967, effectively put into perspective the books just mentioned. Lapide devoted 100 pages of his book to the question "What did Pius XII do for the Jews?" – documenting the magnificent record of the Catholic Church under Pius XII. When he turned to "What Pius XII did not do for the Jews?" he refutes or fundamentally weakens the criticisms of the pope.

Lapide did not stop the onslaught of criticism, particularly from his fellow Jews, which seemed to have been one of his main purposes in writing his thorough account, a rich source of documentation. The articles and books increased and multiplied. Of course there have been books on the other side. There is *Hungarian Jewry and the Papacy: Pius XII was Not Silent* by Jeno Levai (English edition, 1968) and *Pius XII: Greatness Dishonored*, by Michael O'Carroll (1981). But as the attacks multiplied, discussions inevitably began to sound like defenses of someone presumed guilty. The big lie had achieved its propaganda effect. Over the years, the Jesuit Robert A. Graham patiently analyzed and refuted one attack book after another. But the attacks continued. Such sober and documented works as Margherita Marchione's *Pope Pius XII, Architect of Peace* (2000) and Pierre Blet's *Pius XII and the Second World War* (1999) have had little effect. Why? *Because what Pius XII did or not do is no longer the issue.* I will return to this.

CATHOLIC ANTI-CATHOLICS

That a former member of the Nazi *Jungvolk*, after the defeat of Hitler, should have been filled with shame at what the Third Reich had done to Jews and others and sought to rid himself of guilt first by blaming everyone and then, out of resentment at praise for Pius XII's rescue of Jews, created the colossal fiction that Pius XII was the one chiefly responsible for what Hitler and Himmler and Eichmann had done – that is, if not forgivable, in some mad way intelligible. Therapy takes many forms.

That Jewish scholars should bend their best efforts to diminish or deny the fact Pius XII was responsible for the rescue of nearly half the Jews who survived the Holocaust,[6] (if 2 million escaped and the pope was responsible for nearly half that number . . .), that they should scrutinize with a cold eye every aspect of his papacy while remaining silent about the inaction of many Jews and about the fact that Jewish relief organizations were forbidden to help converted Jews – that is, if not forgivable, in some shameful way therapeutic. Such attacks prepared the way for Bruno Bettleheim's bigoted *obiter dictum*. When asked to comment on the American bishops' letter on nuclear arms: "Where [was] the conference of bishops when six million Jews were killed?" Such slanderous attacks on the Church had by then become commonplace. His remark might have reminded some older bishops of the flap created by Cardinal Mundelein of Chicago in 1937, when he wondered how a supposedly intelligent nation could put a paper-hanger like Hitler in charge, along with men like Goering and Goebbels. There was an uproar in Berlin. When the Germans protested to the Vatican, Pius XI was given this advice. "The Holy See should neither correct nor deplore the remarks of Cardinal Mundelein. That would be an act of weakness which would only increase the arrogance of the chiefs of National Socialism and Hitler himself who imagines that the whole world should bow to him." The author of the advice was Cardinal Pacelli.[7]

But that Catholics should have joined the parade of those attacking the Church's record during World War II is worse than shameful. Early on, there was Gordon Zahn's 1963 book, *German Catholics and Hitler's Wars,* the work of a pacifist whose ecclesiastical discontents were perhaps not limited to the wartime German hierarchy. But eventually books like John F. Morley's *Vatican Diplomacy during the Holocaust 1934–1943* (1980) provided aid and comfort to enemies of the Church. Morley was a priest, and his book was systematically dismantled by Father Graham. "He finds a way of cutting down to size the grateful expressions of Rabbi Safran of Rumania and Rabbi Freiberger of Croatia. He discounts the reactions of the international Jewish agencies, thankful for the papal interventions. This is manipulating the evidence and makes the witnesses look like sycophants or uninformed about their own affairs."[8]

There are three recent entries in the genre that might be called "Catholic Anti-Catholicism."

DADDY MADE ME DO IT

In 1997, James Carroll, a laicized priest, attacked Pius XII in *The New Yorker*. He had warmed up for his task by writing *An American Requiem* (1996), a literary parricide, but full of his attitude toward the Church. He tells us he loved being a priest and that his ministry had been "an effort to redeem the cruel myopia of the Counter-Reformation Church. My job was to accompany people on their versions of the journey I was taking."[9] For example, a grief-stricken Alan Tate. And what had Alan Tate been grief-stricken about? A Catholic, he had divorced and remarried and when a child of his second marriage died it was refused a Catholic funeral. An infant. Or so Tate told Carroll, who was ready by then to believe anything awful about the Church. In describing his own ordination, Carroll imagines himself saying to the question, "Do you solemnly promise to respect and obey your ordinary?" "'It depends, Eminence,' I wanted to say. This man and others like him had just sheepishly endorsed the war. And only months before, he and others like him – ordinary indeed – had bowed to the pope's demoralizing edict on birth control, *Humanae Vitae*, published in July 1968." Ah yes. Divorce, contraception, sexual morality. The Church's stand against the sexual *Zeitgeist* lies at the root of this attack on Paul VI.

Carroll's book is a self-serving, prolonged whine, in which his father plays the heavy and Jim the good guy. It presses all the liberal buttons – it mocks the Church, slanders the generation that won the Cold War, turns his father into a parody of Dr. Strangelove. For these and other reasons – he writes well – Carroll's memoir won the National Book Award.

CORNWELL'S GRIEVANCE

"*Hitler's Pope* is the previously untold story of the man who was arguably the most dangerous churchman in modern history: Eugenio

Pacelli, Pius XII, Pontiff from 1939 to 1958 and long controversial as the Pope who failed to speak out against Hitler's Final Solution. Here is the full story of how Pacelli in fact prompted events in the 1920s and '30s that helped sweep the Nazis to unhindered power." Wow! And this is just the dust jacket blurb. Pope-trashing has become a tough market, and authors have to ratchet up the outrage to gain attention.

Needless to say, the book does not deliver on its preposterous accusation – however fuzzily framed: "prompted events" that "helped sweep the Nazis" into power. The reader is led to expect an exposé of Cardinal Pacelli as the *eminence rouge* behind the rise of national socialism, the man who catapulted Hitler into power in the '30s. This turns out to be as historically accurate as the tired and discredited claim that Pius as pope "failed to speak out."

What events did Eugenio Pacelli prompt that swept Hitler into power? In the aftermath of the war and the establishment of the Weimar Republic and centralization, the concordats that the Vatican had with different German states came up for review; the question arose as to whether the Reich as such should have an embassy in Rome. From the point of view of the Vatican, this had the disadvantage that the papal nuncio would be in Protestant Berlin rather than in Catholic Bavaria. The resolution was that there would be a Reich embassy in Rome but a papal nuncio in both Munich and Berlin. But in the event there would be not two men, but one, involved – Eugenio Pacelli, who would commute between the two cities. Here is Cornwell's charge: "Yet, skillful as it seemed, this diplomatic sleight of hand delayed the negotiation of a Reich concordat. And the consequence of that failure, in the view of the German Church historian Klaus Scholder, 'created the fatal starting point from which in 1933 Hitler was to force the capitulation of German Catholicism in a few weeks.' In other words, Pacelli could have achieved a Reich concordat in the early 1920s without compromising Catholic political and social action. A decade later, Hitler cunningly saw the concordat as an opportunity to secure the *voluntary* withdrawal of political Catholicism, confrontation with which he was determined to avoid."[10]

There seem to be a few premises missing in this argument. If a Reich concordat had been negotiated in the 1920s, before Hitler came to power, there would have been no occasion for negotiating one in 1933, when Hitler was in power. What has to be shown is that the absence of a concordat swept Hitler into power and that the collapse of German Catholicism was a result of the absence of a Reich concordat.

The gap between Cornwell's sensational assertions and the support he offers for them is breathtaking.

Even if these arguments could be made, it would have to be shown that the results of not having a Reich concordat were sufficient to sweep Hitler into power.

Absent from Cornwell's demonization of Pacelli's work in Germany is any attention to the factors that had an unequivocal effect on the rise of Hitler, such as the backing of the German industrialists and bankers, many of them Jews. It is noteworthy that William L. Shirer omits any mention of what Cornwell puts forward as prime causes of Hitler's rise. But then neither of them allude to the role of the Zionist party.

These accusations are merely subsidiary to Cornwell's overall complaint against Eugenio Pacelli, and that is that he stood for a strong papacy as the best means of governing the Church in the modern world. Cornwell claims that the diplomatic work that Archbishop Pacelli engaged in while papal nuncio in Germany and later from a distance as cardinal secretary of state "focused not so much on the interests of the German Church but on the pryamidal model of Church authority that had been in the making since Pio Nono."[11] Cornwell's target is not so much Pius XII as the modern papacy itself. Like many dissidents before him, Cornwell imagines that Vatican II did away with that "pyramidal model" and replaced it with the notion of "the pilgrim Church." I have a theological colleague, who should be nameless, who has uttered repeatedly over the years the demonstrable falsehood that Vatican II did away with the hierarchical Church. Cornwell holds a version of this. "The Second Vatican Council was called in 1962 by John XXIII, who succeeded Pacelli in 1958, precisely to reject the monolithic, centralized Church model of his predecessors, in preference for a collegial, decentralized, human community on the move." "The Council signaled, in other words, the end of the ideology of papal power, set in motion by the First Vatican Council and pursued over seventy years to its apotheosis under Pius XII in the 1950s."[12]

A council "signals" through the documents it prepares, votes on, and which are promulgated by the pope. *Lumen Gentium, the Dogmatic Constitution on the Church,* provides as strong a statement of the pope's supreme authority in the Church as was ever made. Collegiality, which Cornwell emphasizes, is not a matter of the pope agreeing with the college of bishops, but vice versa. Bishops have their authority only when they act in communion with the pope.[13] Some signal.

The falsehood that Vatican II redefined the Church and reversed a process that had begun with Pius IX and Vatican I is the basis for criticism of Paul VI and – surprise, surprise – his encyclical *Humanae Vitae*. "Appropriate consultative bodies had been assembled, which, with the majority of the world's bishops [oh?], wanted to sanction the contraceptive pill under certain conditions – a change of course that would have brought spiritual consolation to millions and healed the opening breach between doctrine and practice. Paul, however, resolved the issue by autocratic fiat with his encyclical *Humanae Vitae* (1968)."[14] Cornwell's rhapsody about the benefits of contraception might have been stilled by looking round him at Western society as he wrote his attack on the papacy. Of course there is no attention paid to the encyclical itself, which would have shown him that it is idle to talk about "under certain conditions" when a certain kind of action is as such immoral. And there is no analysis of the etiology of that "breach between doctrine and practice." Thus the attack on Pius XII, which became an attack on the papacy, now arrived at its aim. But that strong papal magisterium is what has held the Church on course when all around her the Western world has been engaged in a self-destructive sexual orgy.

And then we come to the present pope, John Paul II. Cornwell styles him "Pius XII Redivivus" and portrays him as undoing the work of the council and steering the Church away from a collegial model back to the pyramidal model. This is nonsense, of course, but it is not peculiar to Cornwell. Those who truly have undermined and misrepresented Vatican II, the theological dissenters, are Cornwell's ideological comrades. This false view of the present Church – with John Paul II as enemy of the Council, the triumph of reaction, and all the rest – is the basic premise from which Cornwell proceeds to his calumnious portrait of Pius XII.

Scoundrel Time: A Replay

When Lillian Hellman's *Scoundrel Time* appeared in 1976, it had a long fawning thirty-page preface by Garry Wills. Hellman's book told the story of her appearance before the House Un-American Activities Committee which was investigating Communist influence in Hollywood. Wills accepts Lillian Hellman's self-serving account at face value and gives us a Woody Allen version of the proceedings – without the humor. As soon became clear, those who had known the Stalinist Hellman, liberals all, thought she was the scoundrel and accused her of gross inaccuracies. Mary McCarthy, appearing on the Dick Cavett show, was asked if she thought there were any overpraised writers. "The only one I can think of is a holdover," McCarthy replied, "Lillian Hellman, who I think is tremendously overrated, a bad writer and a dishonest writer, but she really belongs to the past." Cavett asked what was dishonest about her. "Everything. I said once in some interview that every word she writes is a lie, including 'and' and 'the.'"[15] Lillian Hellman made the mistake of suing McCarthy and in the ensuing brouhaha the extent of Hellman's mendacity came out.[16]

Relevant to the point of the hearings, which Wills dismissed as fantasy, is a review Mary McCarthy wrote of a film called *North Star*, which had been written by Hellman. The review was called "A Filmy Version of the War," and of it McCarthy wrote that "the Soviet Union appears as an idyllic hamlet with farmhouses and furniture in a style that might be labeled Russian Provincial and put in a window by Sloane." Not on a level with passing over nuclear secrets, but indicative. *Scoundrel Time*, the book Wills had so unctuously introduced, came under scrutiny because of Hellman's libel suit against McCarthy. Earlier criticisms of it were remembered. "It is true that before the lawsuit many readers – Diana Trilling, Allen Weinstein, Sidney Hook, William Phillips, William Buckley, and William O'Neill among them – had pointed out misrepresentations in Hellman's memoir *Scoundrel Time* itself, especially her account of her appearance before the House Un-American Activities Committee. They exposed a number of false statements: that, contrary to her claim, she was not the first witness to offer HUAC only partial cooperation; that she made Alger Hiss look innocent by altering facts about Whittaker Chambers's cache of microfilms of State Department documents; that she called James Wechsler a friendly witness (when, in fact, he was openly hostile to HUAC); and that she accused those connected with *Partisan Review* and *Commentary* of not speaking out against Senator Joseph McCarthy."[17] After the suit was filed, Mary McCarthy presented twenty-two pages of Lillian Hellman's misrepresentations in her various writings.

The moral seemed to be that someone calling others scoundrels is likely to be a bigger scoundrel himself. In *Papal Sin*, Garry Will provides us with a similar performance. In accusing the Church of a "structure of deceit," he exemplifies as well as makes the charge.

The "papal sins" that raise Garry Wills's ire are precisely the magisterial judgments which go contrary to hot items on the secular liberal agenda – contraception (and sexual liberation, in general), the supposed plight of women, and clerical celibacy. In short, what Gary Wills cannot abide is the Catholic teaching on the meaning of sexuality, of the marital act, on the male priesthood, and clerical celibacy. But of course the one that receives most of his attention, two full chapters, is the Church's teaching on sexuality.

Humanae Vitae he calls "the most disastrous papal document of this century." By contrast with Pius IX's *Syllabus of Errors* and the encyclical that accompanied it, *Quanta Cura*, Paul VI's encyclical is "petty and parochial." *Humanae Vitae*, he assures his reader, "is not really about sex. It is about authority." Well, it is an authoritative statement about sexuality. Against papal authority Wills marshals the authority of polls, telling us that five years after the encyclical appeared, 42 percent of the priests in America thought it was an abuse of papal authority and 18 percent thought it an inappropriate use of authority. This is indeed a remarkable fact, if fact it is, but Wills seems without curiosity about why so many priests should have set their face against a papal encyclical. If the encyclical had contained the change many moral theologians expected, it is doubtful in the extreme that there would have been any questioning of its authority. The subversive role of the theological caste was essential in misleading priests and subsequently the faithful into thinking that this authoritative reiteration of doctrine could safely be ignored. Like the other families in the suburbs, Catholics could put acquisitiveness ahead of morality.[18] The treachery of dissenting theologians is behind the confusion that has come over the faithful in matters sexual.

Had Paul VI departed from tradition in writing *Humanae Vitae*? Not at all. He was, in Wills's term, "trapped" by his own and his predecessors' statements, that is, acting within the doctrinal tradition. In responding to the question at issue – had the pill and an advance in biological knowledge provided reasons for questioning the traditional moral judgment on artificial contraception? – Paul VI provided a context for his negative answer by recalling the nature of marriage as well as of the marital act and its procreative and unitive meanings. Wills finds answering the question asked narrowing. "It put the church magisterium, the endangered authority that had been pitted against modernity, at stake on a single issue: birth control." This is disingenuous. While the encyclical unsurprisingly kept to its subject, Paul VI made clear what the implications of separating the unitive and procreative meanings of the marital act were. In so doing *Humanae Vitae* indeed stands against modernity, which more and more had defined itself in terms of sexual liberation.

Wills mocks the ideal of large families and faithful adherence to natural law, yet he is writing at a time when the birth rates of all European countries have sunk far below the replacement rate. It has been below zero in population growth for decades. Sexual liberation has wrought havoc on the societies that embraced it. Families fall apart; children are abused, perhaps because they are regarded as encumbrances and obstacles to freedom; pornography is rampant; sexually transmitted diseases multiply – and Garry Wills finds the *Church* embattled! The one sane voice in a mad world is mocked for its sanity and the circumambient chaos is implicitly defended.

The joke about the man taking the Rorschach test who, when he is chided for finding sexual implications in all the ink blots, retorts, "You're the one showing me these dirty pictures" comes to mind. What Wills regards as a shrinking of Catholic morality to the single issue of sex is a response to the sexually liberated world in which Catholics must work out their salvation. Wills's apparent message is that the Church should have signed on to the sexual revolution and then everything would be fine. This does not rise to the level of arrant nonsense.

Reading *Papal Sin* is like leafing through old issues of *The Watchtower*. It was an amusing spectacle to see Gary Wills on the O'Reilley Factor on the Fox News Network. The host caught the spirit of Wills's book and began to throw in other supposed Catholic absurdities, leaving Wills feebly muttering, "That isn't in my book. I don't say that." For a fleeting moment he seemed to sense the vulgar nature of the Catholic-bashing in which he himself had indulged. But perhaps it was only embarrassment, not repentance.

Mocking the Blood of Martyrs

In a chapter bearing the title "Usurping the Holocaust," Wills discusses the canonization of Edith Stein, which, he says, upset many Jews and quite a few Christians. But the objections are largely from outside the Church, from Jews who hold that Edith Stein, become Sister Teresa Benedicta of the Cross, blessed by the cross, could no longer be called a Jew, and therefore could not be put to death because of her Jewish origins. Wills quotes the hostile remarks of others and finds in them the basis of a suspicion "that Stein is a symbol being manipulated to give Catholics a claim that the Holocaust victimized Catholics as well as Jews."[19] Does he seriously contest that there were millions of non-Jewish victims of Hitler? Or is it forbidden to remember them? His rhetoric enables him to write such things as if he were not saying them. He suggests that such reactions may be extreme or ill-stated, but in effect he endorses them. He quotes Judith Hersschcopf Banki to this effect:

> If Edith Stein had been born a Jew in another time, had converted to Christianity, had joined a Roman Catholic order, had been sent to the Far East or to Africa, and had been murdered there in an outbreak of anti-Christian violence, would her beatification have stirred the same concern among Jews?[20]

Far from pointing out how wildly disanalogous this scenario is to the actual case of Edith Stein, Wills ups the ante, suggesting that in such a case there would have been no question of canonizing at all. Meaning, that there would have been no benefit from doing so.

Wills knows and quotes St. Edith Stein's remark to her sister – he characterizes it as her "supposed remark" – as she was led away by the Gestapo: "Come, we are going for our people." *For,* Wills italicizes, not *with* them. Now if the point is that Edith Stein was a Catholic and no longer Jewish, that she regarded her people "whose scripture was fulfilled in Jesus," as not yet having fulfilled its historic destiny, both are of course true, the one entailing the other. All this comes down to saying that Edith Stein was not a Jewish martyr. But Wills even questions that she was a martyr for her Catholic faith. "She was not killed for being a Catholic." Well, if she was not killed for being Jewish and she was not killed for being Catholic, why was she murdered at Auschwitz? Why was she rounded up in the first place? As a convert, Edith Stein was no longer a Jew. She was exterminated because she was a convert from Judaism.

The sermon of the bishop of Utrecht delivered on the 9th Sunday after Pentecost in 1942, condemning the Nazi treatment of the Jews, brought the reprisal Seyss-Inquart's had threatened: Any such sermon would bring about a round-up of all Christians of Jewish descent. That was the aegis under which Edith Stein was arrested, jammed into a crowded freight car, and transported to Auschwitz where she was exterminated. She was a Carmelite nun, a Catholic, and the daughter of Jewish parents. If the sermon had not been given, the former would have trumped the latter. The sermon being given, she was arrested as a Christian of Jewish descent.

This despicable chapter on Edith Stein is an indication of the lengths to which Garry Wills will go in order to lampoon and mock and ridicule the Church to which he claims to belong. This discussion, and the following one on St. Maximilian Kolbe, show him pandering to

Jewish extremists who are an increasing embarrassment even to their fellow Jews. *Advocatus diaboli*, indeed. He tells his readers that to say Kolbe and Stein died martyrs' deaths is an "invention" whose purpose was to "advance the Pope's thesis that Catholics were the victims of the Holocaust, not the victimizers."[21]

This is a shameful and craven performance. The brash young man who rose to the defense of the Stalinist Lillian Hellman is heading into the twilight trashing heroes of the faith. Wills's book is based on the deceit that he himself is a Roman Catholic. A Catholic is one who accepts the teachings of the Church and gives assent to her dogmas and tradition. But Garry Wills has explicitly denied fundamental doctrines of the faith. *Papal Sin* does indeed exhibit a structure of deceit – the underlying fiction that its author is a faithful Catholic criticizing the papacy. Garry Wills denies a whole menu of undoubted Church dogmas, making his "Catholicism" seem merely a label for the *Zeitgeist* that fills his sails.[22] Only one out of personal touch with the Church could say what Wills does about devotion to the Blessed Virgin Mary. Only someone spiritually severed from the Church would say what he does about two Catholic martyrs.

May St. Maximilian Kolbe and St. Edith Stein pray for him.

These three anti-Catholic Catholic authors make the same mistake about the Church, about its teachings, and about the Council. Whether it is Paul VI who is said to have missed the train of modernity when he issued *Humanae Vitae*, or John Paul II as the supposed foe of Vatican II – that is, the obstacle to the liberated Church of dissenting fantasy – it is the papacy they hate. It is the Catholic Church they loathe. And they hate the Church because she is a lonely voice in the contemporary world upholding common human morality.

6

HITLER'S JEW: The Secret History of David Ben-Gurion. The previously untold story of the man who was arguably the greatest enemy of the Jewish people during World War II. Long controversial as the Jew who failed to speak out against the treatment of European Jewry, Ben-Gurion is here revealed to have prompted events that helped the Final Solution claim millions more victims than it otherwise would have . . . and so on.

ZIONIST SINS: The Lie of the Homeland. The blatant lies of Zionist leaders manifested in the infrastructure of deceit beneath the movement that resulted in the State of Israel. This book tells the hitherto untold story of why the Nuremberg Laws, which codified Nazi racism, permitted only the swastika and the Zionist banner to be flown in Nazi Germany. The inability of Zionist leaders to be honest . . . and so on.

A Jew would react to such titles as any Catholic must to the spate of books defaming and vilifying Pope Pius XII. And if the authors of these imaginary books claimed to be Jewish? How would a devout Protestant enjoy books devoted to showing that Dietrich Bonhoeffer was a double agent of the Gestapo whose treachery foiled plans to assassinate the Führer? Or claims that his long-suppressed diary is studded with anti-Semitic remarks? But it is impossible to find a true parallel to the decades-long, sustained attack on Pope Pius XII, the papacy, the Catholic Church.

In this actual book, sufficient documentation has been gathered from sources available to anyone – no need to spend "months on end" (a minor Cornwell lie) in the Vatican Archives yourself – to disprove what should have been self-evidently false. Here is a little litany of undeniable truths.

Pius XII was *not* responsible for the Holocaust.
Pius XII did *not* make Hitler chancellor of the Reich.
Pius XII did *not* belong to the Gestapo or SS.
Pius XII did *not* condone the Nazi persecution of the Jews.
Pius XII did *not* stand at his window and watch with satisfaction as Jews were rounded up.
Pius XII told the world that the Nazi ideology was diametrically opposed to Christianity. Again and again.
Pius XII told the world that Nazi ideology was opposed to common or natural morality. Again and again.
Pius XII's condemnations of nazism and Jewish persecution were reported in newspapers around the world, including *The New York Times*.
Pius XII carefully weighed his words so that his condemnations would not meet with bloody reprisals.
Pius XII exhausted his personal fortune rescuing Jews.
Pius XII directed the efforts of his nuncios in the occupied counries on behalf of Jews.
Pius XII was rightly thanked by Jewish refugees who benefited from his efforts on their behalf.
Pius XII was responsible for rescuing 860,000 Jews from certain death at the hand of the Nazis.
In word and deed, Pope Pius XII was the best friend the Jewish people had during the Nazi effort to exterminate them.

These are the historical facts. No reasonable person can dispute them.

Why?

So why should wave after wave of books seek to persuade their readers that Pope Pius XII was something other than what in fact he was? That a historian might want to question the wisdom of this or that decision of the pope is not, of course, to defame him. Pius XII acted in what, for those caught up in it, was one of the most difficult periods in recent history. In his efforts to rescue Jews and help them escape the clutches of

Adolf Eichmann, Pius and his nuncios made decisions in circumstances that were unprecedented. Prudential decisions. In contingent circumstances. Might they have acted more wisely or effectively on this occasion or that? Such questions do not amount to defamation. Retrospective alternatives can be proposed. Still, even after half a century during which to imagine alternatives, it is seldom clear that proposed alternatives would have had advantages equal to or surpassing those of the course Pius actually took. Most would have had just the effect Pius sought to avoid – more savage reprisals against the Jews.

Calumny and defamation begin when, in the manner of the pathetic Rolf Hochhuth, vicious motives and objectives are attributed to Pius XII. In a twisted imagination, this good pope becomes a crypto-Nazi. We have seen what psychological need this fabrication filled in Rolf Hochhuth. His efforts after the fact to provide historical justification for his slanders were demonstrably inept. Who would have expected anything else?

Whatever the sources of Hochhuth's fantasies, there is clearly a continuing market for books which escalate the outrage until Pope Pius XII is described as "the most dangerous churchman in modern history!" Nor does it seem to stop the flow of such pseudo-histories when they are patiently refuted. Why do people want to believe such terrible lies about one of the most outstanding churchmen in modern history?

Let this penance be assigned to all those who malign Pius XII: Count from 1 to 860,000, slowly.

The fact of the matter is that such attack-books are really not about Pope Pius XII at all. He is merely a target of opportunity. The real target is the Catholic Church and her unchanging moral doctrine. This is clearest in the books written by *soi-disant* Catholics. Their books express a simmering rage that the Church did not follow their false understanding of Vatican II. Their animus against Paul VI and John Paul II is every bit as great as that they feel against Pope Pius XII. These gentle prelates stand for the road not taken by Catholic dissidents. Hordes of post-conciliar Catholics convinced one another that they could invent their own Catholicism and reject the Church's Magisterium. It began with the revolt of the moral theologians, it spread to seminaries, it ended up in the pulpit and in advice priests gave the laity. A generation has been told that they need not accept authoritative teachings of the Church, solemnly reiterated by the Holy Father.

The turning point was Paul VI's 1968 encyclical *Humanae Vitae*.

Although they themselves were imperfectly aware of this at the time, the dissenters who went ballistic over Paul VI's encyclical were demanding that the Church sign on to the sexual revolution then well under way in the Western world. Sex was to be freed from its link to reproduction. At first, this was seen only as a benefit to married couples, who would thereby be able to limit the size of their families. Proponents of contraception for Catholics would have been appalled then to have their suggestion seen as opening the gates to premarital and extramarital sex, to homosexuality, and to a general divorce of sexual activity from marriage and family. But Pope Paul VI presciently saw the consequences of separating the unitive from the procreative meaning of the marital act, sexual pleasure from the orientation of the act to the transmission of life. Given such a separation, what barrier would there then be to sexual activity by unmarried partners or to sexual activity between members of the same sex?

Those dissidents who took notice of this "domino theory" at the time ridiculed it, denying that they had in mind anything other than enhancing the lives of married couples. But when the domino theory was quickly verified in the contraceptive society, critics of *Humanae Vitae* found ways of blessing all the consequences Paul VI had foreseen. Masturbation, extramarital sex, homosexual activity, abortion – all were given a blessing by dissident moral theologians. They had joined the sexual revolution. But the Church had not. Standing athwart their effort to undermine the moral Magisterium of the Church was the pope – and it did not matter what his name was. Theological dissent has confused the faithful – hence the kind of poll results that Garry Wills cites – but this has not and will not change the moral teaching of the Church. Not even God can make what is wrong right.

It has not mattered in the least that the whole question of the limitation of family size has been revolutionized by Natural Family Planning. Dissidents continue to talk about the rhythm method and Vatican roulette. But Natural Family Planning is a surer method of not getting pregnant than any artificial means. And it does not disturb the natural rhythm of a woman's body. Given this biologically preferable and morally acceptable way of limiting the size of families, only one in the grips of a theory, as Aristotle put it, would continue to agitate for artificial birth control.

Of course, Natural Family Planning is possible only for married couples who have made a permanent commitment to one another. It cannot be used by those who engage in random copulation with various partners. Thus, the continued defense of artificial contraception by theological dissenters is an endorsement of a life of casual sex with multiple partners.

Artificial birth control is part of the package of sexual liberation that dissenting Catholics have bought. Who is surprised when dissenters – Wills is a good example – also reject the Church's teaching on homosexuality and abortion? Soon they will be defending euthanasia. They have become apologists for what Pope John Paul II has called the Culture of Death.

The rebels know this. Hence their rage and contempt for all things Catholic. Having denied the faith, they continue to call themselves Catholics Do they even deceive themselves? How could they not realize that they have joined the other side? They have left the Church. But the Church is still there, teaching as clearly and patiently and lovingly as always.

Similarly, early defamers of Pius XII were content to distort the history of what he had actually done for Jews during World War II. But as the attacks continued, it was clear that authors were after bigger game. They were after the papacy as such. They were after the Church. During the dark days of nazism, Albert Einstein said that only the Church spoke out against the Nazi ideology. The Church continues to speak the same truths now as it did then, but the object of her censure has changed. The Nazis remain as a symbol of evil in the attacks on Pius XII, but what past practices of the Nazis do current critics of the pope in principle condemn?

Are We All Nazis Now?

The Catholic Church's steadfast opposition to abortion has not wavered since the infamous *Roe v. Wade* decision in 1973. That an American society which had regarded abortion as a heinous crime throughout its history should have been turned upside down by a Supreme Court decision that would not qualify as a freshman essay is almost as extraordinary as the way in which the establishment – political, judicial, editorial – quickly became cheerleaders for abortion. Since then, the tide of approval has risen until the taking of innocent unborn life has become a ho-hum topic. The manifest infanticide involved in partial-birth abortion did not prevent the Supreme Court from saying that it too was now covered by the Constitution – that is, the distortion of the Constitution involved in its previous abortion decisions. A woman has a right to choose. So did the Nazi doctors.

Almost alone the Catholic Church has condemned abortion. For this she is hated and vilified. Her enemies understand that the Church's opposition to abortion is more than opposition to abortion – the Church stands athwart the accelerating rush toward decadence. Almost alone she defends the natural-law morality that is being trampled by a society that is paying the price. This is the same natural law to which Pius XII appealed when he condemned Nazi atrocities, most especially the persecution of Jews.

Proponents of abortion do not like hearing it compared to the Holocaust.

The Holocaust lasted less than half a dozen years. The scourge of abortion has been going on for more than a quarter of a century.

It is often asked: "How could Germany, a Christian country – two-thirds Protestant, one-third Catholic – accept the Nazi ideology?"

Try asking: "How could a decent nation like the United States, its citizenry highly religious, adopt the abortion ideology?"

It is often asked: "How could good Germans possibly be unaware of the slaughter of the innocent that was taking place under the Hitler regime?"

Try asking: "How can we be unaware, or unconcerned, about the slaughter of unborn life which takes place, not in this isolated camp or that, but throughout the country?"

It is often asked: "How could good Catholics ignore the judgment of their Church and continue to support the Nazi party?"

Try asking: "How can politicians who are professed Catholics be among the most ardent advocates of abortion?"

Perhaps the Church has not spoken out clearly enough? The Church has spoken out again and again – in the documents of Vatican II, in papal encyclicals, in the statements of the bishops' conference, against the foul crime that is abortion. And Catholic politicians continue to be in the front ranks of those preventing even the slightest regulation of abortion.

Why aren't they excommunicated?

Why indeed?

Were this to happen, such Catholics would immediately become heroes for a day in the media, martyrs to modernity, victims of their obscurantist Church. And they would go on calling themselves Catholics. They would be supported by the aging ranks of theological dissenters. They would be confirmed in their errors.

Abortion is not an isolated evil. It is the fruit of the sexual revolution. At the heart of the sexual revolution is the severance of sexual pleasure from the purpose of the activity it accompanies – by mechanical means. From then on sex could be enjoyed with impunity. Women could be as carefree as men about it. Only a woman can get pregnant, a fact that extends the possible significance of copulation into the future, through the carrying of the baby, and then nursing and rearing it when born. The male, by contrast, could alight where he would and then buzz off, without any thought of consequences. The sexual revolution was to elevate women to this supposedly blissful condition of the male.

It is one of the ironies of the sexual revolution that contraception, which promised to remove pregnancy from the sexual scene, has done anything but. Advocates of contraception are kept busy explaining how it is that young women, indoctrinated, equipped, and sent out to enjoy themselves, keep getting pregnant. The fact is that in the age of contraception there has been an increase, not a decrease, in so-called "unwanted pregnancies." Hence the continued advocacy of abortion, which should have been made obsolete by contraception. Abortion is the necessary back-up for sexual liberation. When all else fails, and contraceptives regularly fail, the unsought fruit of a union can be nipped in the bud. Contraception and abortion are two ends of the same thought.

As Paul VI pointed out in the much-maligned but little-read *Humanae Vitae,* the separation of the two meanings of the marital act, the procreative and unitive, would leave one bereft of the principle according to which pre-marital and extra-marital sex are seen to violate the nature of sexuality. And homosexuality would seem an innocent pursuit of sexual stimulation without reference to the meaning of the act for which the genitals have been designed, procreation having been set aside in favor of pleasure. Those who rose up in defiance of *Humanae Vitae* – theologians, of course – would soon be waffling on all the things that Paul VI saw as entailed by the change they sought. The whole of Christian morality would have become unraveled. And his critics set about proving him right.[1] Here was a veritable *trahison des clercs.*

What the popes condemned in Nazi Germany they continue to condemn.

The popes and the Catholic Church have continued to condemn the notion that there is "worthless human life" of which the state can dispose, whether by official programs or by farming out the right to kill the innocent to abortionists. The Church condemned euthanasia and experimentation on human beings. Once, the Church was praised for this. Once, the Allies identified themselves with the moral stance of the Catholic Church and echoed its condemnation of the Nazi contempt for innocent life. The Nuremberg trials testify to that.

But gradually over the years, we have adopted ourselves what we once saw as the depraved practices of the Nazis. The Final Solution claimed the life of 6 million innocent Jews. In the United States alone, a million and a half abortions are performed . . . every year. Since *Roe v. Wade*, the slaughter of the innocent has surpassed all the victims of Hitler many times over. And it continues to go on even as you read. Infanticide is now defended as a constitutional right.

We are all Nazis now.[2]

But the Catholic Church, and the pope in Rome, continues to judge according to the natural law and the divine law. The judgment of Pope John Paul II is severe. Ours he has called a Culture of Death.

We have adopted the worst practices of the Nazis and others they never dreamt of. Hollow defenses of this decadence and perversion are made. At Nuremberg, the Nazi doctors never admitted guilt and steadfastly defended the practices for which they were on trial.

It would be a tragic and ironic consequence of the campaign to vilify Pius XII if it caused distrust between Catholics and Jews. One cannot read of what Pius XII did on behalf of the Jews being persecuted by Hitler without seeing what unprecedented cooperation there was between the Vatican and Jewish organizations. Jews had no hesitation to turn to Pius and his nuncios for help whenever deportation or worse threatened. Individual nuncios acted with such alacrity and persistence that they were honored in Israel after the war. A grove of trees was planted there in honor of Pius XII. May no Jew or Catholic forget this noble history and the wartime solidarity which resulted in the rescue of almost a million Jews from certain death at Hitler's hands.

> On the flood of sin, hatred and blood let loose by Hitler upon the world, there swam a small ark which preserved intact the common heritage of the Judaeo-Christian outlook; that outlook is founded on the love of God and love of one's fellow men. The demonism of Hitler sought to overturn it in the flood of hate. It was saved by a handful of saints. – Sholem Asch.[3]

Notes

Chapter 2: Diplomat

1   Taken from the release of the Congregation for the Doctrine of the Faith, Vatican City, June 26, 2000.

Chapter 3: Secretary of State

1   I follow here the account given by Lenni Brenner, *Zionism in the Age of the Dictators* (London: Croom Helm, 1983), pp. 87–88.

Chapter 4: A Pope in Time of War

1939

1   Pierre Blet, s.j., *Pius XII and the Second World War* (New York: Paulist Press, 1999), pp. 281–82.
2   New York: Knopf, 1941.
3   Monsignor Tardini says that Pius XI told him several times that Cardinal Pacelli must become the next pope: "[Tardini], looking me straight in the eye with his penetrating eyes, concluded by saying: 'He will be a magnificent pope.' (*Sarà un bel papa.*) He did not say, 'He would be' or 'He could be' but 'he will be' without admitting any doubt.'" Quoted by Pierre Blet, p. 7.
4   I rely here on the portrait of the pope given by Jean Chelini in *L'Eglise sous Pie XII: La Tourmente 1939–1945* (Paris: Fayard, 1983), pp. 89–96.
5   Blet, p. 19. This British optimism evanesced. "Mr. Osborne of the British Vatican legation to Viscount Halifax on May 29, 1939: 'As regards Germany, I assume that the pope's direct influence is negligi-

ble, as any appeal to German Catholic opinion would be suppressed.'"
(Pinchas Lapide, *The Last Three Popes and the Jews* [London: Souvenir Press, 1980], p. 238.)

6 Lapide, p. 127.
7 Ibid.
8 Ibid., p. 217.
9 Ibid., p. 345.
10 Ibid., p. 183.
11 Ibid.
12 Ibid., p. 250.
13 Paul Claudel, *Journal, Tome* II 1933–1955 (Paris: Gallimard Bibliothèque de la Pléiade, 1969), p. 281.
14 Lapide, p. 250.

1940

1 Pinchas Lapide, *The Last Three Popes and the Jews* (London: Souvenir, 1967), p. 127.
2 Ibid., p. 128. In *Pius XII and the Second World War* (New York: Paulist Press, 1999), p. 140, Father Pierre Blet, s.J., reveals how this effort was hampered by the Germans and by the German hierarchy!
3 Lapide, p. 249.
4 Blet, p. 72.
5 Ibid.
6 Lapide, p. 127.
7 Ibid., p. 231.
8 Blet, p. 75.
9 Lapide, p. 184.
10 Ibid., p. 230
11 Ibid., p. 234.
12 Ibid., p. 231.
13 Ibid., p. 245.
14 "Marshal Goering asked me about my opinion on this specific question: whether I considered it possible that the Pope, upon Italy's entry into the war, would take such a contrary stand as to induce him to pronounce some sort of excommunication against the Duce for having tied himself irremediably in belligerent action to the nation in which anti-Catholic doctrines were officially promulgated. . . . [Alfieri answered] in the hypothetical case that it did take place, the official part [of Italy]

would not attach any particular importance to it." Alfieri to Count Ciano, May 23, 1940. Lapide, p. 244.

15   Ibid., 198.

16   Ibid., p. 128. Pinchas Lapide is speaking *in propria persona*. He served with the 178th Transport Company of the British 8th Army.

17   Ibid., 163.

18   Ibid., p. 127.

19   *The New York Times*, March 31, 1940.

20   Lapide, p. 175.

21   "Hitler appointed Arthur Greiser, the former president of the Danzig senate, as head of this region. Under Greiser the policy was one of violent measures against priests and bishops, with an attempt by the Nazis to reorganize the church according to their own ideology. In the mind of the occupying forces, the ultimate objective was a Catholic Church independent of Rome, first in Warthegau [German occupied Poland] and much later in the Reich and its dependent territories." Blet, pp. 77–78.

22   Lapide, p. 183.

23   Ibid., p. 186.

24   Ibid., p. 151.

1941

1   See Blet, *Pius XII and the Second World War* (New York: Paulist Press, 1999), pp. 144–45.

2   Ibid., p. 145.

3   Ibid.

4   Ibid., p. 147.

5   Lapide, *The Last Three Popes and the Jews* (London: Souvenir Press, 1980), p. 198.

6   Ibid., p. 199.

7   Lapide, p. 163.

8   Ibid., p. 180.

9   Ibid., p. 181.

10   Ibid.

11   Ibid., 163.

12   Ibid., p. 250.

13   See Lapide, p. 234.

14   Ibid., p. 236.

15 Ibid., p. 236.

16 Blet, pp. 140–41.

17 Ibid., p. 141.

18 Ibid., p. 142.

19 Ibid.

20 Ibid. p. 143.

21 Blet, p. 149.

22 Lapide, p. 189.

23 *The Palestine Post* (August 31, 1941). See Lapide, p. 177.

24 Lapide, pp. 252–53.

25 Ibid., p. 193. And what did Mauriac himself do? "Revenu à Paris en1942, il est injurié dans la presse, pris à parti dans la rue. De ces quatre interminables années qui ont vu 'le plus grand massacre d'innocents qu'ait enregistré l'histoire humaine . . . Dieu sait ce que j'aurais à dire! Mais il faudrait rouvrir trop de plaies *et j'ai choisi de me taire.'"* Mauriac. *Collection Génies et Réalités* (Paris: Hachette, 1977), p. 172.

26 Lapide, 138.

27 Ibid., pp. 42–43; 138.

28 Ibid., p. 163.

29 Ibid., p. 64.

30 Ibid., p. 173.

31 Ibid., p. 232.

Zionism and the Diaspora – 1941

1 *Diplomacy in the Near and Middle East*, vol. 2, *A Documentary Record, 1914–1956*, edited by J. C. Hurewitz (Princeton, N.J.: Van Nostrand, 1956).

2 Marvin Lowenthal, Diaries of Theodor Herzl, p. 366; quoted by Lenni Brenner, *Zionism in the Age of the Dictators* (London: Croom Helm, 1983), p. 4

3 Chaim Weizmann, *Trial and Error* (New York: Harper: 1949), pp. 90–91; Brenner, p. 4.

4 Patai, *Complete Diaries of Theodor Herzl*, vol. III (New York: Thomas Yoselof, 1960), p. 729; Brenner, p. 5.

5 Weizmann, p. 243; Brenner, p. 11.

6 Brenner, pp. 20–21.

1942

1   Blet, *Pius XII and the Second World War* (New York: Paulist Press, 1999), p. 152.
2   Ibid.
3   Lapide, *The Last Three Popes and the Jews* (London: Souvenir Press, 1980), p. 174.
4   Ibid., p. 196.
5   Ibid., p. 215.
6   Ibid., p. 205.
7   Lapide, p. 199.
8   Ibid., pp. 252–53.
9   Ibid., p. 253.
10 Ibid., p. 139.
11 Ibid.
12 Ibid., p. 140.
13 Ibid., p. 142. See too Blet, pp. 168–69.
14 Lapide, p. 143.
15 Ibid., p. 233.
16 Ibid., p. 142, and Blet, p. 169.
17 Lapide, p. 141.
18 Blet, p. 170.
19 Lapide, p. 143.
20 Blet, p. 170.
21 Lapide, p. 143.
22 Blet, p. 174.
23 Ibid., p. 170.
24 Ibid., pp. 143 and 139.
25 Ibid., pp. 165, 186, 199.
26 Guenter Lewy, *The Catholic Church and Nazi Germany* (New York: McGraw Hill, 1964), cited by Lapide, p. 246. The reference is to July 1942.
27 Ibid., p.165.
28 Ibid., p. 233.
29 Ibid., p. 199.
30 Ibid., p. 164.
31 Ibid.

32 Ibid., p. 173.
33 Ibid., p. 171.
34 Lapide, pp. 197–98.
35 Ibid., p. 200.
36 Blet, p. 148.
37 Cited by Lapide, p. 200.
38 Ibid., p. 205.
39 Ibid., p. 194.
40 Ibid., p. 237.
41 Ibid., pp. 144 and 164.
42 Quoted by Lapide, pp. 189–90.
43 Lapide rightly dwells lovingly on this episode. We have not heard the last from the redoubtable Saliège.
44 Blet, p. 235.
45 Lapide, p. 200.
46 Ibid., 16.
47 Ibid., p. 246.
48 Ibid., p. 185.
49 Ibid., pp. 164. Lapide relies on the accounts of Jews who were involved in these consultations and joint action, notably A. Shafran, *Les juifs en Europe*, published in Paris in 1949, and two books by Theodore Lavi, *The Vatican's Endeavours on Behalf of Roumanian Jewry during the Second World War*, published in Jerusalem in 1961, and *Roumanian Jewry in World War II – Fight for Survival*, published in Jersalem in 1965.
50 Lapide, pp. 191–93.
51 Ibid., p. 197.
52 Ibid., p. 137.
53 Quoted by Lapide, p. 194.
54 Ibid., pp. 255–56.
55 Ibid., pp. 193 and 252.
56 Quoted by Lapide, p. 252.
57 For both these quotations, see Lapide, p. 193.
58 Ibid., p. 186.
59 See ibid., pp. 254–55.
60 Ibid., p. 205.
61 Ibid., p. 174.
62 Ibid., p. 251.

Zionism and the Diaspora – 1942

1 See William Shirer, *The Rise and Fall of the Third Reich* (New York: Simon and Shuster, 1960), pp. 142–45.

2 Ibid., p. 144. The final maneuver is described on p. 178. According to Vitaliano Mattiolo, *Gli Ebrei e la Chiesa* (Milano: Mursia, 1997), Schroeder declared an "honorary Aryan" by Hitler and made a general in the SS. See p. 129.

3 Shirer, op. cit., p 178.

4 Cited by Pinchas Lapide, *The Last Three Popes and the Jews* (London: Souvenir Press, 1967), p. 92.

5 Lenni Brenner, *Zionism in the Age of the Dictators* (London: Croom Helm, 1983), p. 15.

6 Adolf Hitler, *Mein Kampf*; see Brenner, 79.

7 Quoted in Brenner, p. 80.

8 Cf. Ibid., p. 85.

9 The papal Christmas message and the declaration by Cardinal Bertram are cited by Lapide, p. 98.

10 Lapide, p. 101.

11 Ibid., p. 102.

12 Brenner, p. 86.

13 Ibid., p. 87.

14 Ibid., p. 88.

15 Ibid., p. 93.

16 Ibid., p. 94.

17 *Life* 28 (November, 1960), p. 22.

1943

1 Lapide, *The Last Three Popes and the Jews* (London: Souvenir Press, 1980), p. 136. Given the focus of his study, it is understandable that Lapide should concentrate on the number of Jewish refugees helped. Indeed, the Vatican was itself especially concerned with Jews – but not of course exclusively. What stands out is the indiscriminate nature of the papal assistance, based as it was on principles of common humanity and natural morality as well as on the demands of Christian charity and justice.

2 Ibid., p. 166. The treacherous Lecca broke his promise and complained of Cassulo's "incessant interference."

3 The account is by Archbishop Hakin which appeared in what Lapide describes as "an official Israeli publication." See ibid., p. 232.

4   Ibid., p. 206.
5   Ibid., p. 201.
6   Ibid., p. 144.
7   Ibid.
8   Ibid., p. 201.
9   Ibid., p. 253. See Blet, *Pius XII and the Second World War* (New York: Paulist Press, 1999), p. 67.
10 See Lapide, p. 185.
11 Ibid., p. 195.
12 Ibid., p. 176.
13 Ibid., p. 144.
14 Ibid., p. 166.
15 Ibid., p. 145.
16 Blet, p. 66.
17 Ibid.
18 Lapide, p. 201.
19 Ibid., p. 146.
20 Ibid., p. 218.
21 Ibid., p. 202.
22 Ibid., p. 245; second quote is from "La Parocchia" (April 1964).
23 See ibid., p. 44–45.
24 *Osservatore della Domenica*, June 28, 1964, p. 29.
25 Lapide, pp. 175, 172.
26 Ibid., p. 232.
27 Ibid., p. 251.
28 Ibid., pp. 258 and 262.
29 Ibid., p. 257.
30 Ibid., p. 187.
31 Ibid., pp. 132, 258. Lapide quotes Professor Halecki: "Pius XII instructed the Vatican treasurer to raise whatever gold was still required. This was accomplished in less than a day, probably by melting down religious vessels." Ibid., p. 259.
32 Ibid.
33 Ibid., p. 252.
34 Ibid., pp. 132–33.
35 *Osservatore della Domenica* (June 28, 1964), 76, 61.
36 Lapide, op. cit., pp. 132–33, 259, 260–61.

37 Ibid., p. 261.

38 Ibid., 261–62.

39 Ibid., p. 175.

40 Ibid., p. 133.

41 "The Cardinal [Van Roey] also solicited the help of the Secretary General of the Ministry of Justice, who replied to him on December 31, 1943: 'Your Eminence has informed me of the great compassion you feel for our Jewish compatriots, hit by recent decrees of the occupying authorities . . . I have taken steps in order to obtain the release of those at least who have rendered signal services to Belgium.' Moreover, the Cardinal gave his name for an account in the National Bank of Belgium, where three million francs were deposited by the Jewish Aid Committee, for ransom, bribes and other rescue activities." (Ibid., p. 204.)

42 Ibid., p. 238.

Zionism and the Diaspora – 1943

1 Lenni Brenner, *Zionism in the Age of the Dictators* (London: Croom Helm, 1983), p. 228.

2 Ibid., p. 229.

3 Ibid.

4 Ibid.

5 Ibid., p. 231.

6 "If the evidence was played down by many Jewish leaders and the Jewish press, it was not out of the desire to keep the community in a state of ignorance, but because there were genuine doubts. As the worst fears were confirmed, there was confusion among the leaders as to what course of action to choose. This was true especially in the US and caused further delay in making the news public. In Jerusalem, the turning point came with the arrival of a group of Palestinian citizens who had been repatriated from Europe in November 1942. The leaders of the Jewish Agency, who had been unwilling to accept the written evidence gathered by experienced observers, were ready to believe the accounts delivered by chance arrivals in face-to-face meetings." *The Terrible Secret* (Boston: Little Brown, 1980), p. 200.

7 Quoted by Brenner, op. cit., p. 232.

8 Ibid., p. 232.

9 Ibid.

10 Ibid., p. 233.

11 Ibid., p. 234.
12 Ibid., p. 235.
13 Ibid., p. 235.
14 Ibid., p. 236.
15 Ibid., pp. 236–37. See Brenner's discussion of the letter that accompanied Mayer's, one from Nathan Schwalb, which seems to say that the sacrifice of the Jews in Europe is the price that must be paid for being well treated by the Allies who will have spilled so much blood during the war. Weissmandel's interpetation of it was: "In other words: you, my fellow members, my 19 or 20 close friends, get out of Slovakia and save your lives and with the blood of the remainder – the blood of all the men, women, old and young, and the sucklings – the land will belong to us." – pp. 237–38.
16 Ibid., p. 238.
17 Ibid., pp. 238–39.
18 Quoted by Brenner, p. 245.
19 Ibid., p. 149.
20 Ibid.

1944

1 Pierre Blet, s.j., *Pius XII and the Second World War* (New York: Paulist Press, 1999), pp. 255–56.
2 Ibid., p. 186.
3 Lapide, *The Last Three Popes and the Jews* (London: Souvenir Press, 1980), p. 166.
4 Ibid., p. 231.
5 Ibid., p. 230.
6 *Look Magazine* (May 17, 1955): 40–50. See as well Lapide, pp. 167–68.
7 Lapide, p. 150.
8 Blet, p. 187.
9 Lapide, p. 168.
10 Blet, p. 183. Dr. Shafran's name is sometimes spelled Safran. I follow the spelling of the text being cited.
11 Ibid., pp. 187–88.
12 See Lapide, pp. 153, 149, 167, and 150.
13 Ibid., p. 128.
14 Ibid., p. 151.

15   Blet, p. 191.
16   Lapide, p. 151.
17   Ibid., p. 152.
18   Ibid., p. 254.
19   Ibid., p. 218.
20   Ibid., p. 153.
21   Ibid., p. 129.
22   Ibid., p. 219.
23   Ibid., p. 153.
24   Ibid., p. 221.
25   Blet, pp. 194–95.
26   Ibid., p. 192.
27   Lapide, pp. 152–54.
28   Ibid., p. 157.
29   Ibid., p. 156.
30   Ibid., p. 219.
31   Ibid., p. 169.
32   Saul Friedlander, *Pius XII and the Third Reich* (New York: Alfred Knopf, 1966), pp. 226–35. The subtitle of Friedlander's book is: A Documentation. He relies heavily on Nazi accounts of Nazi dealings with the Vatican, so this report of the Cairo meeting stands out. Friedlander effectively ends his book with it – followed by his own churlish complaint that the pope did not do more.
33   Lapide, p. 264.
34   Friedlander, p. 234.
35   Lapide, p. 265.
36   Ibid., pp. 157–58.
37   Ibid., p. 158.
38   Ibid.
39   Ibid., pp. 159–60.
40   Ibid., pp. 140–41.
31   Ibid., p. 264.
32   Ibid., p. 161.

Zionism and the Diaspora – 1944

1   Thomas A. Kolsky, *Jews against Zionism: The American Council for Judaism 1942–1948* (Philadephia: Temple University Press, 1990), p. 59.

2   Ibid., pp. 199–200.

3   Lenni Brenner, *Zionism in the Age of the Dictators* (London: Croom Helm, 1983), p. 229. He supports this with a reference to Yoav Gelber, "Zionist Policy and the Fate of European Jewry (1939–1942)," *Yad Vashem Studies* 13, p. 171.

4   Brenner, p. 229. His source for this is Aryeh Tartakower, who was in charge of World Jewish Congress in America in 1940, who told the story to Shabatei Beit-Zvi.

5   Ibid., pp. 230–31.

6   Ibid., pp. 161–62. He is quoting Maria Syrkin, *Midstream* (May, 1968).

7   Pinchas Lapide, *The Last Three Popes and the Jews* (London: Souvenir Press, 1967), p. 229.

1945

1   Lapide, *The Last Three Popes and the Jews* (London: Souvenir Press, 1980), p. 182.

2   Ibid., pp. 186–87.

3   Ibid., pp. 182–83.

4   Ibid., p. 184.

5   Ibid., p. 185.

6   Ibid., p. 225.

7   Blet, *Pius XII and the Second World War* (New York: Paulist Press, 1999), p. 264.

8   Ibid.

9   Ibid., p. 268.

10 Ibid., pp. 214–15.

11 Ibid., p. 223.

12 These acknowledgments, and others, can be found in Lapide, pp. 224–28.

13 Ibid., p. 229.

Chapter 5: The Defamation of Pius XII

1   Actually, Pius XII condemned the notion of collective guilt twice, on December 24, 1944, and again on February 20, 1946.

2   See Dolores Barracano Schmit, "Rolf Hochhuth: The Man and His Work," in *The Deputy Reader: Studies in Moral Responsibility* (Chicago: Scott Foresman, 1965), pp. 62–67. This quotation is from p. 64, my opening quotation from p. 63 of this essay.

3   John Simon, "The Deputy and Its Metamorphoses," in the collection cited, p. 85.

4   Lapide, *The Last Three Popes and the Jews* (London: Souvenir Press, 1980), p. 266.

5   *Messages from the Underground: Transnational Radio in Resistance and in Solidarity.* Written and edited by Nancy Lynch Street and Marlyn J. Matelski (Westport, Conn.: Praeger, 1997), p.6.

6   "The area of Europe seized by the Nazis during the last war contained some 8,300,000 Jews. Two million escaped Hitler's clutches. Half of these survived by flight, emigration or evacuation into the free world. But at least one million Jews lived on in the crucible of the Nazi hell; lived to see the Nazi threat join the fate of a dozen other would-be destroyers of Israel. The miraculous survival of a million Jews gives the lie to pessimists." [Lapide, p. 212]

7   Louis Chaigne, *Portrait et Vie de Pie XII* (Paris: Editions St-Augustin, 1966), pp. 82–85: "*L'explosion de Chicago.*"

8   *America* (August 9, 1980).

9   James Carroll, *An American Requiem: God, My Father, and the War that Came between Us* (Boston: Houghton Mifflin, 1966), p. 242.

10   John Cornwell, *Hitler's Pope: The Secret History of Pius XII* (New York, Viking, 1999), p. 91.

11   Ibid., p. 85.

12   Ibid., p. 361. The previous quotation is from pp, 7–8.

13   *Lumen Gentium*, nn. 25 and 26, in *Sacrosanctum Oecumenicum Concilium Vaticanum II, Constituiones, Decreta, Declarationes* (Roma: Typis *Polyglottis* Vaticanis, 1977). Consider this conciliar reaffirmation of infallibility. "Qua quidem infallibilitate Romanus Pontifex, Colegii Episcoporum Caput, vi muneris sui gaudet, quando, ut supremus omnium christifidelium pastor et doctor, qui fratres suos in fide confirmat (Cf. Lc 22, 32), doctrinam de fide vel moribus definitivo actu proclamat." And reference is made to Vatican I.

14   Cornwell, p. 363.

15   See Carol E. Gelderman, *Mary McCarthy, A Life* (New York: St. Martin's Press, 1988), p. 333.

16   Chapter 23 of Gelderman's biography is devoted to this sorry tale.

17   Ibid., p. 339.

18   See Ralph McInerny, *What Went Wrong With Vatican II* (Manchester, N.H.: Sophia Institute Press, 1998).

19   Garry Wills, *Papal Sin: Structures of Deceit* (New York: Doubleday, 2000), p. 48.

20   Ibid.

21   Ibid., p. 62.

22   See Robert P. Lockwood, *"Papal Sin* Is Palpable Nonsense," The Catholic League, June 6, 2000. "The level of rejection of basic tenets of Catholic belief within this book is profound, considering that the author firmly claims his Catholic identity and describes himself as a practicing Catholic. There is the standard fare concerning active support for women's ordination, dismissal of celibacy, and embracing of artificial contraception. Wills goes further than many involved in Catholic dissent by also professing unqualified support for abortion rights. But he does not stop there. In the course of the book he rejects the teaching authority of the Church if exercised without lay involvement and agreement, the concept of papal infallibility and any possibility of divine guidance to papal teaching, the ordained priesthood, the doctrine of the Real Presence in the Eucharist, and that the priest has the sacramental power alone to consecrate the Eucharist. Apostolic Succession, the Immaculate Conception and Assumption, and Church teaching on homosexuality are dismissed as well. For the most part, the right of the Church to teach at all in the area of sexual morality are dismissed if it involves the actions of consenting adults."

Chapter 6: Why?

1   See *Human Sexuality: New Directions in American Catholic Thought* (New York: Paulist Press, 1977). A Study Commissioned by the Catholic Theological Society of America. The product of a commission consisting of Anthony Kosnik, William Carroll, Agnes Cunningham, Ronald Modras, James Schulte.

2   See *The Nazi Doctors: Medical Killing and the Psychology of Genocide* by Robert Jay Lifton (New York: Basic Books, 1985) and *The Nazi Doctors and the Nuremberg Code*, edited by George J. Annas and Michael A. Grodin. (New York: Oxford University Press, 1992).

3   Quoted by Lapide, *The Last Three Popes and the Jews*, (London: Souvenir Press, 1980), p. 212.

Index

New York Times, 33–35, 45, 47, 77, 88–89, 95, 161–62, 166, 181, 190
Newman, John Henry Cardinal, 4, 28
Nogara (head of the Vatican treasury), 116
Non abbiamo bisogno, 27, 29, 100
Non-Aryan Catholics, 61
Normandy beaches, 126
Norway, 50
Nos es muy conocida, 27
Notre Dame, University of, 21
Nowowiejsky, Bishop, 151
Nuremberg Laws, 51, 74, 99
Nuremberg Rally, 167

O'Carroll, Michael, 169
Occupied France, 61
Occupied Holland, 51, 55
O'Neill, William, 175
Operation Barbarossa, 58
Operation Pontiff, *50*
Opus iustitiae pax, 42
Oranienburg-Sachsenhausen, 48
O'Reilly Factor, 177
Orsenigo, Archbishop, 33, 43, 49, 52, 60, 61, 84, 88, 97, 107, 153
Orthodox Jews, 70
Osborne, D'Arcy, 43, 131
Osservatore della domenica, 195
Osservatore Romano, 105, 112, 118, 163

Pacelli, Eugenio. *See* Pope Pius XII.
Pacelli, Filippo, 1–2
Pacelli, Francesco, 6
Pacelli, Marcantonio, 1
Pacelli, Monsignor Giuseppe, 2
Pacelli, Virginia Graziosi, 1, 17
Palencia, Ambassador, 113
Palestine, 43, 68–69, 98, 101 ff., 110, 129, 139
Palestine Mandate, 69
Palestine Post, 190
Palestinian Arabs, 101
Palma, Monsignor, 2

Pantheon, 7
Papal Athenaeum of St. Appolinaris, 1, 8
Papal Magisterium, 174
Partial-birth abortion, 184
Partisan Review, 175
Pearl Harbor, 65
Peel Commission, 102
Pereles, Dr. Max, 135
Pétain, Henri, 62, 83, 86
Pfeiffer, Pancrace, 117–19
Phillips, William, 175
Piazza Navona, 7
Piazza Venezia, 7
Pinsker, Leo, 68
Ploesti, 103
Poland, 37, 42–43, 46, 75
Poliakov, Leon, 63
Polish Jews, 34, 66, 160
Polkes, Feivel, 102
Pontifical Academy of Noble Ecclesiastics, 11
Pope Benedict XV, 9, 12, 14, 23
Pope Clement XI, 11
Pope Gregory XVI, 1
Pope John XXIII, 36, 40, 84. *See also* Roncalli, Angelo.
Pope John Paul II, 14, 57, 174, 179, 182
Pope Leo XIII, 3–4, 25, 62
Pope Paul VI, 14, 43, 174, 179, 182, 186
Pope Pius VI, 5
Pope Pius VII, 5, 10
Pope Pius IX, 1–5, 172
Pope Pius X, St., 4–5, 11, 22–23
Pope Pius XI, 22–25, 34, 38, 96, 100–101
Pope Pius XII, *passim*
Popov, 64
Portuguese Jews, 107
Posnanski, Rabbi Gustav, 147
Poznan, 49
Prague, 42
Prinz, Joachin, 101